FURIOUS COOL

FURIOUS COOL | RICHARD PRYOR
AND THE WORLD THAT MADE HIM

DAVID HENRY AND JOE HENRY

Algonquin Books of Chapel Hill

2013

Published by
Algonquin Books of Chapel Hill
Post Office Box 2225
Chapel Hill, North Carolina 27515-2225

a division of
Workman Publishing
225 Varick Street
New York, New York 10014

Library of Congress Cataloging-in-Publication Data
Henry, David, [date]
Furious cool : Richard Pryor and the world that made him /
by David Henry and Joe Henry.—First edition
pages cm
ISBN 978-1-61620-078-7
1. Pryor, Richard, 1940–2005. 2. Comedians—United
States—Biography. 3. Motion picture actors and actresses—
United States—Biography. I. Henry, Joe. II. Title.
PN2287.P77H46 2013
792.702'8092—dc23
[B]   2013019665

10 9 8 7 6 5 4 3 2 1
First Edition

For Clare & Melanie

AUTHORS' NOTE

Intending no disrespect and feeling no need to feign journalistic objectivity, it simply feels false to refer to our subject by anything other than his Christian name. For those of us who first encountered him in the early seventies, he will always be Richard. Even in the days of Nixon, Brautigan, Burton, and Leakey, he was, as the *Village Voice*'s Greg Tate wrote in memoriam, "the only Richard you could possibly be talking about."

And if there is still one hellish, truly accursed thing
in our time, it is our artistic dallying with forms,
instead of being like victims burnt at the
stake, signaling through the flames.

—ANTONIN ARTAUD

ψ

CONTENTS

PRELUDE

He emerges from a side window as though shot from a cannon: exploding free and trailing smoke.

To anyone passing by, he may appear to be following a daily routine as he bounds around to the front of the house and moves down Hayvenhurst Avenue; yet he is dazed, burning, a dim torch that flares and sputters against the flat glare of a summer afternoon.

A call has gone out. Sirens begin to sound in the distance. There are few pedestrians on the sidewalk, but several cars stalled in the crawling traffic begin to take notice:

A man is stumbling alone down the street, disoriented, arms raised, heading west.

There is smoke rising from his hair and body.

He looks familiar.

People cry out when he joins them at a corner, smoldering, waiting to cross. As he moves on between halting cars they call after him, using his first name, as if he were a neighbor or relative.

Hey, wha—? Richard!

But he keeps moving.

Finally, a police cruiser rolls up next to him, keeping pace. When the officers' shouts get no response, the one in the passenger's seat vaults from the moving car into the street and begins jogging alongside him, calmly pleading with the burning man to stop.

"If I stop, I'll die," he answers, making odd sense of a moment that refuses any other kind.

INTRODUCTION | THE FEAR OF BLACK LAUGHTER

> The wise man never laughs but he trembles.
> —Charles Baudelaire

Laughter is anarchy.

"Are they laughing at us?" the comfortable people ask whenever they hear the downtrodden cavort and make merry. They know something must be amiss. They can feel it. The tide is turning. The earth is wobbling on its axis. There's going to be trouble, you can bet your last dollar on it.

Novelist Ralph Ellison tells the story of a fabled southern town where the whites became so unnerved by expressions of mirth among the black populace they installed "laughing-barrels" labeled FOR COLORED ONLY throughout the town square. Any Negro who felt a laugh coming on was behooved — *pro bono publico* — to thrust his head into the nearest one and there relieve himself. Presumably, this was a frequent occurrence. These receptacles not only spared "many a black sore behind," Ellison explained, but "performed the far more important function of providing whites a means of saving face before the confounding, persistent, and embarrassing mystery of black laughter."

Paul Mooney will tell you: white folks love jokes about Mexicans, Puerto Ricans, Chinese, Hindus, Africans, Polacks, guineas, Martians, midgets, Eskimos, vampires, anybody but themselves. Even today, when Richard Pryor's lifelong friend does jokes about white people in his act, he pauses to watch while they gather up their handbags and call for their checks. "There they go," Mooney tells his audience, "like scared little rabbits. They'll get the fuck out of a place. White people can't take it. It ain't funny when it's about them."

––––––––––

We tried not to laugh.

It was a Friday night, August 17, 1973. We had read in the *Akron Beacon Journal* TV listing that Richard Pryor would be hosting NBC's *The Midnight Special*. As the local affiliate's late news ended, we placed both microphones of our new reel-to-reel stereo tape deck (ordered from the Sears catalog and paid for by tag-team summer lawn mowing, assisted by our pal, Jamie Worrell) up next to the single speaker of our family's color console TV (still a big deal at the time) and eased our way back to the couch, careful not to make a sound. We didn't want to spoil the recording. We would laugh later, listening to the playback in our bedroom upstairs.

As a couple of twelve- and fifteen-year-old white kids — sons of the South and sons of an automotive engineer (himself born of Tennessee dirt farmers who migrated to the Carolina textile mills), living in a semi-rural township outside of Akron, Ohio, in the early 1970s — Richard's blunt rants on race ought to have tightened our jaws, left us bristling with indignation. Instead, he did just the opposite. Suburban Ohio alienated us. Richard was a beacon that said, *Take heart. Stay human. You are not alone.*

For us, Richard was a gateway artist, opening the door to worlds of music, storytelling, and poetry that had been thriving just out of sight, humming beneath our radar. Suddenly we were awake to how African American culture had shaped everything we knew and loved. We heard it first in the music: Mick Jagger and Keith Richards, it became clear, desperately coveted the strange fruits of the black man's Delta. Bob Dylan seized upon those same fruits as a juggler might, keeping them deftly aloft while both blurring and affirming the through-line from blues to beat poetry. Eric Clapton, John Mayall, and Jimmy Page viewed them in awe, faces pressed to the glass of some imaginary museum of natural history. Johnny Winter, John Fogerty, Bonnie Raitt, Randy Newman, Janis Joplin, and Captain Beefheart borrowed it as freely as a neighbor would a cup of sugar.

Richard Pryor's genius first blossomed in the steamy whorehouse atmosphere brought north when his grandmother's generation migrated from Louisiana and took root in that most unlikely emblem of middle America, Peoria, Illinois, then a wide-open river town peopled by street-corner storytellers, hustlers, pimps, prostitutes, vaudeville had-beens, high-minded church folk, politicians on the take, itinerant show people, and riverboat tradesmen who all passed through his grandmother's brothel, his grandfather's candy store, or his father's pool hall. By embodying such characters onstage, Richard gave voice to a raucous and jubilant side of life as authentically American as Mark Twain's but one kept hidden away from the majority of white America.

His path led him through a dizzying patchwork of transient Americana, from touring all-black clubs on the midwestern Chitlin' Circuit along with the stripper who inspired Duke Ellington's "Satin Doll," crossing paths with "X-rated" comics such as Redd Foxx, LaWanda Page, Mantan Moreland, Moms Mabley, Skillet & LeRoy, to Greenwich Village coffeehouses of the early sixties where he shared billings with the likes of Bob Dylan, Woody Allen, and George Carlin; from Sunday nights on *The Ed Sullivan Show* and weekday afternoons on *Merv Griffin* to Rat Pack–era Las Vegas; from trendy West Hollywood clubs in the late sixties and guest roles on sitcoms and TV dramas such as *Wild Wild West* and *The Partridge Family* to his self-imposed exile in Berkeley at the dawn of the seventies where he found his authentic, liberated voice through mind-expanding friendships with the founders of the Black Panther Party and San Francisco literati.

The best of Richard's immediate predecessors — Dick Gregory, Bill Cosby, Godfrey Cambridge, Timmie Rogers, Moms Mabley — retreated to relatively safe, homogenized material, scrubbed clean of earthier elements, when we saw them perform for a nationwide audience on afternoon talk shows. But Richard brought out the raw tall tales, mother-rhymes, boasts, toasts, and lies — the "jokes black folks tell on themselves" (Langston Hughes) in the privacy of pool halls, barber-shops, barbecue joints, back porches — and paraded them naked out in front of everybody. There was no telling what he might say.

This was no small breach of the wall. Louie Robinson, writing about Richard's short-lived NBC variety show in the January 1978 issue of *Ebony* complained that one could not sit back and relax while watching *The Richard Pryor Show*. "Instead, you perched on the edge of your seat, ready just in case Richard at any moment did something that would make it necessary for every Black person in America to suddenly drop whatever he or she was doing and run like hell!"

—————

At times, both of us have wondered whether Richard Pryor was truly ours to approach, ours to embrace as a game-changing force, ours to hear as a part of our collective heart's voice, an authentic part of our heritage. When John Cage (another voice in our choir) first began studying Zen Buddhism, he too wondered if it was really *his* to study. "I don't worry anymore about that," Cage came to say, and neither do we. We knew Richard as we did and felt not a racial but a human kinship to his fears and desires, triumphs and failures. Like Dizzy Gillespie said of Charlie Parker, "Bird's music was a gift, and if you could hear it you could have it."

Richard Pryor's gift was Truth. He turned a gritty corner one day as a young man in Peoria, Illinois, and the Truth was on him like a feral alley cat. And he held on to this cat; made a coat out of it and wore it to New York; hid his secret heart underneath it and opened it like a curtain on-stage; wore it when he read Malcolm X, scrapped with Huey P. Newton; when he got high with Miles, sparred with Ali, and went down on Pam Grier. Then he tried to pretend he'd never seen it before . . . swore he didn't know *whose* coat it was; gifted it to girlfriends who all threw it back in his face. When he married up with a freebase pipe, he and his glass bride huddled under that coat for days on end. It kept in the vapors and blocked out the sun until, angry and tired, beset by demons and filled with self-loathing, he doused himself with rum and lit the fuse, melting that animal spirit deep into his own. He tried to swear it off, but by then Truth had gotten under his skin, was a part of him, even if he couldn't live up to its message.

We didn't set out to write the definitive cradle-to-grave biography of Richard Pryor, and haven't. We chose instead to go exploring, to mine the soil out of which he grew, and map the cultural landscape from which he emerged.

What we found more inspiring than the romanticized idea of genius that springs fully formed out of thin air is the evidence that Richard found all the materials he would ever need among the hair clippings, blood-clumped sawdust, and cigarette butts he swept up from the barbershops, meatpacking plants, and pool halls — blowing in the wind, as it were — in his native Peoria. He gathered it all together and deliberately, playfully rearranged and assembled that cast-off detritus into something unexpected, beautiful, frightening, and new. (Even the god of our Old Testament shaped creation not out of nothing but out of chaos.) Richard spun his out of straw. And when he held this thing up for all to see, not only did we all recognize and embrace it, we could no longer remember a time when we had been without it. That this gift came from a broken and tragic figure should come as no surprise. It is the cracks, after all — the holes in the firmament — that let in the light.

The greatest tragedy of Richard Pryor may have been that he was content to be labeled a "comic." We heard this over and over in our interviews with Richard's colleagues and idolaters: he was beyond mere comedy. If you read transcripts of his breakthrough routines, you'll find nothing remotely funny in the words themselves as printed on the page. It was all in his delivery, his empathy, his willingness to give himself fully to the characters he portrayed, and to let them take possession of him — so much so that it seems blasphemous to speak of "other comedians" when discussing Richard Pryor. There are no others. No one else could do onstage what Richard Pryor did. As his friend David Brenner says, "He stands alone."

Stories abound from the early days of radio when white comics would trek uptown to the Apollo, pencil and paper in hand, and help themselves to the best gags. One clear mark of Richard's genius is that his comedy remains absolutely theft-proof. No one else could do his material. No one else would dare.

We watched in real time as Richard's genius outstripped the confines of stand-up comedy, ran circles around it, danced on its grave, even while — in the same way a length of rope can let you know about a knot's design — it was his comic persona that allowed us to see what his genius was all about, which was this: it reflected our flawed and brutal humanity back to us as something we could both love and forgive.

That it still accomplishes this in his absence is testament to the fact that the truth Richard spoke lived outside of his particular alchemy and his frail, fleeting times. But if truth is luminous, Richard was, for a while, the wiry, fragile filament, humming in a glass bulb. A brilliant and ferocious light danced through him. We laughed in private, as he invited us to, all the while vaguely sensing what novelist Walter Mosley would later state plain: Richard Pryor wasn't joking.

FURIOUS COOL

PART **ONE**

A NATIVE SON OF WISTFUL VISTA

"Get *out!*"

That whispery, strangulated voice belongs to an emaciated and prematurely frail Richard Pryor doing a dead-on impersonation of the demonic spirit from *The Amityville Horror.* He was in a good mood, playfully dismissing the questions put to him by Peoria *Journal Star* columnist Phil Luciano backstage at Washington, D.C.'s Constitution Hall on New Year's Eve 1992 midway through a comeback tour that would prove to be his last.

Once upon a time a lanky and loose-limbed Richard had bounded onto the stage with acrobatic grace, shape-shifting himself into all manner of people and things: pious preachers, rum-soaked raconteurs, white guys on acid, drunken brawlers, drooling junkies, angry black militants, bullet-punctured automobile tires, an infant at the moment of birth, a deer alerted by the sounds of hunters crunching leaves in the forest, copulating monkeys, police dogs, an especially potent strain of a Vietnamese venereal disease — even his own heart as it threatened to kill him, forcing him down on one knee to beg for his life. But on this night he made his way across the stage in cautious, shuffling steps, flanked by an alert pair of handlers, one on each arm. Universally hailed as the greatest stand-up of all time, he performed this final tour sitting down.

More than thirty-seven hundred people paid $37.50 apiece to see what reviewers of earlier stops on the tour had warned would be a brief, disjointed performance. During his show at Detroit's State Theatre, he

3

had struggled to read from cue cards fanned out on the floor in front of him while a onetime fiancée in the audience fought back tears. Kicking off the tour in San Francisco months earlier, he had trembled visibly and slurred his words. And when he segued into his most famous character, the street-wizened Mudbone, he barely needed to alter his voice. After a mere twenty minutes, he had to be assisted off the stage to prolonged applause. People were just happy to see him, to thank him. That was all. But on this particular night in D.C., he showed more of his old self, lasting a full forty-five minutes. He seemed stronger, funnier, as he confronted the ravaging effects of multiple sclerosis head-on. "I got some shit here that fucks with me real bad. This is a thing, like, God said to me, 'Slooow down.' Well, fuck, I was going *that* fast?"

Onstage, the man was fearless, prepared to reveal anything. During his show at the Circle Star Theatre in San Carlos, California, a woman in the audience called out, "Does that shit mess with your sex life?" and he ran with it.

It's something when your dick be hard, then look at you and laugh and go away and go, "Aw, fuck it." And it looks like my dick gets scared to death when it sees some pussy. My dick gets hard sometimes, like I get ready to play and masturbate, and my dick will look at me like, "Come on, Rich . . ." It's a bitch when your dick get hard and there's nothing you can do but say, "I can remember . . ." And I have it in my hand. I know I've got it! And the dick be waiting for me to stroke it so it can die. You guys are laughing but I'm telling you this shit fuck with your johnson!

There's something that happens to your bladder. I can be out on Sunset talking with eight or nine womens and I start pissin'. That shit be running down my boots . . . I say, "Damn, baby . . ." She say, "It's alright." How come people always say it's alright when it ain't them? And you have piss trailing a mile and a half.

After the D.C. show, Richard's face lit up when an assistant introduced Luciano to him backstage.

"Really? You're from the *Star*?"

Up close, he seemed smaller than he had on stage. His fifty-one-year-old body scarred by third-degree burns and ravaged by the early onset of multiple sclerosis, his rheumy eyes magnified by oversized glasses that dwarfed his shrunken but still-iconic face. The star seemed genuinely awed that a writer from his hometown paper would come all this way to see his show.

Within moments, though, a swarm of hangers-on invaded the room and he was back on again, performing for the benefit of the room, cracking one-liners in answer to Luciano's questions, killing any chance for a genuine exchange between the two.

Asked about his health, Richard deadpanned, "I'm gonna die one day."

"Do you feel happy?"

"I'm here," he said, "so I'm all right."

And so on.

That final question Luciano put to him was this: "Do you have any message for the folks back in Peoria?"

Richard answered in his horror-movie rasp: "Get *out!*"

That was it. Get out.

———

"My home's in Peoria," he told a sparse crowd at the hungry i in San Francisco's North Beach neighborhood in 1966. "Whatever you think of when you hear the name, that's what it's like."

Usually, people applaud when an entertainer mentions his hometown. If it's Brooklyn, the crowd goes wild. But Peoria? "Last night," he told them, "somebody threw up."

Peoria. That famously average embodiment of Middle American values, three-time winner of the National Civic League's All-America City Award. Peoria has long been a demographer's dream, a city-sized applause meter reliably registering what the great unwashed will embrace or believe, what they will buy and what they won't. As the largest city on the Illinois River, it was a major stop for musicians and vaudeville troupes traveling between Chicago and St. Louis. In the days of vaudeville the old saw was that if an act went over in Peoria, it would play anywhere. Hence, "Will it play in Peoria?" became a catchphrase of the uniquely American theatrical phenomenon that evolved out of blackface minstrelsy, medicine shows, olio, and dime museums and provided a livelihood for itinerant jugglers, plate spinners, ventriloquists, crooners, baggy-pant comics, acrobats, barbershop quartets, hoochie-coochie dancers, human oddities, and animal acts for nearly a century, roughly from the mid-1800s through the 1930s when radio stole America's heart away and held it hostage in front rooms and parlors. Unlike vaudeville itself, the phrase has endured on Madison Avenue and in political campaigns.

Peoria prided itself in being seen as a model city, a coded phrase that meant, "We have our Negroes under control," Richard would often say. Yet things were decidedly more lax on North Washington Street where Richard spent his childhood. Hookers, winos, gamblers, musicians, politicians, and street-corner men populated both Pop's Pool Hall, owned by his grandfather, and the brothels run by his grandmother. From the 1920s through the 1950s, Peoria was awash in gambling halls, speakeasies, whorehouses, and corruption, a haven for gangsters and bootleggers. Known as Roaring Peoria, it was "a wide-open river town in the old meaning of the word," says retired police chief Allen Andrews.

———————

In a 1977 *New York Times* profile headlined "Richard Pryor, King of the Scene Stealers," author Joyce Maynard wrote, "Pryor has been given to saying that he was raised in a brothel, which is evidently not the case."

Maynard gave no reason for doubting the stories Richard told of his upbringing, but she wasn't the only one. Perhaps the idea that a red-light district could prosper openly in America's model city during the wholesome Eisenhower era simply beggared belief. Yet a federal report issued in the early 1950s cataloged 132 brothels operating in and around Peoria's "Aiken Alley" alone.

Aiken Alley was not an alley at all but the popular name given to a notorious stretch of Aiken Avenue that ran west from Briss Collins's tavern at the corner of Franklin and Jefferson, down to where it intersected with Reed Street.

Whorehouses such as the ones Richard's grandmother ran weren't just outlets for illicit sex; they were part of the fabric that held African American neighborhoods together. Playwright and performance artist Jovelyn Richards learned the lore of brothels from one of those prostitutes who went by the name of Satin Doll, immortalized in song by Duke Ellington.

> The madam and the other ladies took care of the community around them, of the families of the women whose men didn't have steady work . . . The madam would pay the grocery store to deliver eggs and milk to families, and loved the fact they didn't know where these were coming from, that they could make up their own stories about how the box of groceries or the coal got to be on the front porch.

As a child of the fifties, Richard felt a mind-messing disconnect between his own surroundings and life as depicted on TV shows such as *The Life of Riley* and *Father Knows Best*. "On television people talked about having happy lives," he wrote in *Pryor Convictions*, "but in the world in which I grew up, happiness was a moment rather than a state of being. . . . It never stayed long enough for you to get to know it good. Just a taste here and there. A kiss, a sniff, a stroke, a snort."

The gleaming postwar automobiles, big as boats, favored by the city's upper crust, would likely have drawn attention in a neighborhood like Richard's had they not been such a commonplace sight parked along the curb. Onstage, years later, Richard would recall playing in his front yard when some untouchable white man would "drive up and say, 'Hello, little boy, is your mother home? I want a blow job.'"

"That," said Richard, "was our mayor."

The joke was barely an exaggeration. Mayor Edward Nelson "Dearie" Woodruff, who served eleven terms as Peoria's mayor over the course of nineteen elections spanning forty-two years, presided over a brazen administration that imposed a strict schedule of "fines" for various illegalities, including, but not limited to, gambling and prostitution. The mayor famously defended the city's thriving brothel trade by saying, "You can make prostitution illegal, but you can't make it unpopular." One December, when the city council authorized a crackdown on the red-light district, the mayor objected on moral grounds, arguing that it would be "unchristian" to shutter the brothels so close to Christmas.

To give Peoria its due, let it be said that Abraham Lincoln publicly denounced slavery for the first time in a speech delivered there in 1854. The first African American ever to vote in the United States cast his ballot in Peoria on April 4, 1870. The original mold strain for penicillin was discovered in Peoria. And, in 1945, early civil rights activist Rev. C. T. Vivian joined forces with Barton Hunter, a white minister at West Bluff Christian Church, in leading a nonviolent direct-action campaign to integrate Bishop's Cafeteria on Main Street. Vivian and Hunter organized their efforts a full decade before Martin Luther King Jr. led the Montgomery bus boycott following Rosa Parks's refusal to comply with a Jim Crow law that required her to give up her seat to a white man. That she did so on Richard Pryor's fifteenth birthday hardly seems worth noting, but there it is. As John Cage said: "Everything we come across is to the point."

Peoria is also the city where Paul Robeson was banned from performing a concert just two days after the House Committee on Un-American Activities cited him a Communist Party sympathizer, where a fourteen-year-old Charles Manson served his first jail time for robbing a grocery store, and where Richard Pryor's 1993 comeback tour abruptly fizzled out for lack of ticket sales.

Buoyed by big turnouts elsewhere along the tour and by the outpouring of affection from his audiences, Richard agreed to an additional string of midwestern dates. Among them was a June 11 show at the Peoria Civic Center, marking what would be his first hometown performance in nearly twenty years. But, then, just three days before the date, Richard abruptly canceled the show, along with the remainder of his tour. Clearly stung by reports of sluggish tickets sales (civic center spokeswoman Amy Blain declined to say how many of the twenty-five-dollar seats had been sold), Richard's spokespeople offered up the hastily concocted excuse that he needed time to prepare for an upcoming television appearance. Transparently false because his next TV role didn't come until 1995 when he received an Emmy nomination for his portrayal of a multiple sclerosis patient on an episode of the CBS hospital drama *Chicago Hope.*

Peoria has yet to make peace with Richard, his street-level profanity, his frank sexuality, his fury, or his wanton drug use. Even today, the town barely acknowledges him.

In October 2001, while Richard languished in deteriorating health in his Encino, California, home, confined to a wheelchair where he spent his days watching a DVD of *The Silence of the Lambs* on repeat play, the Peoria City Council begrudgingly voted 6–5 in favor of renaming a seven-block stretch of a nondescript residential street Richard Pryor Place. In 2011, more than a half decade after Richard's death, when Phil Luciano wrote a column suggesting that the city choose a more fitting site to commemorate its most famous son — the city's new arts center, perhaps, or a major thoroughfare — his readers responded thus:

> I have a perfect suggestion: Match a memorial with his mind and his mouth. In other words, find a nice sewer somewhere and name it after him. — Wally

> He was just like any other foul-mouthed comedian. Some of his stuff was funny, most wasn't. There was absolutely nothing special about him. So he came from Peoria, who the hell cares? At the end of the day he's just another semi funny, dead drug user. — AM

> I'd hate to plan the Pryor exhibit in the new museum. Exactly how does one "honor" this man and still keep the exhibit rated "G"?

Elementary schools will make up the majority of attendees. Do you leave out the facts that he was raised in a whorehouse, that he made profanity funny and that he often joked about his illegal drug abuse? — Anne

To the reader Anne, Luciano replied: "Leave that out? Why? Pryor didn't glorify hookers, drugs or abuse — he put a spotlight on it. Maybe that's why many Peorians never liked Pryor: They didn't like what he made them see."

"I get this kind of crap every time I write about Pryor," says Luciano, a transplanted Chicagoan. "People always say, 'Why don't you ever write about Fibber McGee?' I say, 'Because nobody gives a fuck about Fibber McGee.'"

Fibber McGee, children, was a character created by Peoria native Jim Jordan who costarred with his wife and Peoria high school sweetheart Marian Driscoll in the radio sitcom *Fibber McGee and Molly* which aired on NBC from 1935 to 1959. One of the longest-running and most successful radio shows of its time, it depicted the foibles of daily life in the fictional midwestern town of Wistful Vista.

Peoria was also home to feminist author Betty Friedan, musician Dan Fogelberg, comedian Sam Kinison, and, most happily for our purposes, Charles Correll, the cocreator of *Amos 'N Andy*.

When Correll and his vaudeville partner, Freeman Gosden, were offered the opportunity to create a radio series on WGN in Chicago in 1928, it seemed natural, Correll said, that they should continue to perform in the same black dialect they had developed on vaudeville stages in the South. "We might just as well have done Irish or Jewish dialect," he said, "but we knew that of Negroes." Besides, Correll maintained, he and Gosden were laughing *with* blacks, not at them.

Regardless of who may have been laughing at or along with whom, the fifteen-minute broadcasts of *Amos 'N Andy* drew huge audiences at 7:00 p.m. *every week night* for fifteen years from 1928 until 1943 when it switched over to a half-hour weekly format. It was said, with claims of only slight exaggeration, that one could take an after-dinner stroll through almost any American town and not miss a single line of the show as it wafted from the open windows and front porches of an estimated forty million homes.

When CBS proposed a TV version of the show, the network, in a television first, cast African American actors for all the roles. Chief among them were Alvin Childress as Amos, Spencer Williams as Andy, Ernestine Wade as Sapphire, and Tim Moore as George "Kingfish" Stevens — veteran vaudeville comics all. However tempting it may have been for Correll and Gosden to play the principal roles themselves, their business sense prevailed. The television era, they knew, would not tolerate white actors in blackface.

Despite drawing huge audiences, the TV incarnation of *Amos 'N Andy* survived only two seasons. CBS programmers later acknowledged their miscalculation in airing the series premiere during the 1951 national convention of the NAACP, a coincidence that prompted the group, in a fervor of reform, to pass a resolution condemning the show's depiction of African Americans — or "colored people," as the NAACP preferred — and filed for a court injunction that would have forced CBS to stop the show. (It's worth noting that the NAACP's national office had declined to endorse a similar protest launched by the *Pittsburgh Courier* against the radio show in 1931.)

In a 1975 *Ebony* article titled "Black Humor — Full Circle from Slave Quarters to Richard Pryor," film and broadcast historian Donald Bogle pointed out the irony of an integrationist movement insisting that blacks surrender their own rich heritage as the price of admission into an unwelcoming white culture.

How fitting is it that, after thriving twenty-seven years on radio starring white actors who caricatured black voices, the TV version, featuring the medium's first all-black cast, fell under a storm of civil rights protests? Doubling down on this irony, the Gosden and Correll–voiced program continued to chug along as a weekly radio sitcom until 1955 and then as a nightly disc-jockey show until 1960.

At the time Richard canceled his 1993 hometown comeback performance at Peoria's downtown civic center, it was the only venue in the
town with the capacity to house such an event. Yet, when Richard was
born in 1940, the city of barely 105,000 people boasted more than two-
dozen performance theaters that had sprung up during vaudeville's hey-
day. For longtime Peorians, the names of those theaters — among them
the Duchess, the Majestic, the Deluxe, and the Palace — still conjure up
images of bright marquees and glamorous performers.

Although black performers were sometimes seen in these vaudeville
theaters, black audiences were not. For their own entertainment, they
went instead to taverns, after-hours clubs, and sporting houses.

As the audience for black entertainment grew too large to ignore, a
group of enlightened businessmen in the early 1900s established theater
circuits exclusively for African American performers. Chief among them
was TOBA (Theatre Owners Booking Association — or, if you asked
the performers, Tough on Black Asses), founded in 1907 by Memphis-
based Italian businessman F. A. Barrasso.

Performers on the TOBA circuit might play as many as ten shows
a day while paying their own travel expenses and seeking out their
own accommodations, often staying in private homes since Jim Crow
laws barred them from most hotels, restaurants, and restrooms. Yet
TOBA afforded many the opportunity to play to all-black audiences —
although (nice twist here) some theaters roped off small sections for
white patrons.

Initially, nearly all TOBA comics appeared in blackface, as they had
done since the days of minstrelsy, covering their faces with burnt cork or
black greasepaint and using a white flour compound to accentuate the
whites of their eyes and teeth. In effect, blacks adopted the same techniques whites used to caricature blacks. It was one of the few areas in
which skin color made no difference. Everyone "blacked up" for comic
effect. The first time vaudeville comedian Johnny Hudgins worked the
Apollo without blacking up, he said backstage that he had felt naked
out there.

Harold Cromer, one-half of the famed team Stump and Stumpy, said, "What people today don't understand is why the artists did all the things they used to do. [Performing in blackface] is what you did if you wanted to eat."

The times demanded that black entertainers performing before white audiences restrict themselves to acting in skits or in teams. They could crack wise with each other, exchange banter with straight men, or enact a scene, but black performers on the Keith vaudeville circuit — the largest and most reputable circuit of its day — were explicitly instructed not to address anyone in the audience. Any black performer attempting to elicit a personal response would be making an assumption of equality intolerable to most whites at the time. Not until the early 1950s did black comics, led by Dick Gregory, speak directly to white audiences as peers without the buffer of clownish costumes or in the guise of a character. The few TOBA-era comics who adopted the monologue approach pioneered by the likes of Jack Benny, Milton Berle, and Fred Allen soon found themselves shunned by white booking agents and remained largely unknown outside of black clubs and theaters.

The exception to this rule, and a notable one at that, was Charley Case, an African American songwriter and vaudeville comedian of the late 1800s famous for his monologues, which he performed in blackface while passing for white. Some historians credit Case as having single-handedly invented what we now know as stand-up comedy. (His only likely rival to that claim would be Mark Twain, who began a wildly popular sideline career as an after-dinner speaker with an impromptu address at a printers' banquet in Keokuk, Iowa, on January 17, 1856.)

Because of the restrictions imposed by white theater owners, hundreds of black entertainers — many now recognized as the finest performers of their time — flocked to TOBA, among them Silas Green from New Orleans, Pigmeat Markham, Butterbeans & Susie, Pen & Ink, Moms Mabley, Slappy White, Johnny Hudgins, Miller & Lyles (widely credited as the inspiration for *Amos 'N Andy*), Stump and Stumpy, Dusty Fletcher, and greatest of them all, the Jamaican-born Bert Williams.

Williams was the most popular entertainer of his day and arguably the first African American superstar. Erudite, highly educated, and aspiring to theatrical greatness, Williams quickly learned that he could draw greater laughs if he dropped his refined manners and kept his learning to himself. According to vaudeville historian Trav S. D., Williams found it much easier to lose his inhibitions and play the clown when he donned blackface. W. C. Fields recognized both sides of the dilemma when he declared Williams "the funniest man I ever saw and the saddest man I ever knew."

Williams built his act around a character he described as "the shiftless darky to the fullest extent, his fun, his philosophy. Show this artless darky a book and he won't know what it is all about. He can't read. He cannot write. But ask him a question and he'll answer it with a philosophy that's got something."

Adopting a style of storytelling that recalled Joel Chandler Harris's Uncle Remus tales, Williams recounted the exploits of one Spruce Bigsby, a street-savvy savant. Like Richard's character Mudbone, Williams's Bigsby played off the sentimentalized image of the tale-spinning Negro who had migrated from a bygone South only to find himself beguiled by life in the industrial North.

Bert Williams's most enduring character, however, may be his charlatan minister Elder Eatmore, a direct forebear of Richard's recurring preacher, as evidenced in this excerpt from Williams's recording of "Elder Eatmore's Sermon on Generosity":

> The Lord loveth a cheerful giver. Tonight, my friends, you can omit the cheerful. The truth is the light, and here is the truth: y'all is way back in my salary and something has got to be done here this evening. . . . Because if something ain't done, your shepherd is gone. That's all. THAT IS ALL. I admit that times is tight because when there used to be a ham coming here and fowl or two there from different members of this flock, I managed to make out fair to middlin'. They all comes to he who waits. But you all done learnt

me that self-preservation is the first law of he who gets it. And the Lord helps they who helps their selves.

Everything has got so scientifical nowadays, that they done commenced building such things as smokehouses and hen houses out of pure concrete. And they've invented locks for them the same as the combination on the First National Bank. True, true, that makes it harder for all of us. It's pretty nigh ruint me. And my friends I need, I *need* . . . T'ain't no use talkin' about what I need I needs everything, from my hat *down,* and from my overcoat *in.*

When Richard created his version of this archetypal preacher, the truth poured out of him. And the truth was he had nothing but contempt for the needs of his flock and couldn't be bothered to offer up even a pretense of compassion or moral rectitude.

The Walker family brought in their son and they said to me, 'Can you heal our son?' Well, I apologize because he's a big wally-head boy and I wasn't going to touch the motherfucker, I'm tellin' you that right now. Little nigger had a head about this big and they wheeled him in his head was bobbing back and forth. I was not about to touch the motherfucker because that shit's contagious. Give the nigger a big hat or something — leave me alone!

And some of the deacons come down on me for that. But I'd like to say to the crippled peoples that come here, can't you find another church to go to? Goddamn! You come in here knockin' shit down, breakin' up furniture and shit. Learn how to crawl! Shit! And you deaf and dumb motherfuckers who can't talk, we don't need you here! All that "ah-whoo ah-hah" shit — kiss my ass!

Silent movies wounded vaudeville. Still, the two managed to cohabit peaceably for a time, sharing bills in the same venues, although the performers could not help but notice how many new theatres were being built without stages, only screens. Then radio came along and killed vaudeville completely.

With the advent of radio, people could hear their favorite stars without even leaving the house. Milton Berle and Jack Benny entertained far more people in a single broadcast than they could have in a lifetime out on the road. Those who made the leap to radio found themselves suddenly flush with cash — and frantic to come up with new material every week or, in some cases, every night. In contrast, a vaudevillian could live off one well-honed routine for an entire career.

Such was the case with Clinton "Dusty" Fletcher who performed a solo skit called "Open the Door, Richard" for more than twenty years. The premise: Fletcher's character returns to his rooming house late at night without his key. He pounds on the door and calls out to his roommate to let him in. The audience never sees or hears Richard. He may not even be in there. The skit inspired a hugely popular song of the 1940s and for years remained a popular catchphrase.

Jazz saxophonist Jack McVea had seen Fletcher perform the bit hundreds of times in the early 1940s as the opening act for Lionel Hampton's band. On a rainy afternoon in Portland, Orgeon, McVea, in need of material for his own band, set a simplified version of the skit to music. When McVea recorded the song in October 1946, it went through the roof.

The song's refrain cropped up in routines by Jack Benny, Phil Harris, Jimmy Durante, numerous Bugs Bunny cartoons, in ads for everything from ale to perfume, and generally made life miserable for anyone named Richard.*

---

*When Bob Dylan and the Band reinvented the song during the raucous 1967 recording sessions in West Saugerties, New York, that would come to be known as *The Basement Tapes,* Dylan changed the title to "Open the Door, Homer," even while keeping "Open the door, Richard" as the song's refrain, because, it is said, the Band's keyboardist Richard Manuel detested the original song, having been taunted with the phrase his whole life. And Allen Ginsberg, no less, declared that "Open the Door, Richard" had influenced his poetry during the pivotal road trips he took with Jack Kerouac in the late 1940s: "I would say 'Open the Door, Richard' opened the door to a new sound and music, to new consciousness."

Time magazine reported that radio comedians "had only to mention the word Richard on the air to put their studio audiences in stitches." The phrase became part of the early civil rights movement, as the title of an editorial in the *Los Angeles Sentinel* calling for black representation in city government. In Georgia, college students marched to the state capitol demanding the resignation of segregationist governor Herman Talmadge with banners that read OPEN THE DOOR, HERMAN.

With the song's success, Dusty Fletcher emerged from semiretirement to claim authorship, saying he had written the skit after seeing a drunk thrown out of a railroad station bar in South Carolina. The ejected patron, Fletcher recalled, stood out in the street and yelled for the bartender to let him back in.

Once the song broke, it seemed every singer and band in the country rushed to record it. Within months of McVea's hit, at least eighteen versions were released by the likes of Louis Jordan and his Tympani Five, Dick Haymes, the Pied Pipers, Jo Stafford, Burl Ives, and Bing Crosby. Both Count Basie and nightclub trio the Three Flames scored number-one hits with the song. There was even a Yiddish version by a quartet known as the Yokels.

But, at the end of the day, "Richard" belongs to Dusty Fletcher. The recordings were mere novelty numbers, whereas Fletcher had honed his stage performance to a work of art incorporating pantomime, pratfalls, and an acrobatic balancing act atop a freestanding ladder. Happily, it was captured twice on film, as a ten-minute short directed by William Forest Crouch, and as a vignette in the Cab Calloway movie *Hi-De-Ho.*

Fletcher portrayed his nameless character as a drunk who mutters to himself between shouts up to his unresponsive roommate. In each segment of the routine he peels back layer upon layer of a complicated man gamely soldiering on with his threadbare existence in a harsh, uncaring world.

Critic Jake Austen notes that Fletcher's work, like Richard's, dealt with "fairly horrifying subjects: abject poverty, extreme alcoholism, spousal beating, homicide, and other rib ticklers." Traces of genetic

material from "Open the Door" show up in Richard's "Wino & Junkie,"
the signature piece he developed over a period of several years. It grew
along with him, becoming deeper, ever more fearless, and less dependent on jokes. By the time Richard recorded it for his 1974 LP *That
Nigger's Crazy*, there was nothing overtly funny about it.

> WINO: You better lay off that narcotic, nigger, that shit done made
> you null and void. I ain't lyin', boy. What's wrong with you? Why
> don't you straighten up and get a job?
>
> JUNKIE: Get a job? Motherfucker, you talkin' to the kid, baby. Shit!
> I worked five years in a row when I was in the joint pressing them
> motherfuckin' license plates. I'm a license plate-pressing mother-
> fucker too, baby. Where a nigger gonna get a job out here pressing
> license plates?

Black comics learn their craft on the street corner, Richard once said.
"That's where niggers rehearse. If you want to be a speaker, you rehearse
your speeches. You tell your stories. Singers start there. Players run their
game.... That was my stage."

In communities large and small, African Americans found free expression in games of signifying; playing the dozens; and exchanging
raunchy, rhyming tall tales of "bad niggers" like Stagolee, Shine, Petey
Wheatstraw, the Devil's Son-in-Law and trickster characters hark-
ing back to High John the Conqueror, Br'er Rabbit, and the Signifying Monkey. Richard found genius in this cosmology of language and
humor that, up until that time, had kept sanctuary in barbershops, pool
halls, street corners, front porches, and back rooms. Then, to nearly everyone's dismay, he went and paraded it out in front of company.

"White folks don't play enough," Richard contended. "They don't
relax. They don't know how to play the dozens ... nothing."

> We used to have good sessions sometimes. I remember I came up
> with a beaut, man. I killed them one day. We was doing it all day to
> each other, you know? Bang bang — "Your shoes are run over so

much looks like your *ankles* is broke," and shit like that. And I came up with, I called the motherfucker "The Rummage Sale Ranger," you know what I mean? 'Cause that's where he got his clothes. "The Rummage Sale Ranger" — that was a knockout. I saved that one for the last. That ended it.

Black Panther Party minister of justice H. Rap Brown recalled how he and his friends played the dozens for recreation "the way white folks play Scrabble."

> In many ways, though, the Dozens is a mean game because what you try to do is totally destroy somebody else with words . . . It was a bad scene for the dude that was getting humiliated . . . It was like they were humiliated because they were born Black and then they turned around and got humiliated by their own people, which was really all they had left. But that's the way it is. Those that feel most humiliated humiliate others.

Playing the dozens — aka mother-rhyming — has been known to turn deadly. Most often, though, in the words of British author and blues scholar Paul Oliver, young men play the dozens to "work off their excesses of spirits in a harmless and cheerfully pornographic blues-singing competition."

Black humor as practiced in the community or after-hours clubs seldom, if ever, concerned itself with mainstream or non-black existence, either in imitation of it or in reaction to it. As Henry Louis Gates Jr. put it, these performances carried "an invisible racial warning sticker: For domestic consumption only — export strictly prohibited. . . . You don't want white people to see this kind of spectacle; you want them to see the noble dramas of August Wilson, where the injuries and injustices perpetuated by the white man are never far from our consciousness."

Factor in Richard's observation that "white folks get upset when they see us laughing — 'Wha'd'ya think they're doing, Martha? Are they laughing at us?'" and it's likely that the one aspect of black humor whites would find most disconcerting (were we privy to hear it) is how

largely absent they are. Gates, again, describes a production making
the rounds of the Chitlin' Circuit as recently as 1997: "The subject of
racism — or, for that matter, white people — simply never arises." What
black humor concerns itself with most are the immediate problems and
pleasures of everyday life: love, jealousy, sex, death, rivalries, tall tales,
intoxication, and food — the same territory covered in the blues and
other black music, which, praise be to popular recordings, we have in
abundance.

Although the blues has its origins in the music of West Africa, it is
unique to the United States. The music entered the United States by
the port of New Orleans, then migrated upriver to spawn — mutating,
crossbreeding, and adapting to regional conditions as it spread out
through the tributaries. All manner of love songs, folk legends, feats of
derring-do, murder ballads, conjure tales, ghost stories, courtly Euro-
pean balladry, and blues got passed down and passed around, openly
consorting and cross-pollinating with each other.

It was similar to the way the scattered stories and figures that make
up *The Iliad* and *The Odyssey* had been recited, embellished, and bowd-
lerized by generation upon generation of Ageans before someone like
Homer came along with the wit to see what it could be, gathered up all
the strands, wound them together, shook them up in his sorcerer's hat,
and pulled out those epic twin pillars of world literature.

So it was with Richard. In the truest Homeric tradition, he soaked
up everything around him and, by virtue of wise blood or mother wit,
made of it something new. And if it now seems as though that new thing
had been there all along, waiting for someone game enough to grab hold
and take it for a ride, either to see where it would go or how long one
could hang on, that's because it was.

All of which is just to say, as Black Panther Party cofounder Bobby
Seale observed in ascribing the forces that gave rise to the movement, "It
was already going on." And, as Robert Fitzgerald wrote in the postscript
to his translation of Homer's *Odyssey*, "Our poet came late and had su-
premely gifted predecessors."

Skinny and bearded, Richard Pryor holds the stage of a dark basement club, its brick walls lending it the air of a boiler room fallout shelter where a small crowd nervously laughs and awaits an all-clear of something from somewhere. Steaks and peppers are listed for sale on a chalkboard behind him; chicken curry, beer.

There is a silence that follows each jab of a phrase, the mostly white audience puzzled and uncomfortable as Richard sticks and moves, looks for his way inside . . . talking aches and pains, winos and whores and politicians and pimps; catching the clap, and having sucked another man's dick. These are not jokes he tells but character sketches and vignettes that spool out and surprise like a tablecloth snatched off a birdcage, revealing no living bird but something furry and feral in its place, uncomfortably large for its quarters, grunting and pissing.

Richard seems not to register the quiet and discomfort, or he pays it no mind. He keeps watch over his shoulder, is patient and slow as he lets out his line. He weaves fractured scenes above the heads of those in attendance but seems rarely to glance their way. He is already seeing beyond; over them; out.

"THERE'S A BAD MUTHAFUCKA COMIN' YOUR WAY"

In his 1995 memoir *Pryor Convictions*, Richard told how his grandfather Roy Pryor had been crushed in the coupling of two boxcars while working for the railroad in the 1920s — an incident that should have killed any man on the spot. Instead, Richard tells us, the cars parted, his grandfather made his way to a tavern, downed a drink, and *then* died.

Nothing miraculous about that, Richard explained. The man wanted a drink.

Richard apparently had confused his paternal grandfather, LeRoy Pryor, with his maternal great-grandfather, Richard Carter, whose obituary appeared in the *Decatur Daily Review* of September 20, 1925:

RICHARD CARTER DIES OF INJURIES
Colored Man Crushed between Cars

Richard Carter of 1144 South Jackson street died at 4 o'clock Saturday afternoon at the Wabash Employee's hospital from injuries received earlier in the day, when he was crushed between two cars. He was fifty-five years old.

Mr. Carter was one of the well-known colored men of Decatur. He had been here many years and was well liked by those who knew him. He had been employed in the yards of the Wabash roundhouse for a long time. About 11 o'clock Saturday forenoon he was crushed between some cars that were switching in the yards and was so badly injured that he died five hours later.

Richard's grandmother, Rithie Marie Carter, was one of seven children born to Richard Carter and the former Julia Isabelle Piper. She was born sometime in 1899, perhaps in New Orleans, shortly before her family joined the great migration up the Mississippi early in the century. This first wave of African American migrants, employed as musicians or servants on northbound riverboats, jumped ship in the comparatively free Midwest, and Illinois seemed especially appealing. Marie's family settled in Decatur.*

Marie married LeRoy (or Roy) Pryor, a janitor and apartment building caretaker, in Decatur on a Saturday evening in August of 1914 at the home of Elder T. S. Hendershott, pastor of the Church of the Living God.

Further documented facts of LeRoy Pryor's life include his birth on March 21, 1889, in Mexico, Missouri; his plea of guilty to a charge of grand larceny in Macon County, Illinois, in 1928; an arrest for disorderly conduct in Decatur in 1931; his registration for military service in 1942 at the age of fifty-three; and his death on January 15, 1946, in Decatur, Illinois.

One final documented event in LeRoy's life occurred a little more than a year after he and Marie were married, as shown by an item that appeared in the *Decatur Review* of December 6, 1915:

---

*A second wave migration from New Orleans in 1917 proved beneficial in paving the way for Marie Carter's future occupation. Prostitution had been legal in New Orleans' Storyville district until 1917 when the U.S. secretary of war requested that the law be amended to safeguard the health of the multitudes of seamen who came ashore during the first World War. Many of the Crescent City's girls, madams, and pimps went north in search of greener pastures, resulting in a sudden proliferation of brothels in river towns such as Memphis, St. Louis, and yes, Peoria, where officials found it was easier to control prostitution than to stamp it out. Thus it could be said that Richard's grandmother came by her profession honestly.

CLAIMED WIFE ATTENDED BALL

Roy Pryor, Colored, Fined for an Assault on Spouse

Roy Pryor, colored, 362 East Main Street, pleaded guilty before Justice J. Edward Saxton Monday morning to the charge of assaulting his wife and threatening to kill her. He was fined $5.30. Pryor's assault was provoked, it is alleged, by Mrs. Pryor attending a grand ball some place when Pryor wasn't along.

Marie's next public notice appeared in the *Decatur Herald* of October 14, 1929, under the headline "Three Are Arrested in Raid Sunday Night," wherein it was reported that Marie Carter had pleaded guilty to possession of intoxicating liquor, was fined $28.15 by Justice J. G. Allen, and released.

After divorcing from LeRoy in 1929, Marie moved with her four children to Peoria where she soon married Thomas "Pop" Bryant and went into business operating a brothel and doing some bootlegging on the side. Pop ran a gambling operation, a candy store, and later, a saloon and pool hall.

Marie's eldest son, LeRoy "Buck Carter" Pryor Jr. was a Golden Gloves boxing champion in his teens, spent some time traveling between Chicago and East St. Louis, working odd jobs — including a bit of vaudeville singing — then came back to Peoria to take up the family business. He fell in love with Gertrude Thomas, a part-time bookkeeper who also turned tricks in Marie's brothel, and on December 1, 1940, she gave birth to Richard Franklin Lennox Thomas Pryor III. He was called Frankin for the uncle who had prophesied his birth. Thomas, of course, was his mother's maiden name. And Lennox, he would later learn, had been one of his aunt Mexcine's boyfriends.

Richard professed not to know where his mother came up with the name Richard. An odd claim since his father's younger brother and his great-grandfather on his grandma Marie's side were both called Richard. Odder still considering that biographies, reference works, even his own press materials, often identify him as Richard Franklin Lennox Thomas

Pryor III, although, to reckon him as the third in a line of Richards re-
quires making a few zigzags in his family tree and a slight exception to
the rules. No matter. That piling on of names was heavy enough without
a Roman numeral at the end.

With full acknowledgment of how telling were the circumstances, a
grown-up Richard Pryor recalled how he had come to recognize the
draw and power of physical comedy very early on, when, running across
the yard in his new cowboy suit, he slipped in dog shit and set everybody on the front porch howling with laughter. Realizing he was onto
something, he got up and did it again. "And," he would say, "I've been
slippin' in shit ever since."

Richard found he could use his fledgling comic abilities to ingrati-
ate himself with older, tougher kids in the neighborhood or to worm
his way out of scrapes with bullies. But not always. At the age of five,
while playing alone in an alley behind his house, Richard found himself
cornered and sexually molested by a fourteen-year-old bully known as
Hoss. Despite his efforts to avoid further encounters with Hoss, the assaults continued. "I felt violated, humiliated, dirty, fearful, and, most of
all, ashamed." The humiliation got even worse when an older kid in the
neighborhood pulled him aside and told him he shouldn't be sucking
dick. Who else knew?

At the dinner table a few nights later, his father, out of the blue, began
singing "I'm Forever Blowing Bubbles." Richard was mortified. Did his
father know, he wondered. And if he did, why didn't he do something?
Why didn't he cut off Hoss's dick? Did he think this was funny?

Richard never asked his father if he knew or why he sang that song.
He never mentioned Hoss to anyone until he confessed it in his memoir
fifty years later. "Had me a ghost rattling in the attic. It didn't matter that
I lived in a big house behind a gate in Los Angeles, some half a country
from the bricks and bars of the old neighborhood. My ass was haunted
by the image of Hoss's dick." When he returned to Peoria to re-create

scenes from his childhood on location for his semiautobiographical movie *Jo Jo Dancer, Your Life Is Calling,* someone told him that Hoss still lived in town and wanted to see him. "Even though I was a famous and successful comedian, surrounded by big, menacing bodyguards who would've killed at the snap of my fingers, I was seized by that old sense of fear of Hoss telling me to suck his dick." One day during the shoot, Richard came out of his trailer to greet his fans and there was Hoss with his young son, waiting in line for an autograph.

———————

Other scenes from young Richard's early life include:

Finding a dead baby in a shoebox.

Seeing his father shoot a client who had cussed out his grand-mother. Although Buck emptied the entire magazine of his pistol, not only did the man not die, the multiple gunshot wounds so infuriated him that he dragged himself across the floor and slashed Buck's leg, leaving him with a lifelong limp.

Standing on a chair outside a bedroom door and looking in over the transom to see his mother servicing a client.

Trying to help a man who'd been knifed in the stomach as he stumbled down the street with his guts hanging out. Richard begged the man to lie down and wait for the ambulance, but the man was determined to make it to the liquor store and get himself a half pint.

Seeing his father go running down their residential street clutch-ing his blood-soaked boxer shorts and screaming for his mother. Gertrude, Richard learned, had ripped Buck's nutsack off with her fingernails after he had beaten her.

Yet, when asked, Richard said the most traumatic experience of his early life came when he ventured behind a movie screen at the end of a Little

Beaver western and discovered the show had been a trick, an illusion of light and shadow. "I thought Little Beaver would be there, you know, and I wanted to talk to him."

During his youth, Richard took refuge in the movies, idolizing Tarzan, John Wayne, Jerry Lewis, and especially matinee cowboy Lash LaRue. Exceptionally skilled at using a bullwhip, Lash dressed all in black and enforced the law with the cool aplomb of a film noir gangster. Richard would salvage the theater's discarded movie posters and hang them up on his bedroom wall, pasting his own name over that of the leading man's.

After his parents divorced, Richard went to live with his grandmother at 313 North Washington, just two doors down from his father's home at 317. In between the two houses, at 315, was China Bee's, the most prosperous whorehouse in town.

From the time Richard moved in with her at the age of ten, he always called his grandmother "Mama." To everyone else, by that time, she was Grandma Marie. "Grandma Marie was everybody's anchor," says Richard's onetime sister-in-law, Angie Gordon. "She was the head of it all. Everybody was crazy about her. She looked and talked like Madea. When Tyler Perry came out with Madea, I'm like, 'God, did he meet Grandma Marie?' They were just alike."

Richard's religious upbringing, to the extent that he had one, was Catholic. Although Grandmother Marie attended Peoria's Morning Star Baptist Church, she had been raised in the Creole Catholic tradition and used her influence to enroll Richard in St. Joseph's Catholic School. It didn't take long before the nuns got wind of how the Pryor family came by their livelihood, and a confused young Richard found himself unceremoniously expelled. "Some people just don't know right from wrong," Marie explained, "even though they think they wrote the book."

Despite his expulsion from St. Joseph's, Marie insisted he continue going to weekend catechism where, one Saturday, according to Richard, a priest snuck up and gave him "some smooches on the lips." Richard ran bawling and heaving all the way home. Once his father and uncle Dickie got over their anger at Richard's story, they saw the financial possibilities and hatched a blackmail scheme. "We'll collar him," his father said. The men listened in on an extension while Richard flirted with the priest on the phone — that is, until his grandmother happened to overhear and put a stop to it.

"Richard," she told him, "you've got to understand that everybody's human. Don't ever forget it. No matter what they are. Everybody's human."

Richard, for his part, remembered this as a bonding experience with his father and found it exciting being the center of attention.

After St. Joseph's, Richard enrolled in the overwhelmingly white Blaine-Sumner Elementary School. A chronically truant student, Richard was listless and withdrawn in the classroom on the days he did show up. Yet his sixth-grade teacher, Miss Marguerite Yingst, noticed that he enjoyed making other kids laugh on the playground. So she offered him a deal: if he came to school on time every day, he could have ten minutes to perform in front of the class on Friday afternoons. It worked. His classmates loved him, and having a regular time slot challenged him to come up with new material each week. His family had just bought their first television set, so he mimicked the antics of comics like Red Skelton and Jerry Lewis, freely lifting their jokes until other kids in his class got TVs, too. Richard never forgot the Monday morning he arrived at school to find his classmates all abuzz over Sammy Davis Jr.'s performance on Ed Sullivan's *Toast of the Town* the night before.

"I was jealous," he said. "It was like I'd been home sick one Friday and some other cat had come in and done my act. Now I knew I was going to have to be even better."

Richard was expelled from Woodruff High after he threw a punch at a teacher (and missed). He next attended Peoria Central but dropped out after just one semester. If he wasn't going to school, his father told him, he had to start pulling his own weight. "If you don't put nothing in the pot, you don't get nothing out."

He got his first job mopping floors in a North Washington Street strip club, but did such a poor job the dancers got filthy from writhing on the stage.

Next he tried his hand at robbing stores, but he bungled his first and only attempt when the coins spilled from the register and went rolling all over the floor. Instead of calling the police, the owner kicked him out and threatened to tell his father if he ever came back.

Despite Grandma Marie's faith in Catholic schooling, she had become a devout Baptist and frequently attended revival meetings in hopes of being cured of her arthritis. She took young Richard with her, believing the preacher could "pray the devil out of him."

"It was kind of embarrassing in front of all those people," Richard recalled. "He prayed over me and says for that devil to come out! . . . I didn't feel anything. I couldn't see it. Maybe . . . it's still in there."

BACKING UP WHILE SWIMMING

As it turned out, Richard's salvation came in the person of Miss Juliette Whittaker.

A native of Houston, Texas, Miss Whittaker took a job as director of Peoria's Youth Theater Guild at the Carver Community Center in the late 1940s soon after graduating with a degree in drama from the University of Iowa.

The first time Richard showed up at the community center, they were in the midst of rehearsing a play based on the fairy tale *Rumpelstiltskin*. All the parts had been cast, but Richard was so eager and insistent, Miss Whittaker gave him a role as a servant. He was a "skinny little kid" in his midteens, she remembered, although "he looked about nine."

One day, the boy playing the king was absent and Richard begged her to let him fill in. He knew the king's lines. He knew everyone's lines. "The other kids just broke up, he was so funny. When the original king retuned, even he had to admit that Richard was better in the part.

"So Richard stayed on the throne," she was fond of saying, "and he hasn't come down since."

After that, he won the title role in *Ali Baba and the Forty Thieves* (set to the music of Bizet), and played the lead in *The Vanishing Pearl*.

"You know that label they use now — hyperactive? Well, they didn't have that label then. . . . He had a quick mind, was very good with puns. He could see the biting satire in things people would say. He could take your words, twist them, and throw them back at you. And this used to make the other kids very angry because they weren't used to fighting with words."

Miss Whittaker suspected that Richard hid his talent from the menfolk in his family. "It wasn't quite masculine." Not that his father or uncle had any problem with stage performers. Their world was populated with musicians and comics and female dancers. Buck had done a little vaudeville singing himself. Drama, though, was for sissies. "Nobody from the family, as I recall, would ever come to the plays," Miss Whittaker told biographer Jim Haskins. "They didn't take it seriously."

After observing Richard tell jokes to entertain the kids building sets for one of her plays, Miss Whittaker asked him to be the official host and emcee for the Carver Community Center's talent shows. He took the job seriously, trying out material on the teenagers who hung out in the candy store across the street.

One of his most memorable bits was his takeoff on the popular 1950s TV show *Person to Person* in which Edward R. Morrow interviewed celebrities while touring their opulent homes. Richard's parody had Murrow interviewing a poor black southern sharecropper. Miss Whittaker recalled that he imitated both Murrow and sharecropper to perfection. "Mr. Murrow," Richard-as-sharecropper would say, "this is my table and that there's my chair. And that's my chair and this is my table. Now the table lost a leg in '44 and we put — oh, yassuh, the wall? We papered it with newspaper. Goes all the way back to 1914."

"I've never forgotten this routine," Miss Whittaker said, "because just when you'd think he'd exhausted the possibilities of this chair, this table, and this newspaper, he would say something else. . . . No props. He was just showing it to us. And we were seeing it because he could do that."

In another bit, Richard mimed a scuba diver confronted by a shark. "It was so funny, the way he got out of the water, backing up from this shark," she said. "It's hard to show someone backing up, swimming, but Richard did."

Richard worked whatever odd jobs he could find, mostly through family connections: driving a truck for his father's carting company or racking balls for tips at Pop's Pool Hall at the corner of Sixth and Sheridan. Anytime Richard failed to show up for rehearsal at the community center, Pop's Pool Hall was the first place Miss Whittaker would look. The place would fall silent when she walked in — more out of disapproval than respect, she felt — and Uncle Dickie would say, "Fine. Take him, take him."

"When you walked in that joint to get me," Richard told her later, "they'd be cussin' and fussin', and you'd walk in and that place would be just like a church." Guys who had pool cues "raised in the air to strike somebody would suddenly freeze," she said. "Then the minute I'd leave they'd go back to whatever they were doing."

She could not have known then that his pool-hall loitering would be every bit as essential to his developing genius as the hours he spent rehearsing at the community center. He watched everyone, soaking it all up, holding it in store for future use.

In 1956, Miss Whittaker turned thirty. Having dedicated herself to the Carver Community Center for a full eight years, time seemed to be passing her by. She left Peoria for New York City to take a shot at her lifelong dream of appearing on Broadway. It didn't take her long to decide she wasn't cut out for the fierce competition on the Great White Way. She eventually returned to her post in Peoria, but her absence came at a time that made Richard's life seem all the more desolate.

After a stint shining shoes at the Hotel Père Marquette, Richard landed his first real job in a meatpacking plant as a shaker of cowhides. It was grueling and foul-smelling work, folding and loading the heavy hides onto railroad cars bound for Chicago. At the end of each shift he would walk home — or more frequently to Yakov's Liquor Store — his fingers cramped and frozen and his trousers crusted stiff with slaughterhouse slime.

Richard spent his free time at Yakov's, washing down pickled pigs feet with ice cold beer and contemplating a bleak future which, he began to fear, might well mean buying a pair of steel-toed shoes and lugging a lunch pail to and from the Caterpillar plant five days a week, spending his evenings and his pay "watching TV, getting fucked up, and chasing pussy. Work, pension, die."

One day at the plant, Richard went upstairs to inquire about a better-paying job that had opened up in the beef-cutting department. He took one look at the men in their blood-slicked rubber aprons knocking the brains out of cattle with sledgehammers and changed his mind — as did one of the bulls waiting its turn in line: the bull suddenly bucked free of his stall and, in Richard's account, "ran through the shop, upstairs and downstairs, snorting and butting and kicking everything in his path." Police finally shot the bull as it ran down the street. Perhaps Richard saw parallels between the bull's circumstances and his own.

––––––––––

Gamely attempting to follow in his father's footsteps, Richard entered a Golden Gloves boxing competition. "He won his first fight in the first round," Buck later told a newspaper reporter. "And I think he did it by telling a joke, which made the guy double up. And then he punched him out." If true, that would mark the pinnacle of his brief career.

"I always boxed them niggers that looked like they'd just killed their parents. You know, them rough niggers that could strike a match on the palm of their hand. Niggers would come and be beatin' themselves up. I'd say, 'Well, he don't give a fuck about me. He's beatin' his own ass!'"

––––––––––

As luck would have it, Richard's stepmother operated an establishment on North Aiken Street right next door to Ray LeRoy, "the George Burns of Peoria." LeRoy worked a steady gig as the house comedian at Mike and Mike's Show Lounge and his place was a favorite hangout for black entertainers on the Chitlin' Circuit passing through town.

Richard worked himself into the circle, shyly hanging back, content to listen to the veterans talk trash and tell their stories of life on the circuit and to dream of the day when he would be one of them. "I don't know exactly when it happened, but suddenly he was always there," LeRoy remembered. "We would say to each other, 'Isn't he the politest little fella?' He was about seventeen, I guess — real thin then." Eventually Richard got up enough nerve to ask if he could look though LeRoy's prized gag books. LeRoy was flattered. "I had a lot of material for him to look at — wrote most of it myself. It was mostly stand-up material. He used to sit for hours going through my scripts and books and gags."

At seventeen, Richard fell in love with a girl named Susan whom he described as a Sophia Loren–type from a poor family. They made a secret love nest in the garage of a house his family owned on Goodwin. "She wore me out," Richard told *Spin* magazine in 1988. Susan's orgasms were so intense, he claimed, that "when she would come, she would faint. I thought I killed her." The fun ended, as it often would for Richard, when his girlfriend got pregnant. He went home in tears, he told Barbara Walters in a 1980 interview. "My mother said, 'What's wrong with you, boy?' Father says, 'There ain't nothing wrong with him, he got some girl pregnant.'" This rattled Richard all the more. Did his father know *everything* he did? In this case, his father knew because the girl had told him so herself. Buck had been sleeping with her, too. (Richard's aunt Mexcine cryptically assured him the child was not his. "I was out in the chicken shack," she told him, "and someone else said it was his baby.")

Richard was not present when Susan gave birth to a daughter, Renee, in April 1957. Later in life he came to accept Renee, reasoning that, even if she were not his daughter, she was likely his half sister. Either way, she was family.

His more immediate response was to flee Peoria and enlist in the army.

———————

Military service would not provide the easy way out Richard had imagined. The first time he tried, after bragging to everyone he knew that he was going off to Chicago to join up, he flunked the entrance exam and they sent him back home. He was so embarrassed, he told Janet Maslin of the *New York Times,* he hid in the house for months. When he did venture out, he wore a costume uniform. It fooled his friends but not their parents.

On his second try at enlisting, he got in. After spending eight weeks of basic training in plumbing school — covered in shit, once again — at Fort Leonard Wood, he shipped out to the military installation in Baumholder, Germany, just south of Idar-Oberstein, then the largest concentration of American troops outside the United States. The soldiers' collective buying power had brought about an infusion of bars, dancehalls, and sex-trade workers, prompting the West German government to declare the region a "moral disaster area."

No great student of world history, Richard had supposed that racial attitudes would be more enlightened in Germany. The bars and clubs there, he quickly discovered, were even more segregated than they had been in Peoria. "Out of like 150 bars," he wrote, "only three let in blacks." The worst of it came from his fellow soldiers. Cornered by three guys wielding tire irons in the armory one day, Richard made good use of his basic training. Much to their surprise, he grabbed a length of lead pipe and bashed one of them over the head. ("Really?" David Felton asked him in a 1974 *Rolling Stone* interview. "An enemy or one of ours?" "No, a white cat," Richard said. "One of yours.")

Although Richard had gone into the army with the idea of making it his career, he spent the majority of his two-year stint in the stockade for stabbing a fellow soldier. Prior to his incarceration, he had a love affair with a married woman, a poignant encounter that stayed with him for the rest of his life — so much so that he ruminated on the relationship in the closing pages of his autobiography.

And, as he told Felton in that same *Rolling Stone* interview, the army was where he learned to eat pussy. "I gave some head for the first time in my life when I was in Germany. That was an experience. I'll never forget how it felt on my head, her pussy . . . her hairs and all . . . I knew I would be doing it again."

If it seems improbable that a man of Richard's upbringing would be a cunnilingual virgin at the age of eighteen, consider the African American male's well-documented aversion to going down on a woman. As he described it on *That Nigger's Crazy*: "My family only fucked in one position — up and down. My uncle said 'Boy don't you ever kiss no pussy! I mean that. Whatever you do in life don't kiss no pussy!' I couldn't *wait* to kiss the pussy. He'd been wrong about everything else." And this from . . . *Is It Something I Said?*: "Niggers will not admit to giving up no head. (*in character*) 'Uh-uh. Noooo. Not the kid! Uh-uh. Nah, I ain't no termite.' Be lying their ass off. And black women like head, but they won't kiss you afterwards."

Richard got his first taste of success outside of Miss Whittaker's theater group by performing in amateur shows on the base, developing a routine on army life in which he assumed the role of an incomprehensible drill sergeant, which he included on his first Warner Bros. LP, *Richard Pryor.* But then came the first of what would be a career-spanning string of self-inflicted derailments. During a screening of the Douglas Sirk movie *Imitation of Life,* a melodramatic tear-jerker about a struggling black woman whose light-skinned daughter rejects her in order to pass for white, a white soldier in Richard's unit began laughing a little too loudly at inappropriate times.

As Richard told it, another black soldier started the fight but proved to be "a dumb motherfucker in terms of fighting. The white boy seriously hurt my guy's ass." Richard pulled a switchblade and waited for the right moment. "I stabbed the white motherfucker in the back six or seven times. He didn't stop, though. . . . As soon as I realized he wasn't going down, I ran in the opposite direction, tossing the knife into the bushes."

Richard was fingered for the assault by the victim himself who marched into the barracks later that night, still wearing his shredded and blood-soaked T-shirt, accompanied by an MP. Richard spent the remainder of his stint in an army prison, receiving an early discharge courtesy of a base commander on the verge of retirement who couldn't be bothered with some "silly enlisted man fucking up regulations."

His envisioned military career cut short and again at loose ends, Richard got a job singing and doing impersonations at Harold's Club, a black-and-tan joint (patronized by whites and blacks alike) on Washington Street back in Peoria. Richard claimed he'd had to lie his way onstage at Harold's Club by telling owner Harold Parker he could sing and play piano. His command of the keyboard may have been limited to few simple chords, but his soon-to-be sister-in-law says he had a beautiful voice.

Kelly Jay & the Jamies, a Ronnie Hawkins–inspired rockabilly band out of Toronto — an earlier incarnation, the Consuls, had featured future Hawks (and later Band) guitarist Robbie Robertson — frequently played Harold's Club in the early 1960s. Drummer Peter De Remigis remembers Richard as a mellow, Brook Benton–styled singer who emceed the shows and sometimes told jokes.

Another Canadian band, Freddie Tieken and the Rockers (featuring Little Richard's sometime sideman Byron "Wild Child" Gipson on vocals, piano and guitar) often played week-long gigs at Harold's. It was a fun place, Tienken remembers. In between their sets, from 9:00 p.m. to 4:00 a.m., Richard did stand-up. Some nights they would see a big yellow Cadillac convertible parked outside, and there would be Chuck Berry sitting at the bar all by himself.

"It seemed like everywhere we went, there was Chuck Berry," Tienken says. "In all the years that I ran into the guy throughout the Midwest, I never heard him say two words to anyone."

Patricia Price first met Richard Pryor through a cousin who'd been dating a friend of his. One day they brought him over to the house and she fell in love. "I don't know why," her sister, Angie Gordon, says. "To this day I don't know why."

They married in the summer of 1960, shortly after Patricia's sixteenth birthday. "I don't know if she was pregnant or thought she was pregnant," her sister remembers. "Richard said he thought I had told him she was pregnant . . . that she had a miscarriage, but I told him, 'No, that wasn't me. I don't know anything about a miscarriage.' I think she *thought* she was pregnant and that's why he married her."

Richard certainly thought so. His father advised him against the marriage. "You don't have to do this, son," Buck told him. But he did. "Just to spite him."

The newlyweds moved into a boarding house owned by Patricia's grandmothers. She lived on the ground floor and rented out the rooms upstairs.

"He really had a bad temper," Angie says. "Oh, he was something else. He used to beat her up about the food and have tantrums."

He'd give her money to go grocery shopping — the little money he'd bring in — and she'd buy great big bags of potatoes and chicken wings and things like that. She'd do potatoes in every form you could name and he'd get tired of potatoes. He would come home and she'd fix his plate and he'd throw it across the room and make her clean it up. Grandmother told her, "As long as you let him hit on you, he'll keep doing it, but if you fight back he'll stop." One night he jumped on my sister and she hauled off and knocked him across the floor. He fell at Grandmother's feet and she just pulled her feet back and started laughing at him. After that he never did hit my sister again.

Richard had a special song he always sang to Patricia when she came to see his show. Then one night his gaze seemed to stray. He kept looking past her, just above her head, and his eyes took on an extra sparkle. Patricia turned in her chair to see a white girl smiling up at her man with that same enraptured sparkle mirrored in her eyes.

The club withheld Richard's salary for the next several weeks to pay for the damage Patricia did to the glassware and the furnishings that night. "She tore the place up," Angie remembers. "All of a sudden she was on the stage going after Richard. After that everything was completely downhill."

> He was using — they used to call them bennies. Pills. I remember one time she had a headache and she took one. She thought it was an aspirin. They were lying out on the table by the bed. When he got home she was just cleaning and cleaning and cleaning with all this energy she had. She told him she took one of the pills by the bed and he got on her. He said, "You don't ever take pills you find lying around." He told her what it was and she was like, "That was WHAT!" because she was very naive. He said, "Don't do that. Don't ever take stuff you see lying around." Finally she got calmed down enough that she could go to sleep. He was always taking something.

Richard and Patricia lived together as husband and wife only a few months. Patricia's mother had made him promise when they married that if he couldn't take care of her he'd bring her back home.

Angie Gordon again: "He brought her back home and told my mom that he was living up to his promise, that he couldn't take care of her like she should be taken care of so he was bringing her home, which she wasn't happy about. But then they went on seeing each other, off and on."

When Patricia told him In December that she was pregnant — for real, this time — he moved in with her at her parents' house. For a while. "I felt responsible," he wrote, "which might've been the first and last time I did."

"AIN'T THAT MANY OF US TO GO AROUND"

On Friday the thirteenth of January 1961, Dick Gregory sprinted over twenty blocks of frozen Chicago sidewalk in slick-soled dress shoes to make a club date that would forever alter not only the course of his own life but Richard's, too. And, for that matter, the lives of every African American comedian who followed in his wake.

A call had come in at the last minute that the Playboy Club needed a replacement for Professor Irwin Corey who had canceled his performance that evening in the Carousel Room. Could Gregory fill in for him?

He borrowed a quarter from his landlord for carfare, then, in his excitement, boarded the wrong bus. Realizing his mistake, he signaled for a stop, got out, and ran.

Dick Gregory, along with Nipsey Russell, Bill Cosby, and Godfrey Cambridge, belonged to a new generation of black comedians unencumbered by the deferential buffoonery of vaudeville or minstrelsy. Gregory, especially, did not flinch from skewering white audiences on issues of race: "Wouldn't it be a hell of a thing if this was burnt cork and you people were being tolerant for nothing?" and "Everyone I meet says, 'Some of my best friends are colored,' even though you know there ain't that many of us to go around."

Perched on a stool in a three-button Brooks Brothers suit, Dick Gregory possessed an unflappable cool, taking long, contemplative drags on his cigarette and exhaling well-timed streams of smoke into the spotlight before delivering his punch lines. Not even the inevitable

catcalls of "nigger" could rock his composure. "According to my contract," he replied to one such heckler, "the management pays me fifty
dollars every time someone calls me that. So will you all do me a favor?
Everybody in the room please stand up and yell 'nigger.'"

The pace of his delivery was so dependent upon the draw of his ever-
present cigarette — Winstons only — he once chewed out a stagehand
at the hungry i for buying the wrong brand. "Look," he told the gofer,
"the timing of the drag that I'm using on this cigarette is part of my act.
I can't suddenly change."

When Gregory arrived, out of breath, at the Playboy Club that night,
he was told to go home. A mistake had been made. They were very
sorry, but they hadn't realized the room had been booked by a convention of frozen-food executives from the South — not the best audience
for Gregory to break in with. They offered him fifty dollars and said they
would try to work him in again soon. "But I was cold and mad and I had
run twenty blocks and I didn't even have another quarter to go back
home," Gregory wrote. "I told [the room manager] I was going to do the
show they had called me for. I had come too far to stop now. I told him
I didn't care if he had a lynch mob in there. I was going on — tonight.

"He looked at me and shrugged. Then he stepped aside and opened
the door to the top."

I understand there are a good many Southerners in the room tonight. I know the South very well. I spent twenty years there one
night.

Last time I was down South I walked into this restaurant and
this white waitress came up to me and said, "We don't serve colored people here." I said, "That's all right. I don't eat colored people. Bring me a whole fried chicken."

About that time these three cousins come in. You know the
ones I mean, Klu, Kluck, and Klan. About that time the waitress
brought me my chicken and they say, "Boy, we're givin' you fair
warnin'. Anything you do to that chicken, we're gonna do to you."

So I put down my knife and fork, I picked up that chicken and I kissed it.

At the end of his show, the frozen-food execs gave him a standing ovation. They handed him money as he left the stage. One of them said, "You know, if you have the right managers you'll die a billionaire."

Hugh Hefner came down for the second show to see what all the excitement was about and immediately signed Gregory to a three-year contract, beginning with a three-week run that was held over through March 12.

"And, just like that," Phillip Lutz would write in the *New York Times*, "with little fanfare or protest, nightclub comedy was integrated."

Time magazine of Friday, February 17, featured a prominent article on Gregory, and the following Monday morning a call came from someone on Jack Paar's staff inviting him to appear on *The Tonight Show.*

"My wife took the call and she's so happy," Gregory said. "I got on the phone and said, 'No, I don't want to do this,' and I hung up and started cryin'."

Gregory had long dreamed of appearing on *The Tonight Show,* sometimes practicing for hours in front of the mirror after the show signed off at 1:00 a.m., imagining how he would comport himself and what he would say to Paar when his opportunity finally came, as he was sure it would. Then one night he went out drinking with singer Billy Eckstine who began "cussin' Paar out to me. [He] told me, 'Hey, man, that motherfuckin' Jack Paar, he ain't *never* let a nigger sit on the couch.'

"I was so embarrassed, so humiliated, I never told my wife that I could not do the Paar show. It was just a personal thing."

Fortunately, Gregory's phone rang again. This time it was Paar himself.

"Dick Gregory?"
"Yes."
"This is Mr. Paar. How come you don't want to work my show?"
"I just don't want to work it."

"Why?"

"Because the negroes never sit on the couch."

There was a long pause and he said, "Well come on in, you can sit on the couch."*

While Paar and Gregory exchanged a few canned jokes ("What kind of car you got?" "A Lincoln, naturally"), so many phone calls came in to the NBC switchboard in New York the circuits blew out. The calls, Gregory says, were coming from "white folks who were seeing a black person for the first time in a *human* conversation."

Gregory had been earning $250 a week at the Playboy Club. After sitting on Jack Paar's couch, he said, his salary jumped to $5,000. "What a country!" he would say. "Where else could I have to ride in the back of the bus, live in the worst neighborhoods, go to the worst schools, eat in the worst restaurants — and average $5,000 a week just talking about it?"

———

Back in Peoria, Richard Pryor was watching, stretched out on the couch in his in-laws' living room while his pregnant wife slept upstairs.

---

*While acknowledging the significance of Dick Gregory's appearance on the show, Paar clarified in his memoir *P.S. Jack Paar* that the first black performer to sit on *The Tonight Show* couch had been Diahann Carroll. The young ingénue and singer, who vaulted to stardom on Broadway at the age of nineteen in Harold Arlen and Truman Capote's 1954 musical *House of Flowers,* appeared on the show no fewer than fourteen times during Paar's tenure (1957–62). Paar invited her to sit on the couch after the Jewish American satirist and publisher of the *Charlotte Israelite* Harry Golden had been on the show outlining his "Vertical Integration Plan," by which integration could be achieved simply by removing the chairs from any segregated facility. As Golden explained it, southern whites had no objection to *standing* and talking with black people but would never *sit* with them. "I suddenly realized," Paar wrote, "that in our year or more on *The Tonight Show,* while there were black performers on, I had not actually sat down with one and talked. This may seem a strange thing to say now, but I do it only in the historical context. It just had not been done on any program or panel show that I knew of."

Agitated by deferred dreams, Benzedrine, and the long, leaping shadows cast by the black-and-white TV, he chewed on bits of paper and flicked spitballs until the walls and ceiling were stuccoed with the stuff.

His sister-in-law Angie got stuck with the job of sweeping his dried up spitballs down. "He was just a mess," she says. "He wouldn't go to work. He would just sit around all day making spitballs and throwing them on the walls and ceiling."

One day he went off in the head. I don't know what he had taken, but he climbed out our second floor window and said he was going to kill himself and my sister was pulling him back in and begging him to go lay down. Well, she couldn't do anything with him, so my dad finally got tired of fooling with him and he went upstairs. We had a state hospital here called Bartonville. They would pay you to bring people in, you know. Twenty-five dollars if you brought crazy people in. So my dad went upstairs and he said, "Hey!" He says, "Pat's tired of fooling with you," he says, "so we're gettin' ready to call Bartonville and we're gonna have you picked up and we're gonna get that $25 for you." So Richard's like, "WHAT?" My dad says, "Yeah, because, you know, something's wrong with you." And so he says, "Well, I better stop then, hadn't I?" Daddy says "Yeah." He says, "Pop, I'm gonna lie down and take a nap." We didn't have any more trouble out of him playing crazy after that. But he was just a weird guy. Real weird.

He was real quiet and shy otherwise, though. He had a whole lot of different sides to him, but the majority of the time he would sleep all day and sit up all evening and watch television and chew on paper. But he watched everything around him at all times. That's how he gathered material, you know.

Patricia delivered their son six months into her pregnancy. Born April 10, 1961, Rodney Clay Pryor weighed just one pound three ounces, "the smallest preemie ever to survive in Peoria at that time," according to Angie. "He stayed five weeks in the hospital before he was strong enough for Pat to bring him home."

After his son came home, Richard moved out.

"Why'd I split? Because I could."

Finding himself once again living under his father's roof, Richard doubled down on his resolve and began performing at Collins Corner, another notorious black-and-tan club owned by local businessman Carbristo "Bris" Collins. There he was quickly promoted from opening act to emcee at a salary of seventy-two dollars a week.

Stripper-turned-fire-dancer LaWanda Page, then billed as "the Bronze Goddess of Fire," recalled Collins Corner as the first club she ever played outside of her hometown of East St. Louis. "It was a dump," she said. "It was the kind of place where if you ain't home by nine o'clock at night you can be declared legally dead. They all walked around with knives in there. You better had one, too."

Richard would soon cross paths with Page* when they played the Faust Club together in East St. Louis. "Me, Richard Pryor, Chuck Berry, and Redd Foxx all worked there around that time," she said. "Richard was doing an act where he sang along with doing comedy. He was a very quiet, polite person offstage. Onstage he was doing true-to-life stuff even then, and he was very funny."

Richard later told *Rolling Stone*'s David Felton how his army training

---

*The fire-dancing Page later became a popular stand-up comic in her own right. Billed simply as LaWanda, she was known for her signature line "I'm gonna tell it to ya like it tea-eye-*IS*, honey" and her raunchy, uncut humor.

LaWanda had little interest in crossing over. Like Rudy Ray Moore, Skillet & Leroy, Wildman Steve, and Tina Dixon, she'd found her niche; she never tried to clean up or water down her act for the sake of reaching a wider audience, and she likely would have continued performing X-rated material for predominantly black audiences and recording risque "party" records for the rest of her career had it not been for the intervention of Redd Foxx, her friend since childhood, who saw to it that she got the role of the Bible-thumping Aunt Esther on *Sanford and Son*.

had served him well when he first started out on the Chitlin' Circuit. "Like you'd suck a fire-dancer's pussy in the dressing room, and in her next job she'd try to get you as the emcee. Shit, if I hadn't been able to give head, I'd probably still be in St. Louis at the Faust Club."

———

Given the irregularity of Richard's club engagements, Buck tried to steer his son toward a more stable career as a pimp and, in Richard's telling, even threw in a whore to get him started. For a time, Richard thought he had it made: steady work at two clubs and a woman working for him. Plus, he could have all the sex he wanted with her without any messy emotions or romantic strings attached.

Things quickly fell apart, though, when his woman demanded that he beat her. "I had no idea what she was talking about," he admitted to Sander Vanocur of the *Washington Post*. "I didn't know there was any romantic connotation to physical violence." Richard's stunned inaction only infuriated her. She began screaming at him to hit her and he went crazy, "fighting as if it were a real fight." When his father saw the girl, bruised and battered, he blew up. "What the fuck are you doing?" he yelled. "You don't know how to beat a whore! Get your ass outta here!" He was serious. Buck was so disgusted he banished Richard from his house for good.

The elder Pryor told the story somewhat differently to Jean Budd of the *Peoria Journal Star,* after his son had made it big. "Richard was beginning to run around with the wrong group. So I said one day to my wife, 'Okay, that's it — he goes.' That's probably the best thing we ever did for him — make him go out on his own."

In either case, Richard grabbed up a few clothes, stuffed twenty dollars in his pocket, and hit the streets. He was twenty-two.

By law, Richard was still married to Patricia. He was father to a year-old son and possibly a five-year-old daughter who was just as likely his half sister. Yet the only thing keeping him in Peoria, he said, was the price of a bus ticket.

When Richard told his woes to a troupe of mostly transvestite dancers and backup singers performing with the headliner at Collins Corner,
they invited him to come along with them to their next gig at the Faust
Club in St. Louis.

"I couldn't believe my luck," he wrote. "One minute kicked out of
the house, no prospects. The next I was on the road in show business."

Before leaving town he went and said good-bye to Miss Whittaker at
the Carver Community Center. Recalling his decision years later, she
would say, "I guess he did what Gauguin did." She may or may not have
been the only resident of Peoria who would have compared Richard
to the nineteenth-century postimpressionist French painter who abandoned his family and homeland to pursue his muse in the South Sea
Islands, but she is likely the only one who would've made the comparison a favorable one.

"I believe there was a gift given to me, probably when I was a child,"
Richard would say. "That God searched me out and found me and said,
'Try that one.' Somebody said, 'Uh? *That* one?' And God said, 'Try him,
I'm telling you there's something about him.'" Or, as he explained it after
a few months on the road to a hostile audience in Youngstown, Ohio,
"Hey, y'all can boo me now. But in a couple of years I'm gonna be a star
and you dumb niggers will still be sittin' here."

Richard was ready to shake the dust of Peoria off his feet. He would
go out there and show them all. The ones who'd told him he wasn't shit.
Not least of all, his father.

He pawned a typewriter he'd borrowed from his half sister Barbara
Jean for bus fare and, unbeknownst to Patricia, had their son's name
legally changed to Richard Franklin Pryor Jr.

"Does the champ know this is a benefit?!"

Richard Pryor climbs into a ring with Muhammad Ali who, in answer to Richard's clowning and faux preening, theatrically scowls and mouths carefully constructed words from deep in his corner: "I'm going to kick your ass."

Two equally implausible characters, each of whose rise now feels as inevitable as it once seemed implausible; both slipping through the cracks of trauma and circumstance that helped define an era even as they failed to contain the men they marked; both escaping, skipping out onto a wire — or beneath one — that was sharp, swaying, and electrified. Like Parker and Miles and Dylan and Picasso and Malcolm, they picked at a lock only to find the door already free and swinging, dark and unguarded; sneaking in and onto a vacant seat that had never really been wholly occupied.

Ali literally beat his chosen new name free from the lips of Ernie Terrell who had clamped down on it and refused its utterance and legitimacy. And then he finished him.

Richard made Ed Sullivan's stage a back alley wherein he leaned and hid out, flashing anger and grief; sucking down self-loathing even before it was forced upon him; setting the place on fire and giving away the whole of his secret heart for nothing.

PART **TWO**

"GIVE ME SOME MILK OR ELSE GO HOME"

Down along Manhattan's MacDougal Street, Richard may have felt like a rube with his Jackie Wilson pompadour and shiny, narrow-cut suit that was perhaps a full size too small, but it took more than that to stand out in Greenwich Village in 1963. You could be anything there, and as such, everyone was unfurling a flag in hopes of staking a claim upon outrage and attention. It didn't matter your discipline: it was all theater, and the tiny coffee shops were packed with performers — comedians, musicians, monologists, poets — all eager to survey the competition and glean some deft bits of stage business.

Beat poets, visual artists, and jazz musicians had, since the mid-1950s, become such a potent and magnetic presence in the neighborhood that they'd seemingly reset the clocks, filling the dark cafes and narrow ethnic restaurants with dense smoke at odd hours, spilling with their work from dim rooming houses and co-opted storefronts and animating the street corners of early morning hours, blurring the lines between friendly congregation and performance. Over egg rolls and scorched coffee, writers Jack Kerouac, Allen Ginsberg, Gregory Corso, and filmmaker Robert Frank hashed out an informal manifesto, whereby the most gritty and unabashedly personal of experiences would be thinly veiled in their work, if at all. And just north, Zoot Sims, Mose Allison, and Al Cohn wandered in and out of the frame of the ever-open-and-revolving door of photographer W. Eugene Smith's buzzing loft, nodding their heads through sprawling rehearsals of Thelonious Monk's big band. Smith snapped pictures throughout and kept a reel-to-reel tape recorder endlessly turning, documenting thousands of hours of jam sessions and casual conversation, street noise, radio speeches and staticky baseball games — all with seemingly no thought to judging what of it might be relevant for posterity. At this juncture — where a random satellite photograph revealed Soviet missiles in Cuba, and a crowd member's silent Super 8 footage served as the only recorded witness to an era-defining assassination — there was almost no such thing as irrelevance: something was happening here, even if you didn't know what it was.

The last years of the 1950s had left a flooded gully in its wake, like a psychic borderline snaking through an America that had imagined itself, in the years following the Second World War, to be modern and sufficiently settled: dreams had been assigned and sanctioned — handed out along with your honorable service discharge — and involved new cars, office jobs, pretty wives, and obedient children. But once upon the shore of 1960, it was clear that its sandy banks were trembling and perilous, and that the way forward was dark and overgrown with vines. The boiler room beneath the nation's freshly paved surface was clanging and giving off wisps of rancid steam following decades of brutal violence, deep resentment, and the denying of the very humanity of great segments of the country's population. And now, an imposing and abstractly treacherous cold war pushed back from the idealized future. In a quick few years, a stout crop of popular TV sitcoms sprang up, each a variation on a single theme: something alien is close and secretly among us, and one person is burdened with protecting all others from the unspeakable truth of their presence and power: *My Favorite Martian, My Mother the Car, I Dream of Jeannie, The Munsters, Mister Ed, Bewitched* — they all pointed to the growing anxiety of middle-class whites that nothing was as it appeared, and once the mask slipped, there would be no way of ever securing it back in place.

By the middle sixties, the bohemian subculture would become so per-
vasive that no longer would the flustered secretaries and pressed businessmen cross the street to avoid bearded confrontation, but, rather,
tour buses filled with middle Americans would crawl along Cornelius
and West Fourth streets, craning for a glimpse of the dirty and drugged
radicals they'd read about in *Time* magazine. This transformation had
begun a scant few years earlier, centered in New York's Greenwich
Village. There, a grubby and baby-faced young folksinger named Bob
Dylan was still nicking songs and banter from established acts like Jack
Elliott and Dave Van Ronk, sharing cigarettes and kitchen scraps with
Tiny Tim in the basement of the Cafe Wha? Painters Red Grooms and
Bob Thompson were hustling canvases up Sixth Avenue in a scavenged
baby carriage, and dressing sets for the impromptu theater pieces they
helped stage in an empty shoe store. Ornette Coleman might be dressed
in a burlap sack — like Moses being chased instead of followed — while
Sun Ra paraded his Myth Science Arkestra along East Third Street like a
barnstorming baseball team trying to drum up business en route to their
weekly Monday night gig at Slug's.

―――――――

Into this constantly shifting scene stepped Richard Pryor — straight
from the Chitlin' Circuit and the fading theaters of skittish northern and
midwestern towns that had years before shaken off the dust of vaudeville and the swing era but found little in the grainy, flickering glow of
distant television screens to take its place.

   Looking back on the scene, screenwriter Buck Henry could remember, in his mind's eye, walking along Bleecker or MacDougal streets late
at night and seeing in every doorway someone who would later be famous. On any given night that autumn of 1963, a club hopper might
see the top four stand-up comics of all time — (1) Richard Pryor, (2)
George Carlin, (3) Lenny Bruce, (4) Woody Allen, as ranked by Comedy Central in 2005 — within blocks of each other working the basket
houses, where performers passed a basket or a hat to collect their pay,

or appearing in all-night cafes housed in crumbling basements where patrons were requested to applaud by snapping their fingers rather than clapping their hands so as not to incur the wrath of apartment dwellers farther up the airshaft who were trying to sleep.

As outrageous as the Village characters believed themselves to be, however, they would have turned few heads among the players Richard encountered out on the Circuit, in the days before he made it to New York.

There was the hotel in Toronto favored by gay wrestlers where, after watching them try to murder each other in the ring, Richard was dumbfounded to see the same guys kissing and holding hands in the lobby.

There was the club where Richard opened for a wrestling bear who guzzled beer between bouts. One night when the furry star had a few too many, he pinned a terrified Richard to the floor backstage and gently began stroking him.

There was the Casablanca in Youngstown, Ohio, where Richard, upon learning from a tearful Satin Doll that the performers weren't going to be paid, came to the rescue by pulling a starter pistol on the club's reputedly mobbed-up Lebanese owners (reimagined as Italian for *Live on the Sunset Strip* and again in *Jo Jo Dancer*) and demanded their share of the take.

There was the female impersonator who enticed Richard with a bit of quid pro quo. He was relieved to find, when push came to shove, that she was in fact a she, passing as a female impersonator.

In Pittsburgh, he served thirty-five days of a ninety-day sentence handed down for assaulting a singer he had been seeing. Richard never denied the charge. He'd been talking trash about the woman behind her back, playing the pimp and bragging that she'd been giving him money. When she confronted him backstage, he claimed preemptive self-defense. "I thought she was going to do some serious damage to me so I beat her ass first." It turned out her father was connected. When the cops burst into the rooming house in the middle of the night, Richard feared they'd come to work him over. But, he concluded, they must have felt sorry for this skinny kid with no muscles, trembling in his underwear. Instead, they gave him time to get dressed and then hauled him downtown.

In jail, he struck up a conversation with a fellow inmate who, it turned out, knew his aunt Mexcine and only had a few days left to serve. Upon his release, the inmate contacted Mexcine and she sent Richard twenty dollars, which he parlayed into seventy by playing the numbers. That was enough to buy his way out of jail and out into the freezing cold.

Back on the street, Richard heard that Sammy Davis Jr. was in town. He found his hotel and stationed himself in a chair at the end of the hallway hoping for a chance to meet the man who, along with Sidney Poitier and Harry Belafonte, formed a holy trinity of African American performers of the day.

A hotel security cop gave him the once-over but didn't question his reason for being there. And while no one would ever mistake the twenty-two-year-old Richard Pryor for hired muscle, it might have made sense because Davis had faced continual threats of assassination, lynching, and theater bombings ever since his marriage to the Swedish actress May Britt in 1960, a barrage that only intensified when their daughter, Tracey, was born a year later.

Once or twice, Davis peeked out to see if the skinny guy in the chair was still there. After several hours, someone from Davis's entourage brought Richard a plate of food. The next morning, as Davis was leaving, Richard rose from his chair. "What's happening?" Davis said. The two would become great friends a decade hence, but for now Davis smoked and nodded as Richard stammered out a brief résumé and asked if maybe he would give him a job. Davis gave him a cigarette and some encouragement. "But he was so jive," Richard wrote. "Didn't mind being a star one bit. It was a beautiful thing to see."

And then there was the hooker in Baltimore who invited Richard home with her after his show at the Playboy Club. "I want you to hear something," she said, and pulled out a translucent red vinyl LP from its jacket, set the phonograph arm down on side one of *Lenny Bruce, American,* and for once, Richard forgot all about the pussy.

On the second track, Lenny set the scene wherein a nine-year-old kid inadvertently discovers the mind-altering properties of model airplane glue. Lenny next followed the kid into a toy store where he nonchalantly asks the clerk for a list of innocuous items: a nickel's worth of pencils, Big Boy tablet, some Jujubes, Tailspin Tommy book, and — slipping this in almost as an afterthought — two thousand tubes of airplane glue.

"That destroyed me," Richard said. "I went fucking crazy."

The epiphany of Richard's first brush with Lenny Bruce was akin to what Colombian journalist Gabriel García Márquez experienced when he first opened a copy of Franz Kafka's *Metamorphosis.* "Holy shit!" is what he said, reliving that moment for an interviewer some thirty years later. "The first line almost knocked me off the bed. I didn't know anyone was allowed to write things like that."

Before Lenny Bruce, most comics purchased their jokes from gag writers. And, once those jokes had been performed, there was little recourse against other comics stealing them, so common a practice that Milton Berle, the most famous and highest-paid comic on TV at the time — affectionately known as Uncle Miltie, Mr. Television, Mr. Tuesday Night by viewers — was called the Thief of Bad Gags by his fellow comics. Lenny's brand of comedy changed all that, effectively trouncing the division of labor between gag writer and comedian, rendering the arrangement hopelessly passé, just as Bob Dylan had done to songsters in tin pan alley. ("Bob Dylan killed popular music," an old-time recording engineer at Columbia Records' New York studio was heard to say during an afternoon mastering session in the late 1980s, shaking his head with equal parts admiration and rue. Every songwriter now felt he should sing, and every singer thought he had something to say.) Gag writers and tunesmiths soldiered on, of course, but mainly as remnants of a time that had passed. Comics, like singers — if they wanted to be taken seriously — were expected to do their own stuff.

What Lenny Bruce did was revive the long-neglected tradition of storytellers, balladeers, satirists, and poets who delivered their oratory in the public square. He showed that a comedian standing in front of an audience could roam the same expanse of territory, plumb the same depths of humanity as a novelist, poet, or playwright could sitting over a typewriter.

Richard, in his moment of enlightenment, understood not only the alchemy Lenny practiced, he recognized, too, that he'd already amassed and absorbed everything he needed to work that same spell himself. He knew it better than he knew anything. He'd been learning it all his life from Buck's emasculating tirades, his grandfather's tall tales, Uncle Dickie's boasts, the pool-hall hustlers' mother-rhymes, the prayers of the revival preacher who tried to cast the devil out of him, and the lies told by whichever wizened Peorian it was who planted the seeds of Mudbone as he sent streams of tobacco juice hissing into the barbecue pit.

Where Lenny was cool and detached, standing on the outside looking in, Richard would crawl inside his characters, actually *become* them, and follow them wherever they might go. Which is why the restrictions of TV performance proved so problematic. "I have to *be* that person," he told James Alan McPherson in 1975. "I see that man in my mind and go with him. . . . When I do the people, I have to do it true. If I can't do it, I'll stop right in the middle rather than pervert it and turn it into Tomism. . . . If I didn't do characters, it wouldn't be funny."

Richard's problem, McPherson concluded, was his conviction that objectionable language was essential to the characters he created. To stay within the confines of acceptable practices, he insisted, Richard had to pull back, resist giving himself over to characters who would invariably go where he couldn't follow — not and stay on the air, anyway.

In Buffalo, fellow comedian Donnie Simpson sold Richard on a vision of bigger paychecks and beautiful women awaiting them in Canada.

Finding themselves stranded in Ontario, out of money and with no work, Richard flipped through the June 17, 1963, issue of *Newsweek* to see a full-page article about a young black comic named Bill Cosby.

What set Cosby apart from all other "Negro comedians," the article said, was that he didn't tell Negro jokes. "I'm trying to reach all of the people," he said. "I want to play to Joe Q. Public."

Richard was panic-stricken. "Goddamn it," he told Simpson and anyone else who would listen, "this nigger's doing what *I'm* fixing to do. Ain't no room for two niggers."

If that's what Richard had in mind, Simpson asked him, what was his ass doing in Toronto? "You got to go to New York. That's where all them bit cats are."

———

When he first started out in Philadelphia saloons and New York coffeehouses, Bill Cosby saw himself as the next Dick Gregory, until manager Roy Silver convinced him otherwise. According to *Newsweek*, his act at that time consisted of "one joke about the first Negro President of the U.S. ('Everything is OK. Just a lot of "For Sale" signs on the street') and 30 minutes of gall." Cosby soon conceded that there was only room for one Dick Gregory.

Yet, by the time Richard arrived on the scene, Dick Gregory had all but abandoned his post as the country's designated black comedian, turning his energy and attention more and more toward civil rights and racial justice, working the college circuit and staging hunger strikes that gave him the gaunt face, sunken cheeks, and protruding eyes of a wizened sage. His press conferences, commentator Ralph J. Gleason noted, had become more entertaining than his stage shows.

Never an overtly political animal or even a student of politics himself, Richard nonetheless possessed an acutely intuitive political savvy. He didn't need a weatherman to gauge the brisk winds that sent hats flying and people chasing after them as they rolled down the streets. (Soon enough, men simply stopped wearing them.)

Cosby uplifted the race without ever mentioning the subject. But the ardor of Dick Gregory's activism awoke even Lenny Bruce to deeper currents running through the nation. When Gregory asked him to join a march, Lenny demurred, reasoning that his legal battles stemming from drug and obscenity charges would only bring down more heat on the march. Gregory assured him that would not be a problem. The only thing that mattered, he said, was to "trick whitey, fuck up Boss Charley."

Trick whitey? Fuck up Boss Charley?

Lenny had never heard that kind of talk before. Then it dawned on him that he'd never heard a black man express any type of hostility, ever. If you're in traffic, he said, and you hear some guy yelling, " 'Hey, asshole, move it over dere!' That's never a colored driver, Mack. Isn't that a little strange?"

Still, some in the civil rights movement, such as Whitney Young of the National Urban League, lamented Gregory's activism, believing he could accomplish far more for the cause through performing his comedy on national television than he would in the marches and sit-ins. "We can find marchers and fasters and people who can run for political office," Young argued, "but we don't have many Dick Gregorys."

By contrast, Cosby developed characters that had more in common with Red Skelton's Mean Widdle Kid than with Dick Gregory's cool scathing wit or, later, Richard Pryor's Mudbone. Although Cosby's material was clean and nonthreatening, he made the medium his message. The very notion of a cuddly color-blind black comic in the sixties was radical in and of itself, said critic Gerald Nachman. "He made folks feel good about America. The humor was just the icing on the cake; *Cosby* was the cake."

Richard arrived in New York City in the summer of 1963 with ten dollars in his pocket. He spent fifty cents on a shower at the Port Authority bus terminal, another dollar to have his suit pressed and shoes polished, bought a pack of cigarettes, splashed on some Canoe cologne, and headed uptown to The Apollo Theater in Harlem, the only place he knew to go. The man there took one look at him and suggested he try his luck down in the Village.

On the bus downtown, Richard struck up a hi-I-just-got-to-town conversation with a fellow passenger who offered him floor space in his rooming house on West Thirty-sixth Street until he got his bearings.

Soon Richard had a place of his own on Fourteenth Street and was sharing bills with the likes of Bob Dylan, Richie Havens, and Woody Allen at clubs like the Improv, the Gaslight, Cafe au Go Go, the Village Gate, and the Bitter End where performers would stop by in the afternoon to take a number, just like at a bakery or deli counter, to determine what order they would go onstage that night. Joan Rivers remembers waiting in that line with the skinny and "brilliantly shocking" young comedian whose jacket sleeves had been "lengthened so many times, he looked like an admiral." Rivers would soon join the ranks of an unlikely assemblage of high-profile fans, including Hugh Masekela, Nina Simone, Budd Friedman, and Miles Davis, who took it upon themselves to promote Richard and champion his career.

While writing an article on Joan Rivers for *Life,* Tommy Thompson and the magazine's entertainment editor Richard Meryman accompanied her to see Richard's act at "some awful place in the Village where you walked down two steps — both literally and socially — when you walked into that club." Even though there were only a few scattered people in the club that night, they all three were astounded by Richard's improvisational flights of fancy. He was just incredible, Rivers says. "Funny, funny, funny. And sad. It was acting, it was comedy, it was social comment, it was everything." Her awe only grew over time. Twenty years later (in the early eighties), she spoke of his stand-up characters as though they were actual people. "They're brilliant and they're ugly, but he makes them funny, and by the humor he takes you through the ugliness and into the humor and makes you aware of everything. Nobody can touch him." Then, in a clear-eyed assessment almost unheard-of in a field so fraught with rivalry, she concluded, "In my own way, I may do some comparable things, but on a much more shallow scale. I do what's painful for the middle-class woman. That's a whole different thing. He does what's painful for somebody who has really lived through pain."

During the last week of August and first week of September 1963, Richard shared a broom-closet-sized dressing room at the Cafe Wha? with pop singer Brian Hyland, who'd hit number one on the Billboard Hot 100 three years earlier at the age of sixteen with "Itsy Bitsy Teenie Weenie Yellow Polka Dot Bikini," a novelty song that he followed with more enduring hits like "Let Me Belong to You" and "Sealed with a Kiss."

"Richard projected such an endearing ease and vulnerability," Hyland says, "he had the audience smiling with him from the moment he hit the stage. He was a master of voices and characters." Hyland sat out front every night to watch Richard's act and said he never did the same set twice. "His off-the-wall riffs always left the audiences roaring. He could do anything. I consider it one of the highlights of my career to have worked with the up and coming comic genius."

Nina Simone invited Richard to open for her at the storied Village Gate, a cavernous upscale club twice the size of the Cafe Wha?, where the stage consisted of a simple riser on the floor out among the tables.

On their opening night, Richard was so nervous he shook like he had malaria. Nina stood with him in the wings as he waited to go on. "I put my arms around him there in the dark and rocked him like a baby until he calmed down," she wrote in her autobiography *I Put a Spell on You*. "The next night was the same, and the next, and I rocked him each time. He never stopped being nervous." Or perhaps he just wanted to be rocked in the arms of Nina Simone.

Miles Davis paid Richard out of his own pocket to open for his quintet's weekend shows at the Gate. "He didn't have a reputation yet, but I knew he was going to be a big star. I could just feel it in my bones," Miles told Quincy Troupe. "I just wanted people to know how great this mother-fucker was."

Improv owner Budd Friedman ran a hard business — some called him a benign dictator — but he always had an indulgent spot for Richard Pryor. Richard once accused Friedman of taking advantage of him because he was black. "I was absolutely heartbroken," he told Chuck Crisafulli of the *Los Angeles Times*. Friedman lay awake that night worrying that the kid might be right. Friedman's wife, wanting to get some sleep herself, tried to reassure him: "You should have told him you take advantage of all performers, regardless of race, color, or creed."

"I told Richard that line and he loved it. We had no trouble being friends again." Friedman even played along with a costly gag the night Richard recruited J. J. Barry, and Martin Harvey Friedberg to join him for a bit of silent slapstick that knocked the crowd silly. Inspired as much by the Marx Brothers as the staged happenings and absurdist theater on display in the Village's more high-minded venues, the three comedians set a table onstage and consumed a full meal in silence, grabbing food off each other's plates, licking the dishes, and otherwise cutting up as the improvisational spirit moved them. The performance culminated in a smashing of plates that brought Friedman, on cue, into the act. He came out screaming, "Is this the way you treat my place!" whereupon he snatched away the tablecloth sending what dishes remained crashing to the floor.

Even though Richard drew attention and praise from all the right people, that Bill Cosby article in *Newsweek* still worried him like a bad tooth. His imagination filled with images of Cosby grabbing the headlines, the money, the precious few TV guest slots for black comics. Yet he'd never seen Cosby perform. One night between sets at The Cafe Wha?, Richard went around to the Bitter End to see Cosby's act for himself. He was amazed to find that Cosby's act was nothing like his own. His jokes were clean — no profanity, no politics, no racial axes to grind. As he walked back to the Wha? for his next set, Richard decided then and there that he would refashion himself in Cosby's image. If Cosby did Noah and the ark, Pryor would do Adam and Eve. If Cosby spun stories of his childhood in the projects of Philadelphia, Richard would spin stories that sounded a lot like Cosby's childhood in the projects of Philadelphia but set in Peoria.

On his debut Warner Bros. LP *Bill Cosby Is a Very Funny Fellow . . . Right!,* Cosby had a bit about the free entertainment provided by winos on the New York City subway. So Richard did one about subway drunks and pickpockets. Cosby parodied professional athletes doing television commercials for razor blades and hair tonic; Richard parodied commercials of real housewives captured on hidden cameras gushing about their laundry detergent.

Unfortunately, it worked: The accolades and bookings that came his way when he followed Bill Cosby's lead put a half-decade-long stranglehold on his true genius.

When word got around the Village one night that a TV talent scout had dropped in at the Bitter End, Richard rushed over and begged owner Fred Weintraub to let him get up on stage. That's all it took. And so, on August 31, 1964, Richard made his national debut on a summer replacement TV variety show *On Broadway Tonight,* hosted by Rudy Vallee.

Vallee, an amiable megaphone crooner from the 1930s, famous for his recordings of "The Whiffenpoof Song" and "Brother, Can You Spare a Dime?" had been on the lookout for someone new to feature on his show. Despite mild grumblings from his producer, Irving Mansfield, Vallee saw Richard as just the sort of "out there" comic who would give his ratings a boost.

Despite his avowed determination to go full Cosby, Richard's jokes were drifting toward pure Dadaism, such as this opening bit for the drawling hillbilly, a character that would take up permanent residence in his repertoire:

I heard a knock on the door. I said to my wife, "There's a knock on the door. My wife said, "That's peculiar. We ain't got no door."

Confronting the intruder (who'd presumably knocked before entering), Richard shifted into pitch-perfect mimicry of Cosby's rapid-fire delivery, right down to the elongated vowels:

I grabbed the-eee crook. That was the-eee wrong move. He threw me down. I got up. He knocked me down. I got up. He kicked me down. I got up. He said get up. I said haaaaa! Then my wife threw him across the furniture. She slapped me. The police came. She beat them up. They took her away. Me and the crook livin' happily ever after.

Always more comfortable when he could disappear into a character, Richard fidgeted between jokes and implored the studio audience to hurry their applause lest he run out of time before finishing his act. "Wait," he said, "I've some more to tell you."

The first words Richard spoke to Vallee's nationwide television audience were, "I want to tell you a few things about myself because a lot of you probably don't know me. I'm not a New Yorker; my home's in Peoria, Illinois." Here he paused for the customary applause that greets the mention of almost any American town, and then he let his face go slack when none was forthcoming.

Not that anyone in Peoria was watching. Richard had called home prior to the show to let his grandma Marie know he was going to be on TV, but his grandfather Thomas answered the phone and, assuming that Richard was calling to ask for money, hung up at the sound of his voice. Even his own father missed the show. With three channels to choose from, Buck tuned in to the wrong one.

But they all saw his second TV appearance, nine months later, on *The Ed Sullivan Show.*

Richard left Peoria with a promise to Miss Whittaker that, one day, he would be on *Ed Sullivan*. As dreams go, it wasn't that far-fetched. From the show's very beginning in 1948, Sullivan openly defied social custom, his sponsors, and the wrath of southern network affiliates by presenting black entertainers on the same stage with whites. In the show's first two seasons alone, Sullivan hosted Cab Calloway, W. C. Handy, Nat King Cole, Pearl Bailey (with whom he held hands!), Illinois Jacquet, Ethel Waters, Billy Eckstine, George Kirby, Jackie Robinson, Hazel Scott, and Count Basie, all a dozen years before Dick Gregory took a seat on Jack Paar's couch.

Sullivan was vaudeville for a cool medium, trotting out a weekly lineup of jugglers, dancers, puppeteers, mimes, animal acts, acrobats, fire-eaters, magicians, and comedians — usually propped up by a big-name Broadway, opera, or movie star — at eight o'clock every Sunday night from 1948 to 1971. Marveling at the litany of shows the other networks sent up against Sullivan over the course of his twenty-three-year run, John Leonard compared him to Yankee left-hander Eddie Lopat who "seemed to throw nothing but junk, and still they couldn't hit him." Or, as Fred Allen put it, Ed Sullivan would stay on the air as long as other people had talent.

Comedy was the driving wheel of his show, but comedy, Sullivan understood, usually hinges on subversion, on pushing against the boundaries of decorum and comfort — either by tweaking the nose or rending the mask — and a reassuring punch line isn't always enough to make an audience forget a negative impression. Comedians, then, were risky business. Sullivan insisted on feel-good humor that would build up rather than knock down, entertain rather than subvert. Therefore, every comedian who ever set foot on Sullivan's stage first had to make the trek up Park Avenue to East Fifty-ninth Street where Sullivan and his wife, Sylvia, shared a six-room suite on the eleventh floor of the Delmonico Hotel and audition his or her act — every word of it — while Ed, a late riser who stayed out till all hours scouring the clubs for fresh talent and bits of gossip for his newspaper column, took his invariable midday breakfast of sweetened pears, iced tea, and a seared lamb chop brought up by room service.

Ed never laughed. It just wasn't in his nature. He seldom smiled. ("Ed's the only person who can brighten up a room by leaving it," Joe E. Lewis quipped.) If Ed really thought an act was hysterical, Jackie Mason once advised a young comic, he might part his lips. Curiously, the few who *do* recall getting chuckles from Sullivan never made it onto the show, a kindness, perhaps, intended to soften the blow when Ed's son-in-law and producer, Bob Precht, delivered the bad news.

Generations of comedians count these vetting sessions at the Delmonico among the most excruciatingly ego-bruising experiences of their lives. None more so than Joan Rivers, who lucked into her first appearance, on May 22, 1966, thanks to a slip of the tongue during the closing of the previous week's show. "Next week, we'll have Johnny Rivers," is what Sullivan had meant to say. Instead, it came out as "Joannie Rivers." Broadcast live, with no chance to do it over, they went out and booked her. (Johnny Rivers, meanwhile got bumped all the way back to March 19, 1967, sharing the stage with Cab Calloway, George Carlin, and the Lovin' Spoonful. It would be his only appearance on the Sullivan show, whereas Joan got invited back nineteen times.)

Producer Bob Precht tried repeatedly to book Richard on the show, but Sullivan just didn't like the kid's attitude. Precht was so convinced Richard would be a hit that he turned to Sullivan's longtime golfing buddy, Alan King, for help. The caustic, cigar-smoking comic was Sullivan's go-to guy who could always be counted on to come in from Great Neck for a last-minute appearance if a show was running short. (On one condition: King refused to follow rock 'n' roll bands. The screaming teenagers screwed up his timing and just didn't get his jokes.) Sullivan trusted King so implicitly that he was the only comedian ever granted dispensation from those midweek auditions at the Delmonico.

"Ed, this kid is terrific," King told him. Coming from King, that was all Ed needed to hear. And there Richard stood, fidgeting in his ill-fitting suit while an expressionless Sullivan, seated in his bathrobe, cut into his lamb chop and nodded for him to begin.

———————

"It was a surprise," Richard's sister-in-law, Angie, said. "We knew he was determined to go that route, but we were surprised to see that he had made it." Everyone watched *Ed Sullivan.*

When the Beatles made their first American television appearance on February 9, 1964, it was on *The Ed Sullivan Show.* The hysteria that attended their performance seemed fueled — at least in part — by the nation's edgy fear and the deep desire to shake free the pall of the Kennedy assassination only twelve weeks earlier. The screams were real, even if rooted as much in terror as exuberance, the times growing darker and less predictable, and Sullivan for his part appeared both delighted and unnerved by the implications of his audience's volatility — the audience no longer serving as mannered witnesses to spectacle but suddenly creating it.

Then, in the autumn of that year, Richard went for a walk through Harlem with his old cohort from the Chitlin' Circuit, Redd Foxx. People downtown in the Village often recognized Richard from *The Merv Griffin Show* or *Ed Sullivan,* but up in Harlem it was Redd Foxx who stopped traffic. He caused excitement, like a one-man parade for a returning astronaut. People stepped out of shops and restaurants, leaving their work to come and greet him. They leaned out apartment windows hollering, "Hey, Redd! Zorro!" On that walk, Richard came to realize that the scene unfolding before his eyes contained everything he ever wanted: for people in black neighborhoods to drop what they were doing and come running to greet him, to love him for who he was and for what he did.

That Richard Pryor might find his voice by stepping off the stage and into the lives of his audience — that he might touch a nerve by illuminating the dysfunction and despair that united them all — appears now as inevitable as it was revolutionary. The bloody battles over civil rights and the graphic images flooding in from Vietnam — both finding their way onto family-dinner-hour newscasts — had done much to tear away the facade of warm gentility that most Americans had grown to expect when they flipped on their television sets.

When Cassius Clay emerged in his new identity as World Heavyweight Champion Muhammad Ali, the country seemed stunned to find him as angry as he was lyrical and buoyant, and a boxer with more on his mind than mere sport. Frank Sinatra's hands might always smell of lavender soap, but he was a brute nonetheless, and even he began to stop pretending otherwise. Live recordings of Sinatra bantering between songs with Dean Martin and Sammy Davis Jr. seem almost to quiver with a giddy, high-alert hum. Every joke, every wisecrack or aside from Sinatra and Martin hinges on the plain fact that these guys were sharing the stage with a mulignan. Sinatra and Martin berated Davis without mercy, ordering him off the stage, while Davis begged them to let him stay.

SAMMY DAVIS: Can I sing with you guys? (*apparently placing a hand on Martin*)

DEAN MARTIN: Hey, hey, hey, hey, HEY, HEY! I'll dance with you, I'll sing with you, I'll swim with you, I'll cut the lawn with you, I'll go to bar mitzvahs with you — but don't touch me!

When Davis announced that he would next like to do a few impersonations, Sinatra broke in with, "Why don't you do Paul Revere? Get on your horse, and get the hell out of here?" Then he thought of an even better zinger: "I tell ya what, do James Meredith of Mississippi."

Davis couldn't have cared less, says Kathy McKee, his longtime girlfriend, confidante, and "mistress of ceremonies." "Sammy was in another world. He was high as a kite. They all were. Everybody was blitzed. The money was flowing, the booze was flowing, the coke was flowing. It was all a big party. There was nothing negative to it ever at all. If anything personal went on inside Sammy about this, he didn't show it."

Why would he? As a member of the Rat Pack, Sammy Davis Jr. was a standard bearer for the swingingest kind of postwar, pre-Beatles cool. It was all for laughs. All ring-a-ding-ding. There wasn't a cushier, crazier gig on earth and coon-calling was just part of the shtick.

In the wake of his breakthrough on *Ed Sullivan*, Richard and his new girlfriend, Maxine Silverman, went on the first of Richard's many epic coke and booze binges that would go on for days and culminate in hallucinations of people from his past ganging up on him, casting accusations, demanding their due. In the depths of this delirium, he missed a second booking on the *Sullivan* show.

When Richard didn't show up for rehearsal, producer Bob Precht booked Lou Alexander, a comedian who'd been opening for Tony Martin at the Copa, to take his place. Alexander had a terrific seven-minute monologue about contact lenses that knocked them dead in rehearsal. Fellow guest Myron Cohen came up to him and said, "Tonight's your night, kid. That routine you just did is gonna kill 'em." But the show ran long, and at the last minute, Alexander was told he had to cut the bit by two minutes. "They cut my balls off," Alexander said. "You take out two minutes, you're killing me. I'm doing this in front of forty million people and editing onstage and you can see I'm white as a ghost. It was not a tenth as good as what I'd done that afternoon." Sullivan walked over when he'd finished and said, "Very good job. Very nice." But Alexander knew that was the end of it. He never went back on *Sullivan* again.

Richard's agent smoothed out the no-show with Sullivan's people. Not only was he invited back, Sullivan granted him an unprecedented exception to the strict time limit he usually imposed on comedians. Russ Petranto, who had the job of keeping a stopwatch on the show, recalled Richard coming in and doing a long, semidramatic piece about a wino warning a young kid not to turn out like him. It ran more than seven minutes in rehearsal. "It was so brilliant you couldn't stand it,"

Petranto said. Both Precht and Sullivan refused to cut it, despite calls from the CBS censor objecting to the raw subject matter.

Sullivan paid Richard five hundred dollars — more than he'd ever received for a single performance. He and Maxine went out to celebrate and bought their first hits of LSD.

Later, and perhaps a result of the LSD, Maxine stabbed Richard in the arm during a fight, sending him to the emergency room. The doctor recognized him from TV and didn't believe for a minute his story that he'd cut himself while practicing a knife trick.

He and Maxine both knew they were no good for each other, but when Bobby Darin offered Richard a three-week gig opening for him at the Flamingo Hotel in Las Vegas at twenty-four hundred dollars a week, he asked her to come with him and she went.

———————

A far cry from today's retina-searing wonderland offering the family values crowd package deals on bacchanalian revelries with prix fixe absolution included in the gratuity, Las Vegas of the 1960s (as Tom Wolfe so memorably evoked it in the pages of *Esquire*) was then a nascent low-rise attraction, its skyline dominated by electric signage — neon pink champagne bubbles rising sixteen stories into the empty desert sky — beckoning to pensioners, mostly women, who wandered the casinos wearing hob-heeled shoes and the same shapeless print dress they had on the day before, as though headed down some Mississippi backroad to buy eggs, carrying around Dixie cups filled with coins to feed the slots in one hand, the other sporting, pre–Michael Jackson, a heavy-duty White Mule work glove so their palms didn't callus from pulling the jackpot levers.

A fierce current of Protestant rectitude ran just beneath the surface. This was the same Las Vegas, after all, where George Carlin, opening for the Supremes at the Frontier in 1969, would be suspended for doing a bit about having a small ass. When he was brought back to fill out the remaining dates on his contract the following summer, Carlin was permanently fired for saying this: "Listen, folks, I don't say 'shit.' Buddy Hackett says 'shit' right down the street. Redd Foxx will say 'shit' on the other side of the street. I don't say 'shit.' I'll *smoke* a little of it."

So in Vegas, Richard would need to be on his best behavior, onstage and off. The characters in Richard's head clamoring ever louder to be set free, to speak with their own voices — they would just have to wait. This was Las fucking Vegas. This was twenty-four-hundred dollars a week. He earned more that three-week engagement than he'd ever made in an entire year, even in the army.

Richard loved Las Vegas — the money, the booze, the showgirls, the nonstop parties, seeing his name emblazoned on the marquee — but underneath it all he felt like a fraud. "I knew I wasn't as good as the reviews said I was," he said, "and I knew why." Of course, it wasn't hard for him to figure out why when so many people kept telling him. Don Rickles put it as succinctly as anyone when he came backstage to congratulate him after a show. "It's uncanny," he said, pumping his hand. "You sound just like Bill Cosby."

No matter the criticisms, Richard was now firmly established as a stand-up comic. What he wanted most, though, was to be a movie star. Much like Elvis Presley, Richard's genius blossomed in front of a live audience, alone on a bare stage with nothing but a microphone in his hand. There no one could touch him. Yet he seemed to regard his sublime gift primarily as a stepping-stone to stardom on the big screen. And, again like Elvis, he didn't much care how crappy, inconsequential, or demeaning those movies might be.

"Give Richard the choice between being a stand-up star and a movie star, and he goes for the Hollywood bullshit every time," Paul Mooney would write in his 2009 memoir, *Black Is the New White.*

Richard was, after all, still the same kid from Peoria who had pasted his name on discarded movie posters and hung them on his bedroom wall.

After their Vegas run ended, Bobby Darin threw Richard a Hollywood coming-out party at a posh restaurant in Beverly Hills that led Sid Caesar to cast him as a detective in *The Busy Body,* a loopy, celebrity-laden, cops-and-gangsters comedy that is of interest today only as Richard Pryor's screen debut.

The prospect of acting alongside Sid Caesar made him jittery enough. Richard had idolized Caesar as a skit comic on the NBC variety series *Your Show of Shows* since he was ten years old. Adding to his nervousness was the fact that he didn't have a clue how movies were made. He'd performed in front of cameras on television, of course, but had never *acted* for a camera in a movie before, and he knew enough to know there was a difference. But he knew how to pretend. He channeled a little bit of Bogart, some Robert Mitchum, a dash of Steve McQueen. And it worked, more or less. Richard's performance brought an element of unruffled, world-weary cool to an otherwise frothy concoction, and he more than held his own alongside Caesar and veteran costars Anne Baxter, Jan Murray, Robert Ryan, Kay Medford, Dom DeLuise, and Godfrey Cambridge.

The Busy Body was released in March 1967. One night the following month, when Maxine was nine months pregnant, Richard went out into the backyard and stood gazing out at the moon. It seemed to beckon him. He got in his car and followed it all the way down to Tijuana. He drank and partied with the whores and tried to take his mind off Maxine and the prospect of once again being a father.

On his way back, U.S. customs officials found the remnants of a bag of pot in his car. It was less than enough to roll a joint, he said, but it was enough to keep him from being present for the birth of his second — possibly third — child, Elizabeth.

Richard admitted that he just didn't care. "It's nothing to be proud of. It's just the way it was," he wrote. The concept of fatherhood is one thing Richard clearly did not copy from Bill Cosby. When TV talk show host Mike Douglas asked Richard what he had done that impressed his kids the most, he said, "I admitted I was their father."

W. E. B. DuBois deemed it a necessity for survival that African Americans maintain a dual identity, a double consciousness. One self they presented to white folks — the masters of slavery, industry, or finance — and one — the real one — they kept for themselves, "just between us."

Zora Neale Hurston wrote of how resistant and suspicious black folks in her native Florida were about sharing with outsiders the folk tales and lore they swapped so freely with each other in the evenings on store porches — reluctant to share even with her, Lucy Hurston's daughter Zora, from over in Eatonville, now that she'd gone up north and come back with a college degree and a Chevrolet.

> They are most reluctant at times to reveal that which the soul lives by. And the Negro, in spite of his open-faced laughter, his seeming acquiescence, is particularly evasive. You see we are a polite people and we do not say to our questioner, "Get out of here!" We smile and tell him or her something that satisfies the white person because, knowing so little about us, he doesn't know what he is missing . . . The Negro offers a feather-bed resistance. That is, we let the probe enter but it never comes out. It gets smothered under a lot of laughter and pleasantries.
>
> The theory behind our tactics: "The white man is always trying to know into somebody else's business. All right, I'll set something outside the door of my mind for him to play with and handle. He can read my writing but he sho' can't read my mind. I'll put this play toy in his hand, and he will seize it and go away. Then I'll say my say and sing my song."

Richard's trouble was that he had all but cut himself off from those places where he felt free to say his say or sing his song.

It didn't happen overnight, as Richard often claimed, but he set about tearing down the wall between his two selves with a decisive and defiant act on Friday, September 15, 1967, his opening night at the Aladdin Hotel and Casino in Las Vegas.

It was a move, everyone knew, that once done he couldn't undo.

Gazing out at the crowd, the bullshit reached critical mass. His eyes landed on Dean Martin, of all people, seated at a table down front, his cigarette curling smoke up into the spotlight as he waited for the comic to give him something to laugh about. A realization slammed hard into Richard's chest that Mama — his grandmother Marie — wouldn't be welcome in the room, would not be allowed a seat at the table. "I was looking out at the audience," he would tell Paul Mooney, "and it hit me that all those motherfuckers out there wouldn't make room for Mama if you put a gun to their heads."

And if Mama wasn't welcome in that place, he had no business being there either. As it was, he knew that the only way he could enter that room was by way of the stage or through the kitchen. No matter how glamorous or lucrative, the stage door was still a service entrance.

That's when his inner High John the Conqueror kicked in, his Stagolee, his Bad Nigger. "Every black man harbors a potential bad nigger inside him," psychiatrists William H. Grier and Price M. Cobbs would write in their landmark *Black Rage*, published just nine months later. "The bad nigger is bad because he has been required to renounce his manhood to save his life. The more one approaches the American ideal of respectability, the more this hostility must be repressed. The bad nigger is a defiant nigger, a reminder of what manhood could be."

So standing on that Las Vegas stage, Richard leaned into the mic. "What the fuck am I doing here?" he said, and left the stage.

Moments later, he was trapped. He'd turned the wrong way when exiting the stage and found his path blocked by the theater's soundboard. Recalling the venerable comic gag where a man, filled with righteous anger, storms out of a room slamming the door behind him, only to emerge, sheepishly, moments later from what turned out to be a closet, Richard had no intention of crossing back in front of that audience. He edged his way along a narrow passage in the dark and squeezed through a tiny gap between the proscenium and a soundboard that was so tight he drew blood scraping his face against the brick wall, a scene that conjures up images of passing through a birth canal.

———————

One rumor, started by Richard himself while joking with a reporter, had him running naked through the casino, leaping up onto one of the tables and waving his cock in the air while yelling, "Blackjack!"

The most entertaining account — still current in some circles — has it that Richard whipped out his dick onstage and began pissing either on or in the general direction of a coterie of "very special people" (read high-powered mobsters) who were so incensed that their henchman seized him on the spot and trundled him off to await a swift and certain execution, a sentence rescinded thanks to appeals from a delegation of black entertainers led by Bill Cosby who, as the story was related by novelist Claude Brown, gave the performance of his life, down on his knees streaming crocodile tears. "The boy is sick," Brown had Cosby plead. "We'll look after him. *I'll* look after him. He won't do it again. That's a promise." The mobsters finally relented and delivered a shell-shocked Richard Pryor into Cosby's care.

Richard, in his book, says the mobster incident never happened.

His agent and the Aladdin's management, however, did give him a thorough dressing-down. He would never work in that town again, they told him. He never did.

Two months later, though, he was back on *Ed Sullivan.*

———————

Richard would forever after describe his Aladdin meltdown as his personal and professional epiphany, marking the B.C.–A.D. divide in his life, although the transition was in no way so decisive or abrupt. He'd long been keeping it real, doing real-life material in friendlier venues, yet more than a year after the Aladdin incident, according to Mooney, his transformation was nowhere near complete. He continued channeling Cosby, was still unhappy with himself. He still did not know who or what, exactly, he wanted to be. All he knew was that he had to get over, to keep pushing ahead till he found what felt right. What his meltdown onstage at the Aladdin did was cut off any means of easy retreat.

The Vegas walk-off wasn't entirely driven by artistic angst. The storms were raging all around him. Maxine had filed suit for child support, claiming that they had lived together as husband and wife — a characterization Richard neither could nor would deny. He had often introduced Maxine as his wife and addressed her as such in letters. She had legally taken his last name and would keep it for the rest of her life.

Following his breakup with Maxine, Richard moved into a hundred-dollar-a-month room in the notorious Sunset Tower Motel. Coming in late one night, he got into an altercation with the night-shift desk clerk. Richard claimed he had no recollection of ever striking the guy, but the police report said he punched him in the face and broke his glasses. The clerk successfully sued him for seventy-five thousand dollars.

Richard, at that point, said, "Fuck it." He tried to make himself invisible, at least as far as the System was concerned. He threw away his driver's license and stopped carrying any type of ID. He closed his bank account, stopped cashing paychecks — there is the perhaps apocryphal story of a friend who started leafing through a book in his apartment and found a months-old check for eighty thousand dollars that Richard was apparently using as a bookmark — stopped paying parking tickets or income tax.

———————

Richard's appearances on *Ed Sullivan* and *Merv Griffin*, his run in Vegas, and his movie with Sid Caesar all put him in a caste above all the other climbers he mingled with at bungalow parties around L.A.

It was at one such gathering on Sunset Boulevard that Richard walked up to the drop-dead gorgeous model Carol LaBrea and said to the guy she was with, "Let's all take off our clothes and have an orgy!"

Those were the first words Richard Pryor ever spoke to Paul Mooney.

"Let's go, let's do it, man. Look at these ladies! Let's all get in bed and have a freak thing!"

Mooney's attention had been drawn to Richard from the moment he and his date walked in the door. "Right away I sense he is different," Mooney writes. "He is smiling and laughing. Everything pleases him. He knows there are lots of women and drugs around, and that fills him with childish delight. Like a kid in a candy store. . . . And right away, the first thing out of his mouth, he says he wants to go to bed with me."

Richard's date worked for ex–football star Jim Brown and did some moonlighting on Sunset Strip dancing in the cages at Whiskey a Go Go. So did Carol LaBrea. Maybe that's where Richard had seen her before. He knew her from somewhere. What he didn't know was she was Mooney's half sister.

Despite this questionable first impression, Mooney would become Richard's most trusted lifelong friend, champion, and collaborator.

———

Mooney found it impossible to be angry with Richard. "He's so obviously without guile. He just has no inhibitions. . . . No other considerations figure into his actions, nothing else other than 'I want it.'

"For everybody else in the world, an attitude such as this would come off as totally insufferable. But Richard makes it work because he's completely open and vulnerable. Sure, he's selfish. But he's selfish with the innocence of a four-year-old. . . . He makes me feel protective toward him."

The first time they went to a party together, Mooney sized up the room filled with dope smoke, the cocaine laid out on the table, and told Richard he was cutting out. He'd been to enough parties like this to know that he hated them. "Sometimes it seems like everybody in L.A. is high but me," he writes. Richard was flabbergasted to learn that Mooney didn't do drugs. He didn't drink; at least not the way Richard drank.

He persuaded Mooney to stay. They could just hang out and talk—

and Richard would take Mooney's share of the drugs being passed around.

"I get Mooney's share!" became Richard's cheerful refrain whenever they were out together and someone broke out the powder.

Remembering how often he heard that phrase, Mooney reckons that he single-handedly doubled Richard's drug intake.

When Richard went back to New York to open for Miles Davis at the Village Gate in the winter of 1968, Miles bestowed upon him a magnanimous vote of confidence by flipping the bill. He sent a member of his entourage to Richard's dressing room to tell him there'd been a change in plan. "Miles is gonna play first," he said. Miles had decided to make him the headliner.

After the show, Miles took him to a midtown apartment to meet a woman known as Gypsy Lady who provided them with the best cocaine he'd ever had. They "chopped and snorted until the sun crept through the windows and then we disappeared like vampires."

"From now on you get your coke from her," Miles instructed him.

During that same engagement at the Village Gate, Richard caught the eye, and the fancy, of Shelley Winters who came backstage afterward and offered him a part in her upcoming movie *Wild in the Streets*.* Richard was more than happy to pay the price of admission, according

---

The Green Berets starring John Wayne is often erroneously cited as Richard's second film role by commentators who generally express puzzlement as to why he would be billed as Richard "Cactus" Pryor. They might well be puzzled, too, by the fact that he never once appears onscreen. The role of Collier was, in fact, played by the son of vaudevillian Richard "Skinny" Pryor. Born January 7, 1923, Cactus was a popular Austin, Texas, media personality and a close friend to John Wayne, who, coincidentally, introduced Richard "Cactus" Pryor to the cast and crew of *The Green Berets* as "the funniest man alive," some years before that mantle would be more prominently and lastingly bestowed upon Richard Franklin Lennox Thomas Pryor.

to Mooney, getting "Wild in the Sheets" with Miss Winters, "the most cock-hungry actress in Hollywood."

Richard, for his efforts, was able to get Mooney a job on the film as his stunt double, and his new girlfriend, Shelley Bonus, a role as an uncredited extra playing a "tripped-out hippie chick." With her long blonde hair, miniskirts, white patent-leather go-go boots, and outsized tinted glasses, she fit the part perfectly, although Shelley insisted she was no hippie. Hippies were filthy. She was a flower child.

American Pictures International's *Wild in the Streets* was an over-the-top election year romp in which rock star Max Flatlow (Christopher Jones in a role turned down by Phil Ochs) makes a devil's bargain to deliver the youth vote for Senate candidate Johnny Fergus (Hal Holbrook) and ends up being elected president in a landslide victory at age twenty-four, running as a Republican, by giving fourteen-year-olds the right to vote, spiking the water supply with LSD, and consigning adults over the age of thirty to reeducation camps. Richard played Stanley X, the nonobservant Black Muslim drummer in Max Frost's band (also an anthropologist and author of *The Aborigine Cookbook,* according to the voiced-over introduction). With its pre-Woodstock split-screen sequences, acid-trip camera work, and swirling score by space-age composer Les Baxter, the movie garnered an Oscar nomination for best editing and achieved a cult status that endures unto the present day. Although he made good use of the opportunity to observe firsthand how movies were made, the film itself was a disappointment to Richard, one that sent him spiraling into yet another bout of "What the fuck am I doing here?" soul searching.

———————

On nights when he wasn't performing, Richard liked to hang out with Redd Foxx at his Jazz Go-Go club on Adams off Western, snorting coke and flirting with the cocktail waitresses while Foxx regaled him with stories of the old days, back before he and Richard had worked together on the Chitlin' Circuit.

Foxx told him how, while working in Chicago in the late 1930s, he and three members of a washboard band eager to make their names in show business, hopped a freight train bound for New York, where Foxx — still going by his birth name John Elroy Sanford — became fast friends with a Detroit hustler by the name of Malcolm Little. Because they shared matching "mariney complexions" and red hair, friends took to calling them "Chicago Red" and "Detroit Red," respectively.

The two Reds worked together at Jimmy's Chicken Shack, a Harlem eatery and jazz club at 763 St. Nicholas Avenue near West 148th Street, Little as a waiter, and Sanford — taking over a job previously held by Charlie Parker — as a nine-dollar-a-week dishwasher. The two shared a bed of newspapers on a nearby rooftop.

"We had about 500 pounds of newspapers up there," Foxx told *Ebony* magazine. "Newspapers is some of the warmest stuff going."

"Chicago Red" became famous as Redd Foxx, and "Detroit Red" as Malcolm X. Foxx would point with pride to the passage in the *Autobiography* where Malcolm said, "Chicago Red was the funniest dishwasher on this earth. Now he's making his living being funny as a nationally known stage and night-club comedian. I don't see any reason why old Chicago Red would mind me telling that he is Redd Foxx."

Richard met his future second wife, Shelley Bonis — she preferred to spell it Bonus — at a dance club just before filming began on *Wild in the Streets*. Her father, Harold Bonis, was a show-business Brahman who had managed comedian Danny Kaye for more than three decades.

As husband and wife, Richard and Shelley set out to live as flower children in their own private Eden. Mooney once drove up to the cabin they shared above Laurel Canyon to find them, literally, hugging trees. Shelley arranged flowers in Richard's hair, recited poetry to him. They gave each other rocks as gifts. They gave the rocks names.

Richard would later depict the two of them existing in this blissful state from the stand-up stage. "'Oooh, a rock for me?' If I gave that bitch a rock today, she'd hit me over the head with it."

Shelley took him to task for not being informed or politically aware of his people's struggles, for not reading books. So did Groucho Marx.

At the party Bobby Darin had thrown for him when he first arrived in L.A., Richard found himself cornered by the great comedian, who, to Richard's chagrin, recalled seeing him on *The Merv Griffin Show* when he and fellow guest Jerry Lewis, desperate for laughs, began spitting on each other.

"Do you ever see plays? Do you ever read books?" Groucho scolded. "Do you want to end up a spitting wad like Jerry Lewis, or do you want a career you can be proud of?"

Shelley, being more hip to the literary and political writings that informed black consciousness, encouraged Richard to read young black poets, along with the writings of Angela Davis, Malcolm X, and the prison writings of former rapist and eventual Black Panther Eldridge Cleaver published in the Catholic literary quarterly *Ramparts* and later collected in the best-selling *Soul on Ice.*

In reading *The Autobiography of Malcolm X,* Richard would learn that the One True God first appeared to the Honorable Elijah Muhammad (then Elijah Robert Poole) in 1931 in the person of Mr. Wallace D. Fard, then posing as a seller of silks in Detroit. This was but one of several revelations that Malcolm shares in his book — another being that an evil scientist named Yacub (Jacob of the Old Testament) had created a race of white-skinned devils "6,600 years ago" — that can be jarring to Malcolm's political admirers unfamiliar with the Lost-Found Nation of Islam as preached by the Honorable Elijah Muhammad.

Richard, we can imagine, would have been delighted to learn of Mr. Muhammad's 1931 encounter with God in the flesh on the streets of Detroit. The story melds perfectly with his portrayal of the black preacher who "first met God in 1929, outside a little hotel in Baltimore." (If, in fact, Malcolm's account of Elijah Muhammad's encounter with the One True God on the streets of Detroit is what sparked Richard's routine, he clearly demonstrates how well he knows his craft, as any student of comedy can attest that his elongated "nineteen twenny-nahhhh-nah" is much funnier than 1931.)

"Richard puts on an outrageous character I instantly recognize from my childhood," Mooney writes. "It's the kind of pompous, self-inflated preacher every black churchgoer knows."

Richard performed a nascent version of the routine in May 1968 at P.J.'s, an after-hours club on Santa Monica Boulevard in West Hollywood.

> I was walking down the street eating a tuna fish sammich. That's right, in 1929 you'd eat anything you could get. And I hear this voice call unto me, and the voice has power and majesty. And the voice said, "Pssst . . ." I walked up to the voice and I said, "What?" And the voice got holy and magnificent, and the voice said to me, "Gimme some of that sammich." And every since that day I've been able to heal, because I didn't give up none of my sammich. I said, "If you're God, make your own goddamn sammich. Don't be messin' with me."

(In some performances, God beckons to the preacher from down a dark alley. "However," his preacher concludes, "I did not venture down that dark alleyway, because it might not have been the voice of God but two or three niggers with a baseball bat.")

"I hear the true voice of the preacher in the bit," Mooney says.

Mooney was struck, too, by what he didn't hear.

Richard didn't crack a single joke. No punch lines. No toppers.

"My God," Mooney thought. "He's left jokes behind. Is he going to leave me behind, too?"

———

Nine months later, Richard did a nearly identical version — minus the "goddamn" — on the premiere installment of *This Is Tom Jones,* a TV show taped at BBC Elstree Centre/ATV Studios in Hertfordshire, England, and broadcast Friday, February 7, 1969 on ABC.

Jones had not been familiar with Richard before he came on the show. He believes the network booked him as a way of testing the waters, as they wanted to align themselves with the rising wave of black performers.

"I thought he was really funny," Jones says, "but sort of . . . scared, almost. Very skittish and quiet." Then he made one of the female production assistants cry. "It seems Richard's car wasn't waiting as it was supposed to be after the taping, and he screamed at her that if his car wasn't there in five minutes he would rip her head off and ram it up her ass. Maybe he was just trying to be funny, acting out as if he was outraged by something stupid. But it upset a lot of people."

When the two men met again, many years later, Richard seemed genuinely thrilled to meet the Welsh soul singer saying, "Wow, great to finally meet you, man." Jones was embarrassed to remind Richard that not only had they met before, but that he'd been a guest on Tom's show. "He kind of said . . . 'Oh yeah . . . yeah, man . . . that's cool,' but I'm not really sure he remembered."

So many of Richard's friends over the years — colleagues, cohorts, and business associates — have said the same thing, arriving at nearly identical metaphors, to the effect that there was a big emptiness somewhere at his core, a hole he kept trying to fill with drink and drugs. A pain he kept trying to numb.

"There's something desperate about Richard stuffing his face with dope and drink. Something is bothering him, something deep down at the root of his soul," Mooney writes. "I know if I had an album, a Las Vegas date, or a film role, I'd let myself be happy for at least a little while. Those are the kinds of shots that every stand-up wants to nail. It's what we are all working for. It kills us that Richard has it and it can't make him happy."

Just as the soda fountain and pay phones at Schwab's drugstore became "headquarters" for Hollywood actors and dealmakers in the 1940s and '50s, so Duke's Coffee Shop, at 8585 Santa Monica Boulevard, was to the musicians and comics who performed in West Hollywood clubs during the 1960s and '70s.

Duke's was a greasy-spoon diner on the ground floor of the Tropicana Motel, a haven for actors, musicians, writers, poets, film producers, and rock stars. Owned by Dodger pitcher Sandy Koufax, it became like a West Coast incarnation of New York's Chelsea Hotel but with a motor court and Astroturf around the pool.

It was at Duke's one midafternoon in September 1968 that a morose Richard Pryor, recently returned from his father's funeral in Peoria, sat nursing a hangover with brandy-laced coffee when Paul Mooney came bouncing in and took the seat opposite him.

"Oh, man," Mooney said, "I just saw a lady so pretty somebody should suck her daddy's dick for a job well done."

For a moment, Richard simply stared back at him. Then he laughed.

"You know you can die happy when you make Richard Pryor laugh," Mooney writes. "His laugh is like ripping open a bag of joy."

Richard used the line that very night during his set at Doug Weston's Troubadour, amending it slightly but significantly to "Coming here tonight I saw a woman so motherfucking beautiful gorgeous that it made me want to suck her daddy's dick for a job well done." The place exploded. Afterward, Richard slipped a ten-thousand-dollar watch on Mooney's wrist as payment for the gag.

Richard recorded his first LP on Dove/Reprise during his September run at the Troubadour, but he didn't include Mooney's line on that record. He didn't commit it to vinyl until *That Nigger's Crazy*, nearly six years later, when he incorporated it into the "Wino & Junkie" routine he'd been refining and expanding and digging deeper into for years, dating back to when an awed Ed Sullivan allowed his performance to run overtime rather than ask him to cut it.

Here's how Richard's junkie made use of Mooney's line:

JUNKIE: I saw a bitch, she was so fine. . . . Shot bolts through my heart, baby.

WINO: Nigger, you wouldn't know a fine woman if you tripped over her.

JUNKIE: This bitch was *fine,* pops. I ain't lyin'. Bitch was so fine I wanted to suck her *daddy's* dick. Is that fine enough for your ass?

Richard's junkie blurred the edges of that line, opening it up. There is no longer any quid pro quo. He wants to suck her daddy's dick, not as a reward for a job well done but more like some sort of primal desire to get at the source — the essence — of the woman's beauty. It gets a huge laugh, but it's not really a joke anymore.

The junkie, like many of Richard's characters, seems to know more about life than his creator does. Or perhaps, through his characters, Richard came to know more about life than he could process. They carried him into deeper, more turbulent waters than he could navigate.

———————

Richard was at a stage in his development where, according to Mooney, "he never knows what he's going to say. The words just spill out. I've done enough improv to know how tough it is to do what Richard's doing. Just a man and a microphone, saying whatever's on his mind at the moment, developing it on the spot into a routine."

The title track of his Laff Records album *Rev. Du Rite* includes a young woman's astonishingly emotional testimony of how she sought out the faith-healing Reverend Du Rite to cure her of a runny nose. Richard's trembling, feminine voice is so pitch-perfect, it seems he has disappeared completely into the character. At first, the audience laughs but then falls into a rapt silence until the Reverend reappears to provide what can best be described as comic relief.

Sometimes his spontaneous muse led him into more bewildering territory. In "Boobs," another track released on *Rev. Du Rite,* a stripper stands trial for exposing her breasts in public.

The hapless stripper is asked to describe her boobs ("I dunno. They're just a pair of ordinary ones. They hang kinda low . . .") and further asked if they have a criminal record. The prosecutor then turns on her and thunders, "Is it not true that you took your boobs and touched them on the grave of John Dillinger in 1948? Thus, I hereby say to you that you have had your boobs associating with the underground! If you'll pardon the expression."

There is scarcely a murmur from the crowd.

"Little hip for you folks, huh?" Richard breaks character. "Face it, that was kind of wild. I'll get out of it, though. Don't sweat it."

That connects. He gets an appreciative chuckle, but he doesn't get out of it. When his from-out-of-nowhere gender-reversing twist at the end gets more groans than laughs, Richard hurls it right back at them: "Yeah, well, I'm disappointed in you, too."

Then there is the stunning versatility of "Hank's Place," a nearly eleven-minute ensemble piece set in a Peoria after-hours club patronized by hillbilly johns, thugs, hustlers, a stuttering cop who orders an underage Richard out of the joint, and a carpenter who offers to recushion Hank's craps table in such a way that "the dice always tell the truth."

Richard peoples the stage with no fewer than nine characters who argue, hustle, cajole, and otherwise interact with each other as they pass in and out of the room. And, like a vaudeville juggler, he keeps all the plates spinning. A telling moment comes about a third of the way through when, at the conclusion of his minute-long monologue as "Black Irma," the audience rewards him with a spontaneous outburst of applause. Not laughter for a punch line, mind you, but an ovation of the sort usually reserved for a virtuoso guitar solo or a scene in a play. Stand-up comics don't get this kind of response, but Richard does.

Richard and the audience both seem to know they are witnessing an artist in the process of discovering his genius. Yet, for all his giddiness, Richard is fully in control, letting this fish he's hooked carry the line out, reeling it back in, then letting it out farther.

"He speaks what he hears on the streets, at parties, and during drug transactions," Mooney writes. "What Richard does is knock down the walls between who he is onstage and who he is off it, until there's less of a difference between the two." W. E. B. DuBois's double consciousness. "His routines are no longer comic confections whipped up in some comedy kitchen. They come straight out of his bent life."

It was 1969. The year the Beatles broke up. Judy Garland and Jack Kerouac died. The year Ohio's roiling and oil-slicked Cuyahoga River caught fire, and the United States instituted a draft lottery. American families sitting down to dinner in front of their TV sets were confronted with images of the My Lai massacre, the Stonewall riots, and the Manson murders. It was the year U.S. cities, one after another, began to riot and burn, as Chicago and Paris had done the year before.

It was also the year of Woodstock, where music and drugs and mud created a legend, and then, only a few months later, the Altamont Speedway Free Festival where Hell's Angels were hired to provide security and, on that day, they were the Man. They knew firsthand how the Man conducted his business. They busted some heads, knocked Jefferson Airplane's bassist Jorma Kaukonen unconscious mid-performance and, during the Rolling Stones' spectacularly raw and raucous set, stabbed a spectator to death right next to the stage. The Maysles brothers' terse documentary film *Gimme Shelter* attests to the fact that, aside from the brutality, it was a fantastic show, and most in attendance didn't know about the stabbing until they saw it on the news the next day; but just the same, a curtain had come down, and it signaled the end to a generation's utopian dream. The sixties were over. Anger, violence, and fear dragged the Aquarian flower children into darkness as it always did.

Having burned his bridges in Vegas, dissatisfied with *Wild in the Streets,* and equally unenthusiastic about the few other film roles that had been floated his way, Richard and Shelley decided to make their own movie from a script — or, more likely, an idea for a script — Richard had been kicking around. They convinced themselves that Richard's movie would shake up the world.

Shelley thought, too, that it might save their marriage, and so she sank into it the whole thirty thousand dollars her parents had given them as a wedding present, despite their misgivings about the marriage. It was pretty much all the money they had in the world. Shelley, though, was willing to risk it because, at that time, in that place, everything seemed possible. The heady euphoria of those drug-infused times inclined them both to believe that the plans they made were revolutionary and, once unleashed, would spark a raging fire. That was a common phenomenon of the times, as great creative minds disappeared behind closed doors and into a coke-stoked paranoia that told them all, one way or another, that their visions were potent enough to be dangerous. More often than not, though, the same manic fears kept many artists from completing anything, lest their vivid and grand presumptions about the relevance of what they incubated in dark rooms, curtains drawn and taped together — attended by enabling friends, hangers-on, and sycophants — not be met in kind.

Twenty-two-year-old film student Penelope Spheeris and her boyfriend, Bobby Schoeller, were walking across UCLA's campus toward Melnitz Hall when this black cat crossed their path about thirty feet ahead of them wearing a long brown leather coat and a big wide-brimmed hat, very odd looking for a college campus even then. "Oh my God," Bobby said. "That's Richard Pryor!" Penelope had never heard of Richard Pryor, but Bobby pulled her along saying, "Come on, let's talk to him."

They introduced themselves, curious to know what he was doing on campus. Richard explained that he was looking for some film students to help him make a movie; Penelope said, "You found her."

———————

The movie's title changed several times. Today, it is generally referred to as *Uncle Tom's Fairy Tales*. Few who were involved had a clear idea of what the movie was supposed to be about, but the consensus recollection is of a surreal allegorical tale concerning a white man standing trial before an all-black jury and judge. The man is charged either with raping a black woman or, according to some recollections, for the collective crimes of whites against blacks throughout history. Nobody ever saw a script, although they did see Richard from time to time consulting a spiral notebook of frayed, handwritten pages.

"Richard was crazy on the set, okay? We would assume that," says Penelope. "Pretty screwed up all the time on coke."

The cast consisted of a lot of friends and character types — Paul Mooney and comedian Franklyn Ajaye among them. Members of the jury had plates or mirrors of cocaine in front of them, and the judge swigged from a bottle of booze.

"They all looked like crack heads," Penelope says.

The movie's cast and crew were never sure what sort of domestic mayhem they might walk into when they reported for work at Richard and Shelley's Hancock Park house. Massive amounts of coke coupled with Richard's samurai sword collection did little to calm jittery nerves.

For Franklyn Ajaye, the filming was not a pleasant experience. The first day they met, Ajaye remembers that Richard was screaming at his wife in the kitchen. "It was a pretty rough scene."

When the two comedians came to know each other later on in the seventies, appearing regularly on *The Midnight Special* and *The Tonight Show,* and together on Flip Wilson's show and in the movies *Car Wash* and *Stir Crazy,* Ajaye never mentioned to Richard that he'd been in his movie. "I doubt he remembered me from that, and I never saw it. I don't know if he ever finished it. I didn't even know what it was called."

Ajaye recalls that his character had to wash the man standing trial, "like in a car wash or something. It was kind of a strange-ass fucking movie." Ajaye put in a seventeen-hour day for a fee of thirty-four dollars and Richard paid him with a bad check. "It certainly didn't make you want to be in movies, I can tell you that," he says with a laugh.

———————

A few weeks into the filming, Penelope Spheeris fainted behind the camera. When she came to, Richard was standing over her in his all-white pimp costume. She heard him saying to someone, "Hey, this bitch is pregnant!"

"Oh, Richard, shut up!" she said. "I am *not!*"

Richard knew it before she did. He was psychic about some things, Penelope now says. It stands to reason that any extrasensory powers Richard might possess would naturally be attuned to detecting pregnancy.

———————

In March 1969, Richard took time out from working on the movie to visit his mother, Gertrude, who was gravely ill in Peoria. At her hospital bedside, Richard presented her with the gift of a simple hand mirror he'd bought at the airport, not even bothering to wrap it. He sat on the edge of her bed and looked away with nothing very certain to say, nursing his shame and the bitter memory of his grandma Marie — the only woman he ever called Mama — coaching him, at the age of ten, on what he should say when the custody judge called his name so that he could come live with her in that big bustling bawdy house filled with lust, signifying, knife fights, the groans of hard-earned delight, and the thumping of heavy furniture audible through the walls instead of with this woman, his actual mother. She died a few months later.

———————

After completing filming on *Uncle Tom's Fairy Tales,* Penelope spent more than a year at Richard and Shelley's house, often putting in twelve-hour days cutting the film on a Movieola set up on a table in the den back by the kitchen.

There would always be arguing going on upstairs between Richard and Shelley, "and it would just be — oh, God — it would be so hard to work because I couldn't hear because they were yelling at each other."

A lot of their arguing had to do with Richard's friends. They were always around. Paul Mooney was a "very, very, very smart guy," Penelope says, "but he really got on Shelley's nerves. Paul was like a character out of *Alice in Wonderland,* always sitting around, smug, making brilliant but insulting comments about everything and everybody. She would be cooking in the kitchen and Paul would keep harassing her, doing a southern drawl and saying shit like, 'Miz Shelley, are you gwine to fix us some greens and beans and ham hocks?' It drove her crazy. He and Richard clicked so well because they both had this thing that they were going to erase racism."

In the midst of this frenzy, Rain came into the world.

Rain Pryor was born July 16, 1969. Richard and Shelley took it as a sign that their daughter arrived on the day of the Apollo 11 liftoff, the world's first manned space mission destined for the moon. They called her Rain because it rained that day. It was so weird to have rain in July in L.A.

Rain, her parents believed, was destined to make a mark on the world: a biracial child born in the Age of Aquarius during the Summer of Love, at the dawn of the space age, as the first man embarked to set actual foot upon another celestial sphere, heralding the future, now arrived, where race distinction would be a thing of the earthbound past.

"They both really believed if they both had a child they would start a color revolution," Rain says. "They would change the way America looked at race."

Shelley envisioned her newborn daughter as a window out onto a bright and open field. She may be excused for not knowing that the die had long before been cast, the pattern well established: whenever a child was born unto Richard Pryor, he turned tail and ran.

Richard would follow the same dance steps nearly every time he wanted out of a relationship, as if they were outlines painted on a floor. As he did with other women, Richard did his best (worst) to make Shelley push *him* away. But she wouldn't, and remained, either unwilling or unable to acknowledge as significant any breach of his against her vested vision of their life together. On the day he was to bring Shelley and their infant daughter home from the hospital, he never showed. A nurse finally called Shelley a cab, and when she walked into their bedroom, babe in arms, she found Richard in bed with their housekeeper, as he surely knew she would. But even that wasn't enough. Shelley forgave him. The worse he treated her, the tighter she clung.

Richard returned to New York for roles in two films, *You've Got to Walk It Like You Talk It or You'll Lose That Beat* and *Dynamite Chicken.*

Not released until September 1971, *You've Got to Walk It Like You Talk It* was a disjointed counterculture satire written, produced, and directed by twenty-seven-year-old Peter Locke (who, in 1983 with Donald Kushner, would form Kushner-Locke Productions). *New York Times* reviewer A. H. Weiler described it as the "wacky saga" of a "young, confused middle-class hero tilting against the windmills of the Establishment." Over the course of the eighty-five-minute film, the hero (played by Zalman King) goes up against "his doting mother, a crazy old lady; the Puerto Rican minority municipal madness in the form of a new job ferreting out 'revolutionaries' supposedly out to bomb our highways; group therapy; Madison Avenue advertising; Women's Lib; abortion, and even unrewarding marriage and fatherhood. . . .

"Mr. Locke is partial to more than a few gross sequences," Weiler wrote, "some of which are funny, such as the one involving Richard Pryor, the TV and nightclub comic, who plays a gibbering lush in a men's room." The film is also notable for its sound track, which comprises the first recordings ever released by Donald Fagen and Walter Becker, some two years before they formed Steely Dan.

Richard took top billing in the barely acknowledged and largely forgotten *Dynamite Chicken* — a frenetic hodge-podge of performances, skits, interviews, and archival footage that writer-producer-director Ernie Pintoff presented as "a multi-media movie magazine inspired by the TV generation." The film included rapid-fire clips of John & Yoko, Andy Warhol, Al Capp, Joan Baez, Allen Ginsberg, Muddy Waters, Malcolm X, the Ace Trucking Company, Lenny Bruce, Jimi Hendrix, Sha Na Na, Robert Mitchum, and on and on. Interspersed throughout the movie, a scruffy-looking Richard in a paint-spattered work shirt does perhaps eight minutes of stand-up material outdoors amid the rubble surrounding a boarded-up cinder-block building. A text crawl at the beginning of the film states:

> In the late '60's, Penelope Gill, Chairperson of the Daughters of the American Civil Patrol, filed this special report:
>
> "On June 18, I attended a Richard Pryor performance in the company of policewoman Elsie Schoenberg, #6492. During his presentation, Mr. Pryor used the following words on several occasions:
>
> bullshit
> shit
> motherfucker
> penis
> asshole
>
> The substance of Mr. Pryor's dissertation was primarily based on denouncing the Military, the Pope, the President and the Police.
>
> In addition, Pryor greatly offended us by graphically illustrating how family, friends and luminaries pass gas."

Perhaps being on set for the filming of *You've Got to Walk It Like You Talk It* reinvigorated Richard's resolve to complete *Uncle Tom's Fairy Tales*. Upon his return to California, he arranged to show the movie to Bill Cosby and asked Penelope to reserve a screening room at UCLA.

Penelope Spheeris gave birth to a daughter, Anna, on Saturday, December 13, 1969. Nine days later, she was back on the job at Richard's house with her infant daughter in tow. Penelope fashioned a makeshift bassinet for Anna on the floor next to the Movieola. Richard paced around the room while Penelope worked to finish a cut of the movie to show Bill Cobsy.

"Richard had a whole collection of samurai swords in the living room. He got the swords out and started flailing them around. And I remember going, 'Yeah, those are really nice swords, Richard, but could you kind of do them away from where the baby is.'"

As that first day wore on, Penelope began to worry seriously if the film's dialogue (example: "Eat shit, you pig-faced motherfucker") might inflict emotional or psychological damage on her infant daughter as she ran the scenes over and over and over again to get the edit just right. "And I'd wonder, is this going to screw up my child? Today I think I was right," she says with a laugh.

At some point that afternoon, Shelley came in and announced that she was sick of this shit. Sick of their movie and of the pretense that it somehow mattered or ever would. The money was all gone and, in case Richard hadn't noticed, he had a wife and daughter to take care of.

Richard thought he knew how to placate her.

"He said, 'Well, look at what I did. I got you a present.'

"He brought out a big box and takes out a full-length fox coat — red fox, ironically. I don't know how much it would've cost back then, but thousands of dollars. A lot of animals went into that coat.* Shelley said thank you, and five minutes later they were arguing again."

Spheeris had just shown Richard her edit of the whole film up to that point, about forty-five or fifty minutes on a 16mm reel. The way a Movieola works, as the edited film unspools, it can either go onto a take-up reel or collect loose in a large bin.

"On that particular showing, I let it go into the bin," she says. "The bin was about three and a half feet off the ground and it was full of film.

"They were still fighting. He said, 'You think I love this film more than you? Watch this.'"

Richard grabbed an armload of edited film out of the bin and tore the whole thing up. Literally, he ripped more than a year's worth of work and all their hopes and wedding money to shreds with his bare hands.

"I mean, we're talking little four-inch pieces," says Spheeris. "I'm going, 'No, no, no, no,' because it ain't like the digital age where you've got it stored somewhere."

Shelley at that point retreated upstairs and got in the shower.

"So Shelley's running away. I'm screaming, 'Don't do it!' He finishes tearing up the film, goes out and gets in his car. I could look out the window and see him getting into this Volkswagen Squareback they had. He starts to take off and she comes running down from upstairs and she's naked.

---

*Longtime girlfriend and onetime fiancée Kathy McKee was always suspicious of any gift Richard gave her. He was so sneaky and so deceitful, she says, that unless he actually went with her into a store and bought her something that she picked out herself, she just took it for granted that the fur coat he offered up from his closet or the diamond bracelet he pulled from his pocket had previously belonged to some other girlfriend. He always seemed to have one or two such gifts on hand. McKee herself, on the occasion of one of their several breakups, left behind a twelve-thousand-dollar Siberian silver fox cape that a previous boyfriend had bought for her in Hong Kong. She never saw it again. Richard's house was a virtual fur and jewelry exchange/bazaar. She lost the fox cape but gained a black mink coat she saw hanging on a doorknob in his house in Beverly Hills. "Oh, you like that coat?" Richard said. "It's yours."

"She runs out the door and jumps on the hood of the car. She's beating on the windshield and Richard takes off with her naked on the front of the car. That's what I saw as I looked out the window.

"So I grab the fox coat and I run out to my own car and I follow them. He goes north on Plymouth, hangs a left on Wilshire Boulevard — major street, okay? — and Shelley is still on the front of the car."

At some point Richard decided to pull over and stop.

"Shelley gets off the car. I pull over. I give Shelley the coat. She covers up. Richard takes off again."

Shelley refused Penelope's offer of a ride back home, opting instead to wait for a cab so she could go after her man.

Penelope spent days splicing the pieces of the film back together like a jigsaw puzzle. She reconstructed the forty-some minutes of film by arduously piecing together the mangled pieces, some only a few frames long. The result was so crumpled and patched together that the film danced all around as it ran through the projector gate, adding an unintended element of slapstick to the story.

That's what they showed to Cosby.

At that time the movie was between forty and fifty minutes long.

"My understanding was that Cosby bought the film, but it still wasn't finished. Maybe he just wanted to give Richard some money. Maybe because Richard was his primary competition, he wanted to take the movie and shelve it. But that's pure speculation."

Penelope doesn't know whether or not Cosby ever took possession of the print or the negative. (Richard, in his book, says that he convinced Bill Cosby to pay for a final edit. When Richard screened the completed print for Cosby his only comment was, "Hey, this shit is weird." Richard agreed and stashed it away somewhere.) Wherever the footage ultimately wound up, only four people are known for certain to have seen the film in its final but unfinished form: Richard, Penelope, Bill Cosby, and whoever was running the projector that day at UCLA.

———————

Richard had been paying Penelope an agreed-upon day rate, a minuscule amount by today's standards but not bad for a twenty-three-year-old aspiring filmmaker in 1969. But by the time they screened the movie for Cosby, he hadn't paid her in three months, and now she had a baby daughter to care for. She went to him — he was sitting at the dining room table, she remembers, deep in one of his moods — and said to him, " 'Richard, I don't think I can keep working anymore unless you pay me.' And he said something like, 'Why don't you just take the whole thing and get the hell out?' "

She didn't take his movie, of course. "I knew that wasn't right," she says. But she left and would not see Richard again until the early 1980s when she got a job directing sales presentations and music videos for Warner Bros. Records. She was assigned to do one for Richard's latest LP, a long-form promo that the label would send to distributors worldwide and recut as a thirty-second commercial to promote the album on TV. Richard had proposed doing a skit at Licorice Pizza, a record store on Sunset Boulevard kitty-corner to Whiskey a Go Go. The premise was that he would go into the store and buy his own record. Penelope had the lights set, everything ready. He showed up late ("He was always late") and when he saw her there, his mood turned dark. He was cordial, but there was a palpable discomfort because of how their relationship on *Uncle Tom* came to an end.

The shoot did not go well. Richard's performance was flat, unengaging and uninspired. He complained about having to do multiple takes and clearly just wanted to get the fuck out of there.

As to the story line and possible whereabouts of *Uncle Tom's Fairy Tales,* there are multiple conflicting accounts from which to choose. In Pryor's own telling, the film, which he recalled shooting in March 1969, tells the story of a wealthy white man abducted by a group of Black Panther–type militants who hold him prisoner in a basement and put him on trial for all the racial crimes in U.S. history. For a time, the film was called

"The Trial," although Richard ultimately retitled it "Bon Appétit," a line the chamber maid reportedly shouts at the protagonist as he is being hauled away following an episode of interclass cunnilingus. Penelope Spheeris has no idea why he chose that title. She, of course, shot and spent months and months editing the footage and she recalls no such scene. "Nobody in the film ate anything," she says. She suspects that Richard simply liked the sound of the phrase.

Richard writes that he borrowed money from shady characters to complete the edit, but after a falling out, the unfinished print was stolen and held for ransom. Richard bought it back, but then it disappeared again. Some time later, Paul Mooney saw it advertised at an art house theater in downtown L.A. Pryor managed to get the print back. Flashforward some thirty-five years. Spheeris, while relocating her archives, discovered a reel of dailies from the shoot, approximately thirty minutes of raw unedited footage with no audio, and donated it to the Motion Picture Academy's archive collection. A brief clip was included in a 2005 tribute to Pryor, prompting a lawsuit by Richard's wife, Jennifer Lee, against both Spheeris and Richard's daughter Rain for the return of what Jennifer presumably believed was the only existent print of the finished movie, which, the suit claims, had been stolen from Pryor's home in the mid-1980s.

Listed on the Internet Movie Database under its original and best-known title *Uncle Tom's Fairy Tales,* the film enjoys an 8-out-of-10-star user rating, despite the near certainty that not one of the raters has actually seen it. If the film still exists at all, Penelope's best guess is that it's in Bill Cosby's vault.

After all her stories of cocaine and chaos and samurai swords, the screaming fights and Lady Godiva rides down Wilshire Boulevard, we had to ask Penelope: Was it ever fun working with Richard?

"Oh my God! Hilarious! Are you kidding me? Richard Pryor!"

Penelope remembers he would walk around in his pajama bottoms, a silk robe, and slippers, carrying a plate or mirror of coke and a bottle of Courvoisier, riffing on current events and making fun of people. "It was like having my own private concert right there."

"There was one time when he was in an amazingly good mood. I think he might've been bipolar . . ."

The doorbell rang and Richard sent Penelope to answer it. It was some guy in a suit looking for Richard Pryor.

Acting on a hunch, Penelope told the man she wasn't sure if Richard was there or not. "I said, 'What's this about?' and he said, 'I'm with the IRS.'"

Penelope went back and told Richard. (She didn't know then that Richard had not filed a tax return since 1966.) He said to tell the guy that he'd just left to go to the airport. While she was explaining this to the man from the IRS, Richard came around the side of the house with a pair of gardening shears and started trimming the hedges right next to the guy. Richard grinned and nodded to him like, "I'm just the gardener, suh." It was all Penelope could do not to break up laughing. "He must not have known what Richard looked like because he didn't hassle him or anything, he just left."

The IRS would finally catch up with him in June of 1974. By that time, everyone knew who Richard Pryor was.

———————

In the meantime, Richard devoted himself to woodshedding his new-found voice(s) at the Troubadour, the Redd Foxx Club, and John Daniels's Maverick's Flat, a converted Arthur Murray dance studio that became a symbol of integration in the mid-1960s as Hollywood stars like Marlon Brando and Steve McQueen came to hear musical performers such as Parliament, Marvin Gaye, and Ike and Tina Turner and to see upcoming black comics like Richard and Flip Wilson. The Temptations were the first act to play Maverick's when it opened in January 1966, and the title song on their 1970 LP *Psychedelic Shack* was an homage to the club's funky decor and visionary mindscape artwork on the walls.

———————

On February 8, 1970, Richard was back in New York for his twelfth appearance on *The Ed Sullivan Show*, sandwiched between a chimpanzee and saxophonist Boots Randolph. For weeks after that broadcast, Harry Belafonte recalls that he was liable to burst out laughing at the most random and inopportune times — waiting for an elevator, in a meeting, riding in a cab — recalling the comedian he'd seen on *Sullivan* that Sunday night. Richard had introduced himself as a defiant, in-your-face poet. His first poem consisted of a single word shouted for a full breath as loud as he could: "BLAAAAAAACK!"

He politely acknowledged the audience's applause as he shuffled through his sheets of notepaper, then introduced his next work. His second poem was a street-inflected stanza from the nursery rhyme "Hey Diddle Diddle." However, he explained, his poem had been altered by the establishment, "as are the works of most black artists." The rant that followed is what floored Belafonte: "Now a lot of you out there probably doubt this coming from a black man, but if a wh-wh-wh-white man was to stand up here and tell you, you might believe it." That was why, Richard exhorted his audience, "We got to get together and organize ourselves against wh-wh-wh-whitey, because, if we don't, we gonna be in a lot of trouble." Each time he tried to say the word *white*, Richard's proud, defiant poet was reduced to a wincing, stammering mess, contorting his entire body as he struggled to expel the word. "Now, a lot of you out there, you're sayin' to yourselves right now, Well, if you feel that way about wh-wh-wh-white people, how come you married to a wh-wh-wh-white woman?' That ain't got nothin' to do with it."

At first, Belafonte didn't recognize Richard as the rail-thin comic with the ill-fitting suit who had appeared on the 1967 special he'd produced for ABC showcasing African American humor. That show, a part of the ABC Stage 67 anthology series, was titled *A Time for Laughter: A Look at Negro Humor in America.* Hosted by Sidney Poitier, it starred Moms Mabley, Redd Foxx, Godfrey Cambridge, Diahann Carroll, George Kirby, Harry Belafonte, and Dick Gregory. Richard contributed a skit in which he played a funeral home director who, when the deceased's minister failed to show up, delivered a — this hardly needs saying — crude and irreverent eulogy while perched atop the coffin. He'd come a long way in just three years.

For the remainder of that year, Richard knocked around L.A. with Mooney, landing occasional gigs doing guest shots on TV dramas and sitcoms such as *The Young Lawyers, Wild Wild West, The Mod Squad,* and an interesting episode of *The Partridge Family* intended as a pilot for a proposed series that would have teamed Richard with co–guest star Louis Gossett Jr. as brothers trying to make a go of an inner-city Detroit nightclub housed in an abandoned fire station. In that episode, titled "Soul Club," a booking agent's error has the Partridges showing up at the club instead of the scheduled headliners, the Temptations. The Partridges get busy and organize a block-party fund-raiser that saves the club from being taken over by a local loan shark known as Heavy (Charles Lampkin).

In April of 1971, Richard returned to New York to film his first stand-up movie — perhaps the world's first stand-up performance film — at the Improvisation. Directed by Michael Blum, the forty-six-minute feature, *Live and Smokin',* wouldn't be released for another decade.

Back in L.A. later that spring, Richard sat in Mooney's car, parked on Crenshaw at the corner of Santa Barbara, a block up from Maverick's, just before dawn, drinking Courvoisier from a paper cup.

"I'm losing my motherfucking mind, Mr. Mooney." Richard always called him that, after a character on *The Lucy Show.* "This city is driving me nuts."

The past two and a half years had left him wrung out, strung out, and hung out to dry. Maxine had an arrest warrant out on him for nonpayment of child support. His movie and his marriage to Shelley were both in tatters.

Mooney had been planning a trip up the coast to Oakland to visit his grandmother — his mama — and invited Richard to come along.

Oakland. The Black Panthers. San Francisco. Berkeley. Hippie chicks with no bras.

But most important, Mooney told him, "It ain't L.A."

"It ain't L.A." Richard repeated the words softly, almost magically, as though scarcely able to believe, in that moment, that there could really be such a place as "ain't L.A." It sounded mythical and magic, like Shangri-la or Oz.

A week later, they were driving up Interstate 5 in Richard's blue Buick convertible, with Mooney behind the wheel and Richard behind a bottle of Courvoisier ("I'm getting better mileage than he is," Mooney quips), singing along with the Temptations' song, "Ain't Too Proud to Beg" at the top of their lungs. When the song ended, they switched off the radio and kept on singing a cappella, beginning with "I Heard It through the Grapevine" as they approached Grapevine, California. When they'd exhausted the Motown catalog, they started making up their own songs.

By nightfall, as they descended into the Central Valley, Mooney got quiet and just listened as Richard went on humming off-tune in the dark and, with each sip of Courvoisier, muttering, "Fuck L.A."

It's good to feel the cloying hand of Los Angeles relax its grip, speeding north into the desert. Rather than snake their way along the scenic coast highway, Richard Pryor and Paul Mooney opt instead for the straighter vein of Interstate 5, which takes them quickly over the hills, through the grapevine, and into the cooked flatlands . . . past trailer parks, truck stops, power dams, slaughterhouse holding pens, and many miles of little else. The route offers no sea breezes or glimpses of spouting whales, but they can gun the motor and keep an easy watch for the highway patrol who pay less late-hour heed to this inland stretch than to the quaint beach hamlets. Anyway, it is dark, and a dome of stars arcs above them as they sail, top down, singing along to the radio.

Richard sinks lower into the passenger's seat, nursing a bottle and protecting a continuous string of cigarettes from the wind. Ahead is Berkeley, a series of boldly drawn blurred lines where poets, Black Panthers, tripping musicians, cross-dressers, co-ed radicals, and shaggy scientists launch their test balloons into the ether, their near-religious ferocity largely unmatched by the goal-oriented ethos that keeps the City of Angels to the south staunchly on the grid.

Past three in the morning, and still two hours from the Bay, the music has gone silent, the only thing on the radio call-in program where desert dwellers trade UFO abduction theories.

Richard has gone quiet, too. The fear that had gripped him in L.A. slips from his shoulders like a boxer's robe, only to be replaced by a new one, as he edges himself further onto a tightrope where the fix of the far-end's tether is wholly unknowable.

"Baby, everything is alright, uptight, out of sight," sings Paul Mooney.

Richard lets loose the tail end of his cigarette, lofting it straight above his head and into the wind. It skips with a shower of sparks on the dark flat road behind them.

PART **THREE**

THERE'S A RIOT GOIN' ON

Like Jesus to the wilderness, Robert Johnson to the crossroads, and Malcolm X to Mecca, Richard went to Berkeley.

Berkeley, 1971. A hotbed of free love, psychedelic drugs, and black power. A conflation of scenes as drawn by M. C. Escher, an anthill of revolutionary movements, inverted and swarming in the same space and time; working at cross-purposes and each consumed with such single-mindedness they scarcely noticed the others' presence, let alone the possibility or strength of joining forces: the acid-tripping hippies helmed by Ken Kesey and the Grateful Dead, academia's free speech movement, militant African American groups like SSAC (Soul Students Advisory Council). They were all talking revolution.

Mostly, that's *all* it was. Talk. While Kesey and the Dead spiraled deeper into a satisfied self-indulgence, Huey P. Newton and Bobby Seale — flanked by a few badass cats they recruited off the block — came strutting into an SSAC meeting with shouldered weapons on Malcolm X's birthday (Huey's idea). The leadership freaked at the prospect of actually practicing what they'd preached. So Huey and Bobby resigned the SSAC, went off on their own, and formed the Black Panther Party for Self-Defense.

This was the scene Pryor and Mooney walked in on.

For Mooney, it was a trip back home, a return to his past, a chance to recharge and reconnect. For Richard, it was an escape, a way forward, a self-imposed exile to purge himself of the vicious Hollywood-Vegas talk-show cycle eating away at his soul.

Richard set himself up in a $110-a-month apartment on the city's
west side at the edge of the freeway just blocks from the marina (where,
Mooney noted, freighters would dock every day with kilos of smuggled
cocaine stowed away in their holds). He furnished his place with little
else but a bare mattress on the floor, a portable TV, record player, a few
books, typewriter, and tape recorder.

There Richard got busy, spending his days holed up in his apartment,
writing, desperate to release the "world of junkies and winos, pool hustlers and prostitutes screaming inside my head." Richard would describe
this hiatus, which stretched into two years, as "the freest time in my life,"
marking his full flowering as an artist: "Berkeley was a circus of exciting, extreme, colorful, militant ideas. Drugs. Hippies. Black Panthers.
Antiwar protests. Experimentation. Music, theater, poetry. I was like a
lightning rod. I absorbed bits of everything while forging my own un-
charted path."

When he ventured out, he wandered the street wearing sandals, a
kimono, and a conical hat that made him look, in his words, like a "de-
ranged wizard."

This was Richard's "fuck it all" period, says Mooney, "denying himself for the sake of his art. His job, as he sees it, is to find a way out of
the box that white people want to keep him in. He feels like it's killing
him. He has to get out from under it just to survive as a man." House,
career, clothes, women, friends — he cast them all aside. If he expected
to "find his lost soul," he needed to cast off all but the bare essentials, to
renounce the past in order to discover the future.

No one except Mooney knew how to find Richard. No one entered
his orbit he didn't want to let in. The ones he did admit would include
the brightest stars of the Bay area's literary renaissance, foremost among
them novelist Cecil Brown, author of *The Life and Loves of Mr. Jiveass
Nigger,* who would become Richard's longtime running buddy and
screenplay collaborator; Angela Davis; Claude Brown (*Manchild in the
Promised Land*), poet Al Young (*The Song Turning Back into Itself*); and

Ishmael Reed, who Richard considered one of the most honest people he ever met.

Reed's years-ahead-of-hip-hop technique was to mix and sample borrowings from pop culture — a then-unheard-of practice in the realm of novel writing or anywhere else, for that matter — to create his gumbo-styled prose. Reed characterizes the technique as a defining force running through all of African American culture, making use of gathered scraps to create something whole.

Mooney, on one of his frequent visits to check in on Richard, could see that he was going through a profound transformation, "going all intellectual on me." The most apparent evidence of this was that he had switched from Courvoisier — emperor Napoleon's preferred brand of cognac — to a more proletariat vodka. Either went well with cocaine.

———

Cocaine, coffee, cigarettes, and vodka notwithstanding, Richard's main sources of sustenance were Marvin Gaye's just-released LP *What's Going On* and the published speeches of Malcolm X. "All he does," Mooney writes, "is listen to music and read Malcolm X all day long."

As Richard had grown weary of entertaining Vegas and talk show audiences with his Cosby-lite material while the streets of U.S. cities and college campuses were billowing smoke, so too did Marvin Gaye yearn to move beyond the infectious pop confections churned out by the Motown hit machine. In June 1970, Gaye recorded "What's Going On," a song cowritten by his label mate Renaldo "Obie" Benson of the Four Tops, and Al Cleveland. The record was backed with Gaye's own song, "God Is Love." But Motown president Berry Gordy Jr. refused to release the single. Neither track had that "Motown sound." So Gaye essentially went on strike, refusing to record any more material until Gordy relented, which he finally did, in January 1971. The record was an immediate success. Gaye recorded the rest of the album in just ten days in March, and Motown released it on May 21.

Although Gaye addressed a world of hopelessness in the face of poverty, urban decay, environmental blight, war (Gaye's younger brother, Frankie, had recently returned from a three-year hitch in Vietnam), and police brutality, the LP's title track was not phrased as a question — there is not a single question mark to be found anywhere in the lyric — but issued as a statement. This *is* what's going on. Listen and you will know.

When Richard first read *The Autobiography of Malcolm X*, at Shelley's insisting, he lamented that he hadn't been paying attention when Malcolm was alive and addressing crowds on the streets of Harlem just a subway ride uptown from his Greenwich Village flat. But reading Malcolm's speeches gave him a jolt, a shock to the system. Even in cold print, Richard felt the cadences and rhythms, the visceral way Malcolm connected with and played off of his audiences, and — not nearly enough credit or attention has been given to this — his comic timing and scathing sense of humor. Malcolm saw little advantage in repressing his hostility, although he was always civil. He politely declined an invitation to share a stage with George Lincoln Rockwell, the founder of the American Nazi Party. Neither would he address a rally for the KKK despite its leadership's eager embrace of his calls for segregation. Things had gone topsy-turvy. Time was needed to sort it all out. Most jarring for neophytes listening to recordings of his speeches is how joyfully *funny* Malcolm was. He elicits a surprising amount of laughter from his audiences, usually accompanied by startled gasps of recognition. (In a *Newsweek* review of *Growing Up X*, the 2002 memoir by Malcolm's daughter Ilyasah Shabazz, writer Curtis Harris favorably compares Malcolm's comedic style to Richard Pryor's.) Richard also enjoyed reading Malcolm because "he shows me I'm not out of my mind." Here, for example, in his speech "Message to the Grass Roots," Malcolm lays out the distinction between slavery-era "house Negroes" and "field Negroes."

The house Negroes, they lived in the house with master, they dressed pretty good, they ate good because they ate his food — what he left. If the master's house caught on fire, the house Negro would fight harder to put the blaze out than the master would. If the master got sick, the house Negro would say, "What's the matter, boss, we sick?" We sick!

That was that house Negro. In those days he was called a "house nigger." And that's what we call him today, because we've still got some house niggers running around here.

The Negro in the field caught hell. In the house they ate high up on the hog. The Negro in the field didn't get nothing but what was left of the insides of the hog. They call them chitlins nowadays. In those days they called them what they were: guts . . . The field Negro was beaten from morning to night. He lived in a shack, in a hut. He wore old, castoff clothes . . . When the house caught on fire, he didn't try and put it out; that field Negro prayed for a wind, for a breeze.

You've got field Negroes in America today. I'm a field Negro.

You don't hear field Negroes talking about "our government is in trouble." They say, "*the* government is in trouble." Imagine a Negro [saying] "Our government!" I even heard one say "our astronauts." They won't even let him near the plant. "Our astronauts. Our Navy." That's a Negro that's out of his mind. That's a Negro that's out of his mind.

Malcolm, it should be remembered, admonished his followers to get off welfare, to break the chains of dependency by cleansing themselves of drugs and alcohol — when you unscrew the cap on a bottle of liquor, he reminded them, that's a government seal you're breaking — to form their own businesses and to patronize each other's.

"Of all of our studies, history is most prepared to reward all research," Malcolm often said, and "the white man made the mistake of letting me read his history books." He spoke with equal passion of the revolutions in Russia, China, Cuba, and colonial America, of how the Viet Minh overthrew the French at Dien Bien Phu while at the same time exhorting his followers to heed the examples of free enterprise as practiced by General Motors and the F. W. Woolworth Company.

After a time, Mooney became anxious to resume his career in L.A., even if he had misgivings about leaving his friend in Berkeley, holed up all alone in that "shitty little studio apartment" where he might go for weeks on end without seeing anyone except coke dealers and food-delivery boys. Before leaving town, Mooney made sure Richard had at least a few acquaintances he could reach out to. So he took Richard to meet his mama, who still lived in his old Oakland neighborhood on Eighteenth Street. She fed them a meal of butter beans and neck bones that Richard declared the best he'd ever eaten in his life. As Mooney recalls:

> Mama thinks he's fooling with her but he's not. That meal isn't the first beef neck bones Richard eats in his life . . . He chows down on possum, rabbit, whistle pig, fat-back, garden greens and chitterlings like the best of us. Black folks developed a taste for food like this in slave times. The massa always takes the choice cuts for himself. We are left with snouts, ears, neck bones, feet, rectums, and intestines. But we make a silk purse out of a sow's ear. The discarded cuts turn out to be the best eating.

Mooney also introduced Richard to his old high school pal, Black Panther Party minister of defense Huey P. Newton. Newton graduated from Berkeley High a functional illiterate but then doggedly taught himself to read by struggling through Plato's *Republic*, plowing all the way through it no fewer than five times until he understood it. The book, and his accomplishment in learning to read it, fueled his aspirations to become a political leader.

By the time he and Bobby Seale formed the Black Panther Party in October of 1966, Huey Newton had completed two years of law school and was well known on campus for his spirited discussions on the finer points of constitutional law. Bobby Seale was an engineering design major who had spent three years in the air force doing structural repair on high-performance aircraft and had worked on the *Gemini* missile program. Yet the press and political forces portrayed the Panthers as armed hoodlums and drug thugs who roamed the streets looking to gun down white people. J. Edgar Hoover's counterintelligence unit regarded even the Panthers' free breakfast program a threat to national security. The free breakfast program, which by 1969 served more than ten thousand Oakland children every morning before they went to school, was but one of the party's "survival programs," along with clothing and food giveaways, escort services for the elderly, and health care services that included testing for sickle-cell anemia.

Still, the only thing that mattered to the media and to a majority of Americans — the only thing they *knew* about the Panthers, apparently — was that they had guns. At that time, white America could scarcely imagine anything scarier than "armed Negroes."

The scariest thing they *couldn't* have imagined would be Negroes with unconcealed weapons operating out in the open and entirely within the law — angry young militants brazenly availing themselves of their legal and constitutional rights the same as everyone else. "They were registered guns," Newton pointed out. "Just like the NRA's guns. Just like Charlton Heston's guns."

This wasn't what the Establishment had in mind when they advised minorities to work for change within the system. They meant casting ballots — with proper ID and no outstanding warrants — every couple of years for either candidate R or candidate D. That didn't mean exercise your rights to peaceably assemble, to engage in free speech, or bear arms and, when challenged, demand the courts to either uphold those rights or announce to the whole world, point-blank, that those rights didn't apply to people like you. But that's what they did.

Here, as they so often did, the Panthers followed the example set by Malcolm X, who, through the auspices of his Organization for

Afro-American Unity, dedicated what was left of his brief life toward bringing charges of human rights violations against the U.S. government before the United Nations. Malcolm didn't expect a reversal of fortune, he wasn't asking for reparations. At that point, he hoped for nothing more than an acknowledgment of what had been done, a public reckoning of how the United States had made itself the most powerful nation on earth and at what cost. It remained, in his eyes, the only way anyone involved could ever get over.

Exercising their constitutional right to bear arms was but one weapon in the Panthers' arsenal. Along with their guns, they carried tape recorders, cameras, and law books as they patrolled the streets on their mission to "police the police," to observe and document law enforcement's volatile interactions with Oakland's black citizenry.

Prominent white leaders were willing to concede, for the record, that even though there was no legal basis for denying African Americans their full civil rights and liberties, society was simply not ready for an upheaval of such seismic proportions. In other words, blacks would just have to wait until whites were ready to grant them their rights, although none were prepared to say just when that might be.

Huey, Bobby, Stokely, Hubert, Eldridge, Sherwin — who would've guessed that such bookish, even nerdy-sounding names could strike apprehension and fear in the hearts of white America more than midway through what was supposed to be its greatest century?

Congress went so far as to pass a law against the party's minister of justice Hubert "H. Rap" Brown — the "Rap Brown" Federal Anti-Riot Act, tacked onto a fair housing law at the last minute by Senator Strom Thurmond, making it illegal to travel from one state to another, write a letter, make a telephone call, or speak on radio or television with the intent of encouraging any person to participate in a riot.

An alarming headline on page 1 of the April 30, 1967, *San Francisco Examiner* read: "It's All Legal. Oakland's Black Panthers Wear Guns,

Talk Revolution." "If a Hollywood director were to choose them as stars of a movie melodrama of revolution, he would be accused of typecasting," the story began. The writer marveled that the Panthers' "lithe, slender, saturnine and handsome" leader — his good looks marred by the "blunt, ugly riot gun" in his hands — was "a Negro who doesn't use that word but calls himself black."

"What man in his right mind," the reporter asks parenthetically, "would call himself black?"

———————

Eldridge Cleaver, the Panthers' future minister of information, famously recalled undergoing a personal transformation during a meeting of the Bay Area Grassroots Organization Planning Committee at a storefront on Scott Street in San Francisco's Fillmore District when four armed members of the Black Panther Party — Huey P. Newton, Bobby Seale, Bobby Hutton, and Sherwin Forte — entered the room dressed in their uniform black berets, powder blue shirts, black leather jackets, black trousers, and shiny black shoes.

> From the tension showing on the faces of the people before me, I thought the cops were invading the meeting, but there was a deep female gleam leaping out of one of the women's eyes that no cop who ever lived could elicit. I recognized that gleam out of the recesses of my soul, even though I had never seen it before in my life: the total admiration of a black woman for a black man.

A black woman gazing upon a black man with a look of total admiration. That was a look Richard Pryor longed to see for himself. How many of his most biting (and most hilarious) routines describing his relations with women were laced with a crippling fear that he was despised in their eyes, that he was something less than a real man, whether manifest in the shame he felt at a black woman's accusing glare when he went out in public with a white woman on his arm, or the indignities he suffered at the hands of police in the presence of any woman, black or white?

Richard makes the point plainly in his routine about a black couple going out for a night on the town only to be pulled over by a cop and ordered out of their car at gunpoint:

"GET OUT OF THE CAR THERE WAS A ROBBERY. A NIGGER LOOKED JUST LIKE YOU. PUT UP YOUR HANDS, TAKE YOUR PANTS DOWN, SPREAD!"
Now what nigger feel like having fun after that?
"Uh, let's just go home, baby."
You go home, beat your kids and shit. . . . You wonder why a nigger don't go completely mad.

Richard would find much to admire in Eldridge Cleaver's story involving a car donated to the Panthers by a white man in Berkeley who sympathized with the work the party was doing. The car was a big help to the party but also a headache, because it had Florida license plates. All of the Panthers' vehicles were well known to the Oakland police. It took only a few days before word got around and they began routinely stopping the car. Cleaver usually took responsibility for driving the car because he had multiple forms of valid identification, including a driver's license, draft card, Social Security card, and a variety of press credentials from *Ramparts* magazine. He even had a press card issued by the United Nations. Once, an Oakland cop stopped him demanding to know whose car it was. Cleaver told him that a white man from Florida had donated it to the Black Panther Party. "You expect me to believe that story?" the cop said. "No white man in his right mind would give the Black Panthers a car." Cleaver had a ready reply. "Maybe this white man is crazy."

"Police put a hurtin' on your ass," Richard told the crowd at the Purple Onion, a cellar club in San Francisco's North Beach area. "They really degrade you. White folks don't believe that. . . . White folks get a ticket, they pull right over (*white voice*) 'Yes, officer, glad to be of help.' A nigger got to be talking 'bout, 'I am reaching into my pocket for my license, 'cause I don't want to be no motherfuckin' accident.' "

When he recorded the routine as "Niggers vs. Police" on *That Nigger's Crazy,* it spread throughout the country. Richard realized how big the record had become when he was out working on the road and people in the audience started speaking the lines right along with him.

He was understandably startled when two policemen were ushered into his dressing room before a show in Detroit. But they merely wanted to share with him their story of having pulled over a black motorist who gave them Richard's line word for word.

THE WORD MADE FLESH

Berkeley in 1971 wasn't Hollywood. There Richard had been *too* black. It wasn't even Greenwich Village where a no doubt well-intentioned comedy writer had counseled him, "Don't mention the fact that you're a nigger. Don't go into such bad taste." Here militant black men were arming themselves, taking it to the streets, excoriating him for his show-biz ambitions and exhorting him to be black above all else.

Richard was intrigued by the Black Panthers' emphasis on education. Like Malcolm, they prized their knowledge of history. They studied not Malcolm but Frantz Fanon's *The Wretched of the Earth* and *White Skin, Black Masks;* the quotations of Mao Tse-tung; Marcus Garvey; and Toussaint L'Ouverture's 1794–1803 Haitian revolution, the uprising that became the model for third-world liberation movements from Africa to Cuba.

As much as he admired the Panthers' ideology and courage, Richard had to confess he could never be a for-real revolutionary. He liked white women too much. He even admitted to having an erotic dream about Tricia Nixon. "I woke up. I was like 'What the fuck?' I mean you know you got the white-woman disease bad when you're having dreams about Tricia Nixon, right? Cause Tricia, she can't give her pussy away. Even the Secret Servicemen, they be like, 'Uh, not now baby, I gotta go wash the car.'"

Shelley had once berated Richard that he was incapable of loving anyone.

Not true, he said. "I love Miles."

Now word came that Miles and Shelley had been hanging out. Richard convinced himself they weren't sleeping together, but still, the thought of it tore him up inside. He bought a pawnshop trumpet and started blowing it on street corners. "Only I didn't know how to play," he said. "Not a fucking note. But I blew the motherfucker as if the shrill, discordant sounds that went screaming into the darkness would let everyone know how unhappy I felt inside."

His performances in Berkeley clubs could be just as bizarre. Some nights, he went onstage and made strange animal noises. "Other nights I repeated a single word like 'bitch' or 'motherfucker,' but gave it fifty-seven different inflections. Each outing was like playing jazz, searching for that one perfect note that would carry me into a higher state of bliss. I never thought about what I was going to do until I did it." In Berkeley, he might find an audience for that sort of thing, but whatever it was, it wasn't stand-up comedy.

And then one night he stepped onstage and tried it with the word *nigger*. Just flat-out said it, like a man committing himself to a 12-step program.

"Hello. My name is Richard Pryor. I'm a nigger."

He said it again.

"A nigger."

Again and again. Just that one word, over and over, he recalled, "like a preacher singing hallelujah." It gave him strength, he said. It robbed the word of its wretchedness and made him feel free.

"What we both like about the word," writes Mooney, "is that it demonstrates a simple truth. White people cannot say it in front of black people without declaring themselves to be racist. . . . We are saying something that white people can't. It's forbidden to them but allowed to us. Ain't too many things like that. It's liberating."

Flip Wilson had a similar awakening, sparked by a white friend who told him, "Look, I think you've got a lot to express. But you're inhibiting yourself . . . well, because you're a nigger. Now that's a word I don't use, but I want you to understand. I think black people are too self-conscious about having been slaves. All nationalities have been slaves, and nobody has come back faster than you people . . . I'm amazed at black people, yet they spend all that time feeling sorry for themselves. The point is, it's over. It's over! Damn what anybody thinks of you. Say what you have to say and help open up somebody else's eyes."

That, Wilson said, is when he realized how interesting being black is. "Niggers is fun!" he would say.

Not everyone felt the euphoria. Some were mortified, accusing Richard of self-hatred and "running down the race," as if that word, in his hands, had the power to undo the decades of racial progress. What rankled others was the way he took the folkloric language of the street corners, neighborhood bars, barbershops, and pool halls and paraded it out on a public stage before mixed audiences. John A. and Dennis A. Williams, authors of *If I Stop I'll Die: The Comedy and Tragedy of Richard Pryor*, described the reaction as "like hearing a language that might be spoken only at home being shouted through the streets."

Jabari Asim, author of *The N Word: Who Can Say It, Who Shouldn't, and Why*, similarly observed that Pryor had "devised a new style that was raw, obscene, and often delivered while its creator seemed to teeter on the verge of weeping or violence. . . . To blacks with middle-class sensibilities . . . he was as embarrassing as he was funny, like a witty but uncontrollable cousin who you just knew was going to act up in front of audiences."

It didn't help that white commentators were nearly universal in lauding his new raw and racial style. Mark Jacobson declared Richard's use of the *n*-word a "masterstroke."

"When Pryor says it, it means something different," *Time* magazine insisted.

Depending on his inflection, or even the tilt of his mouth, it can mean simply black. Or it can mean a hip black, wise in the ways of the street. Occasionally nigger can even mean white in Pryor's reverse English lexicon. However he defines it, Pryor is certain of one thing. He is proudly assertively a nigger, the first comedian to speak in the raw, brutal, but wildly hilarious language of the street.

Today, forty-some years after his N-word epiphany, audiences and middle American hip-hop listeners are well versed in the N-word's variant spellings and nuanced meanings. In commentaries penned by scolds and advocates alike, the N-word's prevalence in contemporary popular culture is traced back to Richard Pryor.

Harvard Law School professor Randall Kennedy sets the stage in his book *Nigger: The Strange Career of a Troublesome Word:*

> While the hip comedians of the 1950s and 1960s — Dick Gregory, Nipsey Russell, Mort Sahl, Godfrey Cambridge, Moms Mabley, Redd Foxx — told sexually risqué or politically barbed jokes, *nigger* for the most part remained off-limits.
>
> All that changed with the emergence of Richard Pryor.

It's not that Richard was the first comedian to embrace the N-word. Dick Gregory hoped to declaw the slur in 1964 when he titled his memoir *Nigger,* though Gregory's use of the word had nowhere near the impact that Pryor's would. Gregory's was a powerful and influential book, but as Woody Guthrie said when asked about the success of his 1943 memoir, *Bound for Glory,* no book, no matter how good, could ever get a hall full of people shouting and stomping and clapping along the way his songs could. Richard served the word up live, playing off the highly charged reactions of integrated audiences. Some nights the crowds were hostile, sometimes jubilant, sometimes chilly, but never lukewarm. Richard's move was a spontaneous one, hatched in the moment, with no thought of the outcome. Inspired by the black poets' use of vernacular rhythms and street language, and the Panthers' insistence on being authentically and unapologetically black, he seized the word with the same heedless urgency the French dramatist Antonin Artaud had demanded of creators in his time, "like a victim burning at the stake, signaling through the flames."

Lenny Bruce, in his own way, got there ahead of Gregory, once pausing between nightclub bits to ask, "Are there any niggers here tonight?" He filled the stunned silence that followed saying, "I know that one nigger who works here — I see him back there. Oh, there's two niggers, customers, and, uh, *aha!* Between those niggers sits one kike — man, thank God for the kike! Uh, two kikes. That's three niggers, two kikes, and one spic. One spic — two, three spics. One mick. One mick, one spic, one hick, thick, funky, spunky boogey." He went on like an auctioneer, tallying up the kikes, spics, guineas, greaseballs, Yids, boogies, and Polacks before he got to his point. "The point? That the word's suppression gives it the power, the violence, the viciousness. If President Kennedy got on television and said, 'Tonight I'd like to introduce the niggers in my cabinet,' and he yelled 'niggerniggerniggerniggerniggerniggernigger' at every nigger he saw, 'boogeyboogeyboogeyboogeyboogey, niggerniggerniggernigger' till nigger didn't mean anything any more, till nigger lost its meaning — you'd never make any four-year-old nigger cry when he came home from school."

Maybe.

Richard knew it would take more than familiarity or frequency of use to scrub that particular word of its bloody history. Sure, if you say almost any word enough times in a row like that the sheer monotony of repetition will drain it of its sense and meaning. But not *nigger*. It just digs in deeper. "That word," Dave Chappelle would attest, "is a doozy."

It all came back to what Malcolm X had said when a "'token-integrated' black Ph.D. associate professor" stood up during a question-and-answer period to challenge his characterization of white attitudes, accusing Malcolm of being a "divisive demagogue" and practicing reverse racism. Finally, Malcolm asked the professor if he knew what whites called black people with Ph.Ds.

"He said something like, 'I believe that I happen not to be aware of that' — you know, one of these ultra-proper-talking Negroes.

"And," Malcolm said, "I laid the word down on him, loud: Nigger!"

That was it. No matter what Richard or any other black person at that time might achieve, no matter how much white people might praise or pay him, Richard Pryor knew that, behind his back, he would always be a nigger.

———————

By the end of Richard's time in Berkeley, Huey Newton had begun his downward spiral, demoralized by party infighting that was only exacerbated by FBI efforts to divide and conquer the Panthers through a campaign of misinformation. Eldridge Cleaver, then living in exile in Algiers, received mounds of FBI-forged letters, supposedly from party members, challenging Newton's leadership and urging Cleaver to take control before Huey decided to force him out.

Speaking in the 1980s, Huey recalled that, during this time, he would often have spurts of brilliant clarity but then would become entirely incoherent and rambling, that he was committing reactionary suicide, killing himself with cocaine and heroin.

———————

After leaving an Oakland party together late one night, Huey and his girlfriend went back to Richard's apartment, doing more blow and making big plans, when Huey fell into a dark mood. The tension had begun mounting, Richard recalled, when Newton's girlfriend started coming onto him and he did nothing to discourage her. Huey was convinced that, by and by, he would surely end up behind bars. He was terrified of prison. "Everyone's going to want to fuck me," he said. "But if they put their dick in my mouth, I'll bite it off." "That's a plan," Richard said, "but right before you bite, you know, you're going to taste that dick in your mouth and wonder whether or not you like it." Newton leaped up from his chair like — well, like a panther — fists flying, pummeling Richard about the head.

It could have been a lot worse. Both men were high, both had guns. In that moment, Richard knew it was time to pack up what he'd found in Berkeley and take it back to L.A. Why force himself into the mold of a radical poet or militant activist when he knew he could "stir up more shit on stage"?

In truth, he'd been moving in that direction ever since his Las Vegas walk-off — a personal awakening that the press agents and keepers of the cultural narrative had labored to characterize as a breakdown, a disaster, a tragedy. A career once bright with promise reduced to ruins.

The Catholic writer, mystic, and Trappist monk Thomas Merton made the observation that "there is not so much new in your life as you sometimes think." Keeping a journal showed him that his latest spiritual insight or self-discovery generally turned out to be a repeat of something he'd discovered years before.

Richard had already awakened to the same self-discovery several times, going back at least as far as those late nights watching TV in Peoria while spattering his in-laws' living room with spitballs and scheming how he would ever get up from that couch to take his place alongside Redd Foxx and Dick Gregory on the other side of that screen. Same thing when he heard a Lenny Bruce LP for the first time. Same as when he stared out at that Las Vegas crowd and opened his mouth to find nothing would come out but "What the fuck am I doing here?"

He always awoke to the same thought: cut the bullshit, speak the truths he had the gift to see, give voice to those characters in his imagination clamoring to come out and say their say.

But after each revelation, he backslid to the safety of easy money and easier laughs. The irony, of course, is that when he finally did give free rein to his voice, he would get bigger laughs than anyone. And the money would be insane.

He reached the same awakening in Berkeley. Only this time it would stick. The times were right and he was ready. The times were calling for a Richard Pryor.

Perhaps he had heard about Eldridge Cleaver's embrace of Brother Merton, while reading *Seven Storey Mountain* in solitary confinement at Folsom prison, Merton who averred that all sin is "the refusal to be what we were created to be."

Motown president Berry Gordy Jr. invited him to audition for a role in a movie he was developing with Paramount, a biopic of Billie Holiday starring Diana Ross. The part was so small the script didn't even give him a name. He was simply "Piano Man."

Right around that time Paul Mooney came knocking at Richard's door, rousing him from his stupor, telling him to get his shit together. Enough with the wizard hats and dashikis and tie-dyed flower power. It was 1972. L.A. was the place to be. Johnny Carson had just moved *The Tonight Show* from New York to Burbank. And a new club had opened on the Strip where Ciro's used to be. The place was owned by TV skit writer Rudy De Luca and old-school gag man Sammy Shore, whose regular gig was opening for Elvis in Las Vegas. They called it the Comedy Store. Sammy Shore didn't know the first thing about running a club, but his wife Mitzi, did.

TV and movie producers were at the Store every night, booking talk-show slots and tossing out deals left and right to a whole new breed of comics. And, in case Richard didn't know it, he could run circles around them all.

On Friday, January 14, 1972, NBC broadcast the first sitcom — the first
network show of any kind — to star an all-black cast since *Amos 'N Andy*
was taken off the air in 1953.

Producers Norman Lear and Bud Yorkin based the show on a British
sitcom *Steptoe and Son* set in the Shepherd's Bush area of West London
featuring Albert Steptoe, a crusty old rag-and-bone man who mocks,
belittles, and actively sabotages the social aspirations of his thirty-seven-
year-old son, Harold. For their version, set in L.A.'s Watts neighborhood, Lear and Yorkin cast Redd Foxx in the father's role and gave the
character Foxx's birth name, Sanford.

After thirty years as a top comic in black clubs and on adults-only
"party" records, Redd Foxx became a star overnight. (It's fun to imagine
fans of the show who'd never heard Foxx do stand-up before — and that
would include most of them — picking up one of his Laff LPs at the
mall and hearing this on side 1, track 1: "Did you ever stop to think that
if the Pilgrims had shot bobcats instead of turkeys we'd be eatin' pussy
on Thanksgiving.")

Right away there was trouble with the network. Despite having the
full weight and support of Lear and Yorkin and their hit series *All in the
Family* behind him, Foxx ran into a brick wall when he insisted that black
writers be hired for the show. Specifically, he wanted Richard Pryor and
Paul Mooney. NBC wouldn't budge, despite both their track records

and the unassailable authenticity they would lend to the show.* None of that mattered. The network insisted on using "established" writers. As Mooney has often observed, racism trumps capitalism. And nobody, it seems, likes being told that they don't understand the black experience.

When Richard returned to Los Angeles from Berkeley, in the spring of 1972, he came back inspired to speak truth, using the raw language of the streets. He embraced *nigger* as an empowering term of endearment and spoke with startling candor about things many people at that time were uncomfortable admitting even to themselves: his homosexual experiences, masturbation, racial anger, his physical abuse of women, drug addiction, feelings of self-loathing, and the guilt he felt as a conflicted champion of black pride who also had an irresistible lust for white women.

> I'm nervous up here. I ain't had no cocaine all day. I love cocaine.
>
> People don't talk about nothin' real, like jackin' off. A lot of people didn't jack off. I did! I used to jack off so much I knew pussy couldn't be as good as my hand.
>
> You go out with a white woman and sisters look at you like you killed your mama.
>
> You can't talk about fucking in America, right? People say you're dirty. But if you talk about killing somebody, that's cool. I don't

---

*Eventually, Richard and Mooney were hired to write a total of two episodes during the show's second season: "The Dowry" (September 29, 1972) and "Sanford and Son and Sister Make Three" (December 1, 1972). Comedian Daryl Mooney fondly recalls the times Richard came to their house to work on those scripts with his father. Richard would be at one end of the table with his Courvoisier and cocaine, while Paul Mooney sat at the other end with a secretary stationed between them, taking it all down. "Our father would have to temper him and make it clean," Daryl says. "Richard would throw out lines like, 'We'll have Redd say to Aunt Esther, "Bitch, shut the fuck up. Eat your own pussy"' ... My father would be like, 'Richard, TV, bro — we can't do that, Richard, this is TV.'"

understand it myself. I'd rather come. I've had money and never felt as good as I felt when I come. Nothing else matters when you're gettin' the nut. Especially if it's a girl.

Never fuck a faggot, 'cause they will *lie*. They always say, "I won't tell." They lie. They can't wait till you finish fucking them. (*miming telephone*) "Well, guess who was here, honey. Girl, looka here, the nigger got more bitch in him than me."

And the punch line? There wasn't one. He wasn't telling jokes, he was telling the truth: "Y'all act like you ain't never sucked a dick or some-thing. Y'all be, (*white voice*) 'No siree, bob, never touched a penis in our life, we're real men.' I sucked a dick. You can get a habit from sucking dick. Become a dick junkie. You can only do it maybe three times. You do it more than that you get a habit." It slipped the noose of anything that would have previously passed for nightclub comedy. To his amaze-ment, audiences of all races loved it — and loved him for it.

Richard had planned to kick off his return with a performance at the Apollo. Mooney suggested he woodshed his new act at the Comedy Store first. With one caveat. The Store was full of white comics, Mooney warned, who would steal his best lines and run with them to Vegas or *The Tonight Show*. Richard knew better. "Ain't nobody gonna steal noth-ing off me," he said. "Motherfucker wouldn't know what to do with it."

No other comic ever used Richard's material. It simply couldn't be done. It wasn't a matter of repeating his words but of taking possession of them. One would have to capture the genius of his performance. One might just as well caution Caruso or Michael Jordan against performing in public lest competitors try to copy them. Anyone was welcome to try. The exception proving the rule came when Eddie Murphy, employing his extraordinary skills at mimicry, included some ten or twelve minutes of vintage Pryor in his early concerts and called it homage.

When Richard took the stage at the Comedy Store, it was as if, in Mooney's words, all the "copycat Cosby bullshit" had been burned off while he was in Berkeley. He had rid himself of all the impurities, like firing up some base. "This was the pure shit."

Bill Cosby himself attended a pivotal performance: "Richard took on a whole new persona — his own — in front of me and everyone else. Richard killed the Bill Cosby in his act, made people hate it. Then he worked on them, doing pure Richard Pryor, and it was the most astonishing metamorphosis I have ever seen. He was magnificent."

It was a metamorphosis Richard had labored over for years. Over the previous decade and a half, Richard had crossed paths with so many masters, stumbled onto so many pivotal scenes, and soaked up so many influences, from the African American traditions of boasts, toasts, and signifying that he'd learned from street-corner raconteurs and vaudeville holdovers in the clubs of Peoria, to touring the "black belt" nightclub circuit opening for the singer who inspired Duke Ellington's "Satin Doll," to sharing bills with the likes of Bob Dylan, Woody Allen, Richie Havens, and George Carlin in the Greenwich Village of the early sixties, to Sunday nights on *The Ed Sullivan Show* and weekday afternoons on *Merv Griffin*, to mingling in Rat Pack–era Las Vegas; from West Hollywood clubs of the late sixties and guest roles on sitcoms and TV shows such as *The Young Lawyers, The Mod Squad, Wild Wild West,* and *The Partridge Family*, to his eye-opening and mind-expanding friendships with the Black Panthers and literary lights in Berkeley at the dawn of the seventies.

There had been glimpses of a new Richard Pryor in the monologue sequences scattered throughout *Dynamite Chicken,* for the few who ever saw the movie. A still-rough-around-the-edges version of his new self could be heard on his second LP, *Craps (After Hours),* an underground hit for West Coast indy label Laff Records, best known for the bacchanalian cover photos, replete with comic-strip speech balloons, that graced "adults only" party records such as Wildman Steve's *Eatin' Ain't Cheatin!!!* and *That Ain't My Finger . . . It Just Ain't Your Day* by the team of Mantan Moreland and Livingood. Laff producer David Drozen went through hours of material recorded live at the Redd Foxx Club in Hollywood in January of 1971 and spliced together a ragtag assemblage of thirty-one tracks, sixteen of which were less than a minute long, with some clocking in under twelve seconds, such as "Being Born": "I'm one of the few people that remember being born. And I'd like to do it for you. (*beat*) Could I have a lady volunteer?"

But when Richard reemerged on the scene in West Hollywood, he blew everything wide open. As when Dylan released "Positively 4th Street" as a single, a whole crop of young songwriters saw that songs could be about anything. Joni Mitchell remembers it was unlike any song she had ever heard: "I remember thinking 'the American pop song has finally grown up.' You can sing about anything now. 'You've got a lot of nerve to say you are my friend.' Just in that statement was a different song than any I had ever heard. . . . The potential for the song had never occurred to me. . . . But it occurred to Dylan. I said, 'Oh God, look at this.' And I began to write."

Stanley Kubrick undertook *2001: A Space Odyssey* in part to test his conviction that "if it can be written or thought, it can be filmed." Kubrick believed that filmmakers should grant themselves the same freedom a novelist has when buying a ream of paper. Young comedians began to see their craft in the same light. Freed from the conventional setup–punch line–topper formulas that had been around since vaudeville, the world of stand-up opened wide, as the music world would for hip-hop artists a decade later. Stand-up comedy was suddenly the freest art form ever, able to absorb and incorporate any and all of the performing arts from dramatic acting, mimicry, burlesque, music, magic tricks, improvisation, mime, buffoonery, confessional memoir, poetry, Pentecostal preaching, social commentary — they could take it anywhere. Comics could lip-synch to a phonograph playing the *Mighty Mouse* theme song, if they wanted, or smash watermelons with sledgehammers.

———————

Change was in the air. Everyone could feel it. The old ways were unraveling. And there was plenty more excitement where that came from. On the other end of the continent, nighttime security guard Frank Wills noticed that someone had put tape over the latch of an office door to keep it from locking. He peeled off the tape, closed the door, making sure the latch caught, and thought little of it until he came back around an hour later. When Wills saw that the same door had been taped back up again, he called the D.C. police. Something fishy was going on at the Watergate complex. It would prove to be the single greatest gift this generation of TV and nightclub comics could ever hope for.

It's cold-blooded in jail. Nixon wouldn't have lasted two days. They'd have turned him out. Niggers was waitin' on Nixon to come to jail. "What's happenin' Tricky Dick? Ha-ha-haaa. Yeah. I'm gonna see how tricky you are." Can't you just see Nixon? "Let me make one thing perfectly clear . . ."

The divide between so-called serious art and popular entertainment — between high and low culture — fell apart, revealing itself as a sham, a figment, a judgment. *Village Voice* columnist and downtown theater critic Laurie Stone had this epiphany while sitting through yet another solo performance in some forgotten loft space. The show's absurdist confessional humor wasn't working. No one in the theater was buying it. She could almost smell the tang of flop sweat emanating from the actor onstage, yet everyone sat there, silent and respectful. Stone endured it for the duration only because she was getting paid, and the thought occurred to her, "There are comedians in clubs doing better monologues than this." She persuaded her editors at the *Voice* to allow her, henceforth, to review stand-up comedy in the same space as serious solo theater.

"NIGGER, COME OUT OF THAT BLACK SKIN
AND BE BLACK, NIGGER"

Al Bell couldn't believe his ears when this skinny guy started his set at the Comedy Store. As the head of Memphis-based Stax Records, Bell commanded one of the largest African American–owned businesses in the United States, second only to Berry Gordy's Motown.

Richard did this one bit — a routine he'd continue to refine over the next few years — where he imitated a guy on an acid trip. "I couldn't believe what I saw," says Bell. "The story he was telling as he played out the character was really penetrating as far as black people are concerned." At the end of the routine, as the guy was coming down, his last line was, "Nigger, come out of that black skin and be black, nigger."

"It left the audience stunned," Bell recalls. In that one line "he had exposed so much about black people."

The line was not some bumper-sticker slogan. It was mind blowing, like some kind of Zen koan. No matter how you turned it over in your mind, or it turned your mind over in you, you could never plumb its depths. The line kept turning in on itself, refusing to be translated into anything other.

"This man is a genius," said Bell. "When you listen to the intelligence behind what he is talking about you really realize you're talking about a literal genius."

Bell had gone to catch Richard's act at the behest of Forest Hamilton, son of jazz drummer Chico Hamilton and the head of Stax West, the record company's new division based in Los Angeles. The twenty-six-year-old Hamilton's job was to scout West Coast talent and establish

Stax within the motion picture and television industries. Bell was in town to organize a daylong concert commemorating the seventh anniversary of the 1965 Watts rebellion.

Wattstax, as the concert came to be known, took place on Sunday, August 20, 1972, at the L.A. Memorial Coliseum featuring Stax recording artists Rufus Thomas, the Staple Singers, Kim Weston, Albert King, Little Milton, William Bell, Carla Thomas, The Bar-Kays, Luther Ingram, and Isaac Hayes among others. The Reverend Jesse Jackson flew in from Chicago, landing with less than an hour to spare, to deliver the invocation and to lead the crowd in his "I am somebody" call and response.

With more than one hundred thousand mostly African Americans sitting out in the hot sun all day in celebration of Watts, local media were just waiting for the whole thing to blow up. Security was minimal. Stax had requested that the LAPD assign only African American officers to work the event. It all went beautifully. The Stax organizers were pleased and relieved that not so much as a scuffle had been reported, but it didn't necessarily make for engaging cinema.

Stax had hired director Mel Stuart (*Four Days in November; If It's Tuesday, This Must Be Belgium; Willy Wonka and the Chocolate Factory*) to helm a documentary of the event. The music was superb, of course, but even when interspersed with documentary footage and interviews filmed in area restaurants, barbershops, and on front stoops, the movie still felt incomplete. What the movie needed, Stuart decided, was "someone who would sum up what the picture was about, would lead us on to the next step, would really be the voice of the community." A chorus, like the one in Shakespeare's *Henry V* — "O for a muse of fire, that would ascend / The brightest heaven of invention."

Al Bell knew just the guy. "Hey, man," he told Forest Hamilton, "go find Richard Pryor."

Hamilton tracked him down at a small club in Watts. When they first walked in the place, Stuart recalls, "this rather big gentleman walked over to me and grabbed me and said, 'What is this honky doing in my club?' I thought my life was over. . . . Forest Hamilton, who weighed about three hundred pounds, grabbed this man, threw him against the wall, and the guy went *down*. Forest went over to him and said, 'He's got expertise, motherfucker!' The guy looks up at me and says, 'Shit, man, I didn't know you had expertise. Come on in, man, come on in.'"

Less than five minutes into Richard's set, Stuart knew that he was in the presence of a comedic genius. "I knew this was the chorus. Everything you see in this film is improvised by Richard. There's no script. And he is the soul of the film."

The decision to cast Richard as the film's "wickedly funny commentator" was a superb stroke, according to *Newsweek* magazine's reviewer. "Perhaps not even Dick Gregory can shape accumulated black experience into such biting bits of humor. [Pryor] is reason enough to see *Wattstax*."

Richard's role in the film was to spin documentary straw into comic gold. In one of the documentary segments shot in a Watts restaurant, a man tells how his "high yellow" brother made him first realize he was a nigger. The two had been playing with a group of white kids who excluded him, yet bonded with his lighter-skinned brother. When they got home, his brother called him a nigger and declared himself white. "I didn't know what a nigger was," the man says. "But my mother's bad. Check this out. She said, 'Cool. All right, then, I ain't your mother because all my kids are niggers.'"

Richard wraps up the segment with this:

I think, like, niggers are the best of the people who were slaves, you know what I mean? That's how we got to be niggers. Cause they stole the cream of the crop from Africa and brought them over here. And God, as they say works in mysterious ways and so he made everybody "nigger." Cause we were arguing over in Africa about the Watusi and (*riffing on African-sounding tribal names*) the Ojuomboo, and Zamunga . . . in different languages. So he brought us all here. The best. The kings and queens. Princes and Princesses. Put us all together and called us one tribe: Niggers!

Watergate notwithstanding, the single greatest stroke of luck to ever befall the new wave of stand-up comedians came in December 1973 when Sammy Shore, called back to Las Vegas for a months-long engagement at the Hilton, left his wife Mitzi in charge of the Store.

In her husband's absence, Mitzi Shore found her life's calling. She put young comics to work painting the entire interior black — black walls, ceiling, tables and chairs — so when the single spotlight hit the comic on stage, there was nothing else to look at. She had them move the bar back by the kitchen. From now on, customers would order drinks from cocktail waitresses.

Mitzi Shore made the Store a place where comics could be seen, get exposure, commune and confer with their comic brethren, and workshop their material in front of an audience. She did it all for the comics. Which is why she thought she didn't need to pay them.

By the end of the year, Mitzi took full ownership in a divorce settlement from Sammy. He must've known he was losing both his club and his wife when he made a visit to L.A. after only a month in Vegas. He barely recognized the place. Everything had been painted black. The floor was packed. And where was the bar? Sammy told his wife he wanted to do a few shows while he was in town. She said she would try to fit him in the next night's lineup but couldn't make any promises.

Back when Sammy Shore had been in charge of the Store, he gave his old-school pals full run of the place. There was no lineup or schedule. They went behind the bar to pour their own drinks and commanded the stage for as long as they pleased. The younger, less-known comics had to hang back and hope for a chance to go on. Mitzi turned that system upside down, giving preference to young up-and-coming comics and scheduling them in strict fifteen-minute time blocks.

The stream of young comics flowing into L.A. behind Johnny Carson's move of The Tonight Show to Burbank swelled to a tidal wave after nineteen-year-old Freddie Prinze made his television debut on Thursday, December 6, 1973. So impressed was Carson with Prinze's five-minute performance that, as Prinze started to leave the stage, Carson waved him over to the couch. Never before had a first-time comic been granted a sit-down chat with Johnny.

Over at the Comedy Store, jaws dropped. The comics crowded around the TV "recognized that they were seeing history," writes William Knoedelseder in *I'm Dying up Here: Heartbreak and High Times in Stand-Up Comedy's Golden Era*. Their reactions "ranged from 'Holy shit,' to 'I can't fucking believe this,' to 'Right on, Freddie!' "

> Few comics failed to notice one more thing about Prinze's *Tonight Show* debut: Johnny introduced him as "a young comedian who's appearing here in town at the Comedy Store." That statement put the Comedy Store on every comic's map and created a new equation in their heads: One set at the Comedy Store plus one appearance on Carson equals the whole world. If it happened to Freddie, then it could happen to any of them. You could almost hear the suitcases being packed.

A young Jay Leno, sitting on his sofa in Boston, watched the same equation play out for his pal Jimmie Walker who was immediately signed to the new Norman Lear–Bud Yorkin series, *Good Times*. Leno had worked the same clubs with Walker. He was a better comic than Walker. He got bigger laughs. Yet there was Walker on TV, and there sat Leno watching him. He got up off his couch, booked a flight to L.A., packed a single suitcase, took his entire savings (fifteen hundred dollars) out of the bank, left his apartment unlocked, and, on his way out the door, told the neighbors in his building to help themselves to anything inside.

———

Lily Tomlin remembers improvising a scene for her upcoming TV special at Richard's house when Berry Gordy called to praise his performance in *Lady Sings the Blues*, guaranteeing him he would be nominated for an Oscar. After he hung up the phone, Tomlin remembers, Richard suddenly became the six-year-old boy from his "The Primpce and the

Primpcess" fairy tale he'd performed the first time she saw him on *The Ed Sullivan Show* — "shy, hopeful, and suddenly terrified, as if he had pulled off something he'd never expected."

Although the Oscar nomination Gordy predicted never came to pass, Richard received universally outstanding reviews for his revelatory portrayal of Billie Holiday's heroin-addicted piano player, a characterization inspired in part by his old friend Jimmy Binkley, the house pianist at Collins Corner back in Peoria. The movie brought him much attention but few acting offers. Perhaps he'd played the heroin-addicted piano man too convincingly. Along with the accolades, Richard earned a reputation for his erratic behavior, violent temper, and heavy drug use.

That reputation was not wholly undeserved. During filming of *The Mack,* now regarded as a blaxploitation classic (perhaps the most sampled movie in hip-hop and one of Quentin Tarantino's acknowledged touchstones), Richard as "Slim" played sidekick to Max Julien's pimp "Goldie." Following one of many altercations with producer Harvey Bernhard, a coked-up Richard told Julien that he was going to kill the man. Julien declined Richard's invitation to take part but stood back and watched from down the hallway as Richard, carrying a lead ball in a sock, knocked on the producer's hotel room door. Because the production, filmed on location on the streets of Oakland, California, had been plagued with threats, interference, and outright assault from local gangs, Bernhard kept an around-the-clock bodyguard in his room and a .45 in his belt. As Bernhard recounted the scene to Julien the next day, he pulled his gun on Richard and challenged him to make his move, at which point, Richard wisely collapsed in laughter and assured Bernhard it had all been a joke. Richard and Julien, who contributed heavily to the script, both pushed back against Bernhard and director Michael Campus (who likewise shot *The Education of Sonny Carson* on the streets of Brooklyn's Bedford-Stuyvesant) for their depiction of pimps and urban street life. In one instance, Richard went off script to create what turned out to be the film's most riveting scene. Rather than play the scene as written, which called for him to turn his back on a pair of corrupt white cops (Don Gordon and William Watson) — an act that anyone with a lick of sense would recognize as suicidal, they protested to Campus — Richard's Slim stands his ground, breaking down in real tears as he bitterly curses the two cops while allowing Goldie time to slowly walk away unscathed. After viewing the dailies, Campus had no choice but to use the scene as Richard had improvised it. It was too good not to.

The movie's second-most-memorable scene comes when Slim and Goldie take prisoner a rival pimp (Dick Anthony Williams) who'd had Goldie's mother killed, and order him, at gunpoint, to stick himself with the long stiletto he carried concealed in a walking stick. Richard's smiling, near-hysterical command that the pimp stick himself — "Stick yourself, nigger. One more for me, now. Stick yourself! I'm tryin' to help you. Don't get angry. Be cool. Again!" — is still harrowing to watch. And it was all Richard's idea. Williams's character had previously pulled the stiletto during a confrontational pool-hall scene. In his commentary on the DVD release, Williams laughed, marveling, nearly thirty years later, at the workings of Richard's mind. "I knew the dude was gonna come up with something from the pool table scene. He's got a mind . . ."

Richard similarly threw himself into every role that came his way during this time and, in 1973, turned in some of the finest performances of his career, mostly in films that had poor showings at the box office. Not one of them was a comedy. As would most always be the case, Richard did his funniest and most incisive work when he embodied broken or conflicted characters from within and played them in earnest instead of for obvious laughs. There's no better example of this than the "Juke and Opal" sketch written by Jane Wagner for *Lily,* Tomlin's comedy-variety special that aired November 2, 1973, on CBS.

Tomlin, without benefit of complexion-enhancing makeup, plays Opal, the black owner of a cafe frequented by Juke, a scruffy young drug addict played by Richard in a green fatigue jacket. Opal serves him potato soup ("something nourishing") and talks with him about getting on methadone.

Their teasing, flirtatious banter — "You irritate the lining of my mind,"

Opal tells him — is interrupted by the entrance of a couple of social workers doing community research. "We'd like to ask you a few questions," the young woman announces as they come through the door.

Juke openly admits, when asked by the survey takers, that he's addicted to drugs but objects when the young woman makes note of his answer. "Don't write it down, man. Be cool. That's not for the public. I mean what I go through is private." Before he answers any more, Juke has a few questions of his own: "Who's Pigmeat Markham's mama? You ever been mugged in the same neighborhood more than once? Do you know who 'Boo' Diddley is?"

When Opal gives Juke ten dollars from the register, the young man tries to intervene. "You really shouldn't give him the money. You know what he's going to do with it." Opal covers for Juke by saying he's going to buy her more potatoes.

After the couple leaves, Juke gives the ten back, saying he's not buying any more potatoes. He's going to try. "You know, I think I'm kinda crazy about you," he says. "You a sweet woman." As he leaves, he hesitates at the door and says, "I'll think about you. Be glad when it's spring." Then one last word: "Flower!"

Writing for the *New Yorker* in September 1999, Hilton Als said the nine-and-a-half-minute sketch "remains, a little over a quarter of a century later, the most profound meditation on race and class that I have ever seen on a major network."

Perhaps the greatest testament to how convincingly Tomlin embodied the black cafe owner Opal can be found in the lack of viewer outcry when she and Richard's Juke exchanged a brief kiss on the lips as he put up his hood to head back out into the cold. It was rare — and risky — for a black man to kiss a white woman on primetime television in 1973. In this instance, no one seemed to notice.

———

The troubles — and triumphs — that would mark the entire of Richard's sketchy TV career were fully on display when an improvised skit pairing Richard's little-boy character Billy with Tomlin's rocking-chair preschooler Edith Ann wandered afoul of program practices. Director Rick Wallace called, "Cut!" when Richard's character remarked that he had "bigger titties" than Tomlin's Edith Ann.

Lily followed Richard to his dressing room and tried to talk him back, but he said he just couldn't do anymore. It was as though the ordeal of fully embodying and then abandoning or being less than true to a character caused Richard psychic distress, if not physical pain.

"You can't stop a guy like Richard Pryor when he's on a roll," says Richard's friend David Brenner. "If you interrupt him, he's done. It'd be like if you went down on the track when someone's running and said, 'Listen, I want to change your sneakers. I think you'll do better with these.' You can stop a guy like me and I can be back in an instant. I'm being the real me — the funny me — but I don't get into these great characters, these dimensions."

"I felt ridiculous," Richard told David Felton of *Rolling Stone*. "My kid couldn't get into it. So I can't go onstage and it be in my mind that this kid can't say something, 'cause the kid is wrecked, as a kid. I mean, I was ready to cry as a kid, 'cause I *was* the kid, you dig?

"That's the way I see kids. I just get fascinated talking to 'em, 'cause it'll be honestly sweet and whatever they say is innocent. And if they say 'tittie,' you can't tell a kid they can't say 'tittie.' They deal with real shit."

Lily scored big in the ratings, got great reviews, and won its writing team (including Richard) an Emmy for Best Writing in Comedy-Variety, Variety or Music category. CBS never aired the show again.

Richard, Billy Dee Williams, and director Sidney J. Furie were all riding high on the success of *Lady Sings the Blues* when they regrouped for the action-thriller *Hit!* about a federal agent (Williams) who seeks revenge after his teenage daughter dies of a drug overdose. Knowing that his superiors would never allow such an operation to proceed through official channels, Williams takes it upon himself to recruit, finance, train, and transport to France a small band of private American citizens who have each suffered personal tragedies as a result of illegal drugs. They seek vengeance not against street-level junkies and pushers but by going up against the nine leaders of a Marseilles drug syndicate who control product and distribution.

Mismarketed as a blaxploitation film, *Hit!* confounded the genre with its ensemble cast of multiracial and cross-generational heroes. Even the wealthy French villains are portrayed in identifiably human terms. One French kingpin, for example, disappointed by his sumptuous lunch, rails against big oil polluters, the "pigs who use the sea for a sewer," doing such harm to aquatic life that "it will soon be impossible to eat a decent bouillabaisse."

With its tagline "To pull off a job no one would ever dare you need a team no one would ever believe," the movie's lineage can be traced to *Dirty Harry* and *The French Connection* by way of *The Seven Samurai*.

The cautiously mistrustful camaraderie between the characters played by Richard and Billy Dee Williams is palpable throughout the movie, drawing method inspiration from their off-screen friendship. Williams enjoyed hanging out with Richard and Mooney but was so uptight about his career he avoided being seen with them in public. He wanted to be a leading man. Richard had a reputation for the kind of trouble that could screw that up.

There's a scene — one of several — in which Richard clearly goes off script while flirting with fellow vigilante Gwen Welles in the backseat of the van driven by Williams. As they approach the Seattle Ferry dock, Richard chuckles, reading aloud from a sign at the entranceway: "Seattle Ferries from eight to six." Then, affecting an effeminate lisp: "My, my . . . business must be brisk." Williams shoots Richard a scathing look. Richard doesn't let up. "Why don't they name a ferry boat the *Lesbian*? (*lisping again*) 'I'm taking the *Lesbian* to the island.'"

Williams mutters something incomprehensible as he climbs out of the van. Whatever he says seems intended for Richard's ears, not ours. Richard, for his part, reacts with a bewildered, what-the-fuck's-bugging-him expression. Then, playing to Welles, he foppishly slaps a glove

across the back of the driver's seat and, lisping again, delivers this: "He's
gone to ask the Marquis de Sade who we should recruit."

Later, while piloting a boat across French waters, Richard half mutters half sings, "I gotta get laid, I gotta get laid . . ." then breaks into a
blues-inflected sea shanty, sounding a bit like the later-day Tom Waits:

> *I bet they have some weird bitches here*
> *I bet they have some weird bitches here*
> *I bet they got some Eskimos*
> *and all they do is suck your toes*
> *I bet they have some weird bitches here*

He doesn't play it for laughs. It's all completely in character, a man labor-
ing to cheer himself against a sense of impeding doom. No one else is
even listening. His somber cohorts down on deck are staring out across
the water, grimly contemplating the illegal and potentially suicidal nature of the mission they are about to undertake.

As he docks the boat, Richard calls down to the man shagging their
line, "Tie it off there, me lad. Where's the pussy?" When he gets no reply,
Richard looks at his hand and says, "Well, Rosie, looks like it's you and
me again tonight." Then, planting a kiss on his gloved palm, says, "I love
ya, baby."

As the climax approaches and the bodies of French kingpins begin
piling up, Richard even coaxes a teary laugh from the heroin-addicted
character played by Gwen Welles as she begins to fall apart, crying to
him that she can't go through with the other hits. She's scared and she
doesn't like killing people. Richard, whose scuba-diving character had
surfaced alongside a drug lord's yacht with a speargun and harpooned
him in the chest, barks back at her in the voice of a shit-talking hustler,
"You think you got troubles, nigga? I lost a motherfuckin' spear. Cost
me forty-seven boxtops. I saved for six months. Shit! Had a gold tip on
it and everything."

The few critics who bothered to give *Hit!* any notice complained that
the film provided a scant twenty minutes of thrills, and only after the
audience had endured an hour and fifty minutes of setup and character

development. All true. For audiences expecting a blaxploitation thrill ride, Furie's art-house pacing, often disorienting camera work, and generous attention to character and detail made for slow going. It would not be released on DVD until April of 2012 and has yet to find the audience it deserves.

In *Some Call It Loving,* an oddly sad and atmospheric film inspired by John Collier's much livelier satiric short story, "Sleeping Beauty," jazz musician Zalman King becomes obsessed with a spellbound woman (played by Mia Farrow's younger sister, Tisa) on exhibit in a carnival sideshow. Richard, for the most part, is wasted as King's drug-addled friend who is insistent in explaining the deeper meaning of a lopsided heart he has painted in glow-in-the-dark red on the wall above a urinal in the men's room of a jazz club where King is performing. Midway through the film, Richard's character dies of an overdose for no apparent reason (story-wise) other than perhaps writer-director James B. Harris's concern that he might bring more oxygen and light than his otherwise claustrophobic fantasy could bear. This was, after all, the same James B. Harris who, nine years earlier, walked away from his production partnership with Stanley Kubrick over what he believed was Kubrick's misguided decision to adapt Peter George's cold war novel *Red Alert* as a comedy and call it *Dr. Strangelove, or: How I Learned to Stop Worrying and Love the Bomb.*

Although Richard is onscreen for less than five minutes of Sidney Poitier's *Uptown Saturday Night,* he manages to steal the scene — if not the entire movie — out from under Bill Cosby and Poitier both. (Screenwriter Richard Wesley had originally envisioned Redd Foxx and Richard in the Cosby and Poitier roles.) Penelope Gilliatt, reviewing the 1974 comedy for the *New Yorker,* calls Richard's performance as private detective Sharp-Eye Washington masterly: "He takes not the faintest notice of his clients' shy attempt to hire him." While they regard his quick-wittedness as the mark of a good detective, his "mind is obviously more on making a quick exit, which he does by way of window and a fire escape — or possibly a water pipe — waving goodbye professionally as if he had everything under control."

What's so striking about these movies — however uneven or ill-conceived — is that directors and producers cast Richard Pryor because of his brilliance as an actor, because of what he could actually *do*. They allowed him to bring his rage, his mischief — his badass self — and they gave him room to occupy his characters with pathos and human foible. That's why they hired him. As Pauline Kael wrote, "Pryor shouldn't be cast at all — he should be realized. He has desperate, mad characters coming out of his pores, and we want to see how far he can go with them."

This was the artistic capital he would trade on a few years later when his name had become a box-office draw and studios began throwing millions at him. At those rates, the stakes were too high. He had to tone it down. Instead of going inside and embodying his characters, he had to stand outside where he could keep an eye on them.

"The movies that they had him ultimately do were very forgettable," says Franklyn Ajaye. "Hollywood always takes the bite out of any comedian. If you're a comedian they just bring you on to do something silly. Woody Allen did the best because he did his own thing. Richard was a phenomenal comedian, but they softened the edges when they brought him the money for the movies. But, look, I don't know how anyone can turn down three, four million dollars."

If the studios and networks weren't willing to risk his mayhem, it was only because they didn't need to. His name — the Richard Pryor brand — was by that time worth more than any performance, worth more than they were paying him. All he had to do was show up and hit his mark. By then, there was no going back.

"LET IT STAY HEAVY IF NOT HARD"

Mel Brooks initially turned down the chance to do *Blazing Saddles* when his agent David Begelman showed him the screen treatment — then titled "Tex X" — written by fellow Begelman client Andrew Bergman. Brooks was only interested in developing projects of his own. But he was at a career low. No acting jobs were coming his way, he couldn't get his own projects off the ground, and Warner Bros. would pay him well to shape the treatment into a script that he would then direct. "I figured my career was finished anyway," he said.

To help him with the script, he hired Bergman and the team of Norman Steinberg and Alan Uger, writers he had worked with before. The script would also need the contributions of an authentic black voice. After Dick Gregory turned him down, he went to Richard Pryor.

Richard, by all accounts, threw himself into the project with abandon, spinning out gags and situations like an inspired Rumplestiltskin — even offering up bits from *Black Stranger,* a cowboy screenplay he'd written while in Berkeley. What's most impressive, he showed up every day and on time.

"I decided this would be a surrealist epic," Brooks told Kenneth Tynan in a *New Yorker* profile. "It was time to take two eyes, the way Picasso had done it, and put them on one side of the nose, because the official movie portrait of the West was simply a lie. For nine months we worked together like maniacs. We went all the way — especially Richard Pryor, who was very brave and very far out and very catalytic. . . . They wrote berserk, heartfelt stuff about white corruption and racism and Bible-thumping bigotry. We used dirty language on the screen for the first time, and to me the whole thing was like a big psychoanalytic session."

Impressed by what he'd seen from Richard during their months of writing the screenplay together — the way Richard would jump up and act scenes out — Brooks became convinced that he would be outrageous in the title role of "Black Bart," as the script was then called. Brooks had been delightfully surprised when the studio accepted their profane, illogical, irreverent, madcap script, requesting only a few minimal changes to rein in the running time. So he was perhaps more stunned than he might have been when Warner Bros. flatly refused to consider Richard for the part. He lacked acting experience, they said. What they didn't expressly say was that he had a reputation for being erratic and uncontrollable and was known to have drug problems. There was no telling what he might do.

Richard was dumbstruck when he got the news from his friend Cleavon Little that he'd signed on for the role. That Richard would later share a Writers Guild of America award for Best Comedy Written Directly for the Screen did little to ease the pain. His name was inadvertently left off the early prints of the film.

"Richard wrote it and Mel Brooks chased him out," director Michael Shultz said at the time. "Mel Brooks was trying to get total credit for the picture. . . . To be outmaneuvered and ripped off at that early stage in his career is something that's a little hard for him to get over. I'd feel the same way."

Knowing that Richard had been slated for the role makes watching the movie a bit of a disappointment, says film scholar James Monaco. "You keep thinking what Pryor could have done. He is exactly what's missing from *Blazing Saddles*. He might have injected the necessary evil gleam. Little was too rational and simply too attractive to energize the film." Had he played the role, Pauline Kael wrote, Richard would have made the sheriff "crazy — threatening and funny both."

Besides all that, it would have teamed Richard with Gene Wilder two years before *Silver Streak*.

Cleavon Little did a fine job, Mooney allows. "He's okay, but he's not a genius. On the other hand, can you picture *Blazing Saddles* with Richard Pryor in the lead? Ridiculous, right?"

Take a look at the televised performance of Richard playing both a man and a woman going through a breakup in his routine "When Your Woman Leaves You" or embodying all participants in a bar fight in "Nigger with a Seizure," and then imagine what he could've done with the scene in *Blazing Saddles* where Bart holds off a mob of angry townspeople by putting a gun to his own head and taking himself hostage, barking them back with, "Hold it! Next man makes a move, the nigger gets it." The crowd recoils with a collective gasp. The town doctor says, "Listen to him men, he's just crazy enough to do it." Bart then embodies both hostage and hostage-taker simultaneously.

AS HOSTAGE-TAKER: Drop it or I swear I'll blow this nigger's head all over this town!

AS HOSTAGE: (*terrified "darkie" voice*) Oh, lordy, lord! He's desperate! Do what he say, do what he say!

It broke Richard's heart that he never got to play it. It was his scene.

Richard was further devastated to learn that the studio wanted to cut his cowboys-farting-around-the-campfire scene and that Brooks had agreed to it.

Yes, Brooks agreed to cut the fart scene — and the scene where the horse gets punched in the face and all derogatory references to black people — but he never had the slightest intention of following through. "It's what I always tell young filmmakers," he said. "Say yes, yes, yes to every damn fool thing the producers ask, then ignore it all. No one ever notices."

After the heartbreak of *Blazing Saddles,* Richard fell into a dark and bitter depression. Mooney urged, pestered, and cajoled him to get back

up on his feet. Stand-up was the only forum in Hollywood where a
black man could speak his mind without the town "going all Frankenstein on his ass." Frankenstein's monster was their in-joke metaphor for
Hollywood:

> Just like Dr. Frankenstein, producers want to stitch together body
> parts and build their own stars, their own monsters. . . . I always
> thought of Frankenstein's monster as a black man. All the white
> people are always chasing him. "Get him! Get him!" . . . The villag-
> ers are terrified of him, just like crackers are terrified of the black
> man. And when they catch him, he whups villager ass, just like a
> black man. He throws motherfuckers all over the place.

But Richard had to be a movie star. Anything less would be failure in
his eyes.

Contemplating the spectacle of Richard Pryor — a solo performer
without peer — setting his true gifts aside to perform in such arid fare
as *Adiós Amigo*, incomprehensible camp like *The Phynx*,* and nearly

---

*If you must know, the evil ruler of communist Albania has kidnapped a multitude
of America's bygone stars — among them George Jessel, Butterfly McQueen, Guy
Lombardo, Andy Devine, Ruby Keeler, Edgar Bergen, Colonel Harland Sanders (believe it), Jay Silverheels, Johnny Weissmuller and Maureen O'Sullivan (aka Tarzan
and Jane) — who all make cameos. The leader of the SSA (Super Secret Agency) wears
a cardboard box over his head but sounds like Richard Nixon (courtesy of Rich Little).
He responds to the crisis by assembling his legions of undercover agents — whole divi-
sions of them — who pose as bikers, hookers, Black Panthers, Klansmen, Boy Scouts,
and so on. He consults a supercomputer called MOTHA (Mechanical Oracle That
Helps Americans), a female-shaped contraption with blinking lights and cone-shaped
breasts. SSA hatches a plan to recruit four young men selected by MOTHA to form a
rock group (the Phynx), make them into international stars, and then wait until they
are invited to play a gig in Albania. As part of the group's training, Richard (who introduces himself as "Richard Pryor"), dressed as a chef, is onscreen for all of eight seconds, just long enough to say that his job will be to teach them "soul." Unbelievably, the
Phynx's songs were penned by Jerry Leiber and Mike Stoller, composers of "Jailhouse
Rock," "Hound Dog," and "Yakety Yak," among others.

everything he did after 1979 is even more mind numbing than that of Elvis Presley abandoning his country-stewed brew of roots, blues, and gospel rhythms to star in insipid teen movies with barely functioning story lines held together with bubble-gum pop confections and rear-projection backdrops. (On the flip side, consider that Shakespeare, according to a theory put forth by professor Felix Schelling, wanted most of all to be a poet, only resigning himself to writing crowd-pleasing plays because he couldn't make a living from his verses.)

And then in February, while Richard grieved through the theatrical release of *Blazing Saddles* and the attendant reviews praising Cleavon Little, he got a call from Forest Hamilton at Stax West. Buoyed by the success of *Wattstax,* and perhaps egged on by Motown's *Lady Sings the Blues* — if Berry Gordy could make Oscar-caliber movies, then Stax owner Al Bell figured he could, too — Stax produced *Darktown Strutter's Ball,* directed by William Witney and starring Trina Parks, under the Stax-Netter Films banner (a partnership with former MGM vice president Doug Netter, despite Netter's having threatened Stax with a lawsuit over the inclusion in *Wattstax* of Isaac Hayes's performance of the MGM-controlled "Theme from *Shaft*"). *Darktown Strutters* (as it was eventually released, then reissued in the 1980s as *Get Down and Boogie!*) turned out to be not at all what Stax's vice president of advertising and publicity Larry Shaw had envisioned when he read the script.

As the head of Stax West in Los Angeles, Forest Hamilton was tasked with monitoring the progress of the film. He called Shaw up and said, "This film is crazy. It ain't going nowhere we thought it was going."

"It was going into very white folks comedy," Shaw concurs. "Slapstick, pies in the face, weird Batman sounds — horrible. We couldn't stand it."

Everyone agreed that Richard had elevated *Wattstax,* taking it from being a mere document of a historic event and turning it into a genuine *movie.* Shaw wondered if maybe Richard could work the same magic on *Darktown Strutter's Ball.* Hamilton arranged a special screening for him. Shaw was there, watching from the back of the projection room and, at some point, noticed that he didn't see Richard's head anymore. He found him on the floor, crouched down below seat-level, crawling toward the door. He said, "Please, Shaw. I know I owe you a few favors, but don't ask me to do this."

Fair enough, Shaw said. How about doing a record instead?

Stax's new comedy label Partee Records had released only a handful of LPs, mostly minor efforts by major comics such as Timmie Rogers, Moms Mabley (*I Like 'Em Young*), and the now highly collectable *At Last . . . Bill Cosby Really Sings.*

Richard gave them *That Nigger's Crazy,* recorded live at Don Cornelius's *Soul Train* studio in San Francisco with all new material he'd been developing at the Store.

> My uncle said, "Boy, don't you ever kiss no pussy. I mean that. Whatever you do in life, don't kiss no pussy."
>
> I couldn't *wait* to kiss a pussy. He'd been wrong about every-thing else. Woman had to beat me off. "That's enough, that's enough! Please. Two days . . ."

> "You crazy!" some guy in the audience yells.
> "Huh?"
> "YOU CRAZY!"
> "Yeah!" Richard agrees. Absolute glee in his voice.

That Nigger's Crazy was a phenomenon, marking the emergence of Richard in full possession of his genius, the Richard Pryor we know today. Greg Tate, looking back on the LP in an obituary piece for the *Village Voice,* wrote:

> You have to go to Chekhov or Edward P. Jones to find small lives rendered with as much epic detail and epiphanal force as Pryor un-veils on "Wino & Junkie," a hellacious and ruthlessly hilarious vi-sion of life beneath the underdog that erects a totem to Black male

oblivion out of the parsed lines his Boswell wino relates about his junkie Johnson.

James Alan McPherson wrote that Richard "enters into his people and allows whatever is comic in them, whatever is human, to evolve out of what they say and how they look into a total scene. It is part of Richard Pryor's genius that, through the selective use of facial gestures, emphases in speech and movements, he can create a scene that is comic and at the same time recognizable as profoundly human."

Richard renders his downtrodden characters in purely human terms, unsullied by any trace of sentimentality. "These portraits were wonderfully specific," writes Richard Zoglin, "yet evocative of a whole community — unmistakably black yet too recognizable to be mere instruments of a racial agenda.... stand-up comedy had never seen anything like it."

JUNKIE: Pops...nigger, listen to me!

WINO: Don't you hit me no more, boy. I'll dust your junkie ass off. You know I will, nigger. You rile me, boy. I'm ashamed to see you like this.

JUNKIE: Ashamed to see *me*? What about this shit out here? Niggers just fuckin' with me, man...
(*trails off, long silence*)
Was I finished?

The self-validating logic of Richard's junkie at times recalls Shakespeare's Sir John Falstaff.

JUNKIE: I went to the unemployment bureau, baby. Bitch sittin' behind the desk—ugly motherfucker come tellin' me talkin' 'bout, "You have a criminal record." I say, "I know that, bitch! I'm a criminal!"

(In *Henry IV, Part 1,* when Prince Hal chides Falstaff as a rogue and a stealer of purses, the corpulent and debaucherous knight reasonably answers, "Why, Hal, 'tis my vocation, Hal; 'tis no sin for a man to labor in his vocation.")

His junkie goes from comedy to pathos with whiplash-inducing abruptness.

> JUNKIE: My father say he don't want to see me in the vicinity. Just 'cause I stole his television. That's the politics, baby. I'm sick, pops. Wonder can you help me? My mind's thinking about shit I don't want to think about. I can't stop the motherfucker, baby. Movin' too fast for the kid. Tell me some of that ol' lies of yours, make me stop thinkin' about the truth.

Richard Lewis remembers Richard workshopping these routines at the Comedy Store. "He was absolutely fearless. He would say anything." And reveal anything.

> You ever be with a woman you wanted to be with for a long time, man, and you finally get with her and you come in about four seconds? And you be panicked, jack, trying to be cool. "Oh, God! Lord don't let her know . . . just let it stay heavy if not hard." (*as woman*) "You're not moving as much as you were . . ."
> "Uh, I'm just resting a little. I want you to enjoy this."

Richard's characters were no less "real" when confronting vampires or space aliens. As metaphors, they really were not that much of a stretch.

> Nothing can scare a nigger, not after four hundred years of this shit. A Martian wouldn't have a chance. A nigger would warn a Martian. (*as old man, foreshadowing Mudbone*) "You better get your ass away from around here. You done landed on Mr. Gilmore's property."
> If he land in New York, a nigger would take his shit from him. "You got to give up the flyin' saucer, baby. Cause I'm a macaroni." Nigger'd be cruising, "Oh, yeah, this sweet! How much is petrol? Eighty-two million a gallon? Fuck this machine!"

Al Bell and Forest Hamilton knew that with Richard's new recording they had a crossover hit on their hands, but Stax's distributor CBS recoiled at the very idea of taking *That Nigger's Crazy,* based on nothing more than the title. And once they listened to it, John Smith says, "They were absolutely certain. They didn't want anything to do with it."

Partee released the LP through independent distributors in April 1974. Richard, at that time, was out on the road. He got his first inkling of how huge the record was when people in the audience started calling out requests, speaking lines along with him, or even beating him to the punch.

Girls weren't givin' up no pussy in the fifties. It was very seldom you got any parts of pussy. You'd be tongue-kissing and shit, your dick get harder than times in '29. Nuts get all up in your stomach . . . You ever have that? You'd be like, "Ooooh, you gotta give me some now."

(as *girl*): "I'm not giving anything, I'm on my period."

"You on your period again?"

(*now everybody, in unison . . .*)

"You gonna bleed to death, bitch."

"It was quite a surprise," Richard said. "Niggers was in the audience doing my shit. And you better not change nothing, cause they be like, 'Wait, motherfucker, you didn't say that on the album. Don't bring us no original shit. Bring the shit on the record, motherfucker!'"

White folks do things a lot different than niggers do. They eat quiet and shit. You be over there they be, "Pass the potatoes. Thank you, darling. Can I have a bit of that sauce? How are the kids coming along with their studies? Think we'll be having sexual intercourse this evening? We're not? Well what the heck."

The album quickly went gold and took that year's Grammy Award for Best Comedy Album, despite the then-common record store practice of keeping X-rated or potentially inflammatory titles under the counter. This presented an additional hurdle to Bell's hoped-for hip young white record buyers faced with the prickly — and quite possibly dangerous — dilemma of having to ask for the record by name. The break-through sales came too late for Stax. Within just a few months of its release, the album had sold out, and there were no more copies to be had. Facing foreclosure from Union Planters National Bank, trouble with the IRS, and an injunction from CBS, Stax simply couldn't find a pressing plant willing to fill its orders. Reluctantly, on September 23, 1974, the company returned the master tapes to Richard in lieu of two hundred thousand dollars in royalties it had no hope of paying him. Richard turned around and licensed it to Warner Bros. — but not before he had, in frustration, shot up his framed gold record with his .357 Magnum. It was, for Richard, the first of at least a half-dozen inanimate objects he would take down with that gun.

Back in 1970, finding himself in dire financial straits, Richard had signed an unvetted deal with Louis Drozen's Laff Records for "a substantial four-figure advance." From that time on, Laff seemingly recorded every club date Richard played, and they kept the tape rolling. In crafting its contract with Richard in 1974, Warner Bros. allowed Drozen to retain the rights to the trove of tapes he had stored away in Laff's vaults. It turned out to be massive.

Over the next decade and a half, every time a Richard Pryor movie came out or Warner Bros. issued a new Richard Pryor LP, Laff rode the coattails of free publicity and released a Pryor album of its own, culled from their apparently bottomless trove of archived recordings, sometimes repackaging the same material for a second go-round. Three of those Laff records were nominated for Grammys — perhaps a reflexive action on the part of nominating members in response to seeing the name Richard Pryor on the list of considerations, despite the junior-high-school-newspaper-quality cover illustrations (that's assuming they actually saw the LPs in question). The first time that happened, with *Are You Serious?*, released in 1976, Richard bought full-page ads in the trades thanking the Recording Academy for the honor of being nominated but asking members not to mark their ballots for something he believed did not represent his best work. Eventually, one Laff title — happily, the most deserving one, *Rev. Du Rite* — won Richard his fourth gold award in 1982. (*Live on the Sunset Strip* would be his fifth and final Grammy winner the following year.)

The cover of *Rolling Stone* dated October 10, 1974, pictured Richard and Lily Tomlin as personifications of theatrical comedy and tragedy masks — Richard cackling, Lily sobbing — under the headline "Jive Times: The Comedy, Theater and Routine Lives of Richard Pryor and Lily Tomlin," the first of a two-part feature by David Felton. For this issue, Felton wrote three separate pieces on Richard: the most in-depth biographical profile yet published, a fanciful musing on the inner workings of Richard's imagination, and the most candid, unguarded — and, one might guess, manipulative — interview Richard would ever give. (Felton's piece on Tomlin appeared in the following issue.)

Felton certainly fared better than the *National Observer* interviewer who found Richard in an especially pissy and combative mood when Richard claimed, with a straight face, that J. Edgar Hoover had been his most important influence. He feigned not to know who Charlie Chaplin was. Insisted he'd never even heard his name before. When the exasperated reporter started packing up his things, Richard told him, "Say hi to your boss, Buckley, for me." So that was it. The reporter patiently explained that he was with the *National Observer*, not William F. Buckley's *National Review*. Oh. In that case, Richard told him, sit back down and he'd submit to a proper interview.

By contrast, Richard gave Felton eight separate interviews over the course of several months, allowing Felton to witness him sobbing in a restaurant as he tried to describe the guilt he felt for having let people down and letting him observe as he workshopped the material that would become *That Nigger's Crazy*.

Richard even allowed Felton to quote extensive passages from his autobiographical screenplay "This Can't Be Happening to Me" that he'd begun writing in Berkeley, including a remarkable scene in a cathedral in which Christ begs Richard to help him down from the cross. "I've been hanging around here two thousand years," Jesus says to him, "and they ain't buried me yet, and I'm tired." Richard pulls the spikes from his hands and feet, and helps him, limping, out of the cathedral. As soon as they reach the street, sirens go off. Richard and Jesus are set upon by a group of monks who beat them up, haul Jesus back inside, and nail him back on the cross. As Jesus wails in agony, Richard vows to tell the world what just happened, to which one of the monks replies, "Who's going to believe you, nigger?"

———————

While on a late-summer cross-country tour, Richard stopped in Peoria to attend a ribbon-cutting ceremony dedicating the new sliding board — apparently a very elaborate sliding board — that he had donated to Miss Whittaker's new day-care center. The mayor proclaimed it "Richard Pryor Day." A band played on the back of a flatbed truck, and the YMCA put on a show in his honor at the Shrine mosque. Following the ribbon cutting, Richard presented the Emmy he had won as a writer for the second Lily Tomlin special to the woman who had inspired and believed in him when he needed it most. As he ceremoniously unveiled the trophy, which he had hastily wrapped in newspaper, he told Miss Whittaker, "If it hadn't been for you, I would not have learned anything about the theater. And I certainly wouldn't have learned how to write."

(On his next visit to Peoria, he shyly asked Miss Whittaker if he could have the statuette back. But it was adorable the way he did it, she insisted. "Miss Whittaker," he said, "when I say I won an Emmy, people don't believe me.")

———————

Richard cohosted *The Mike Douglas Show* for the entire week of November 25–29, 1974. Introduced as "the Pride of Peoria," his stint featured guest appearances by Sammy Davis Jr., Freddie Prinze, Harry Belafonte, Joe Frazier, and a memorable performance by Sly Stone. (Memorable to everyone except Sly, that is. When an interviewer complimented him on his appearance, he didn't know who Mike Douglas was.) At the end of the week, in what Richard would often say had been the proudest moment of his life, his grandmother Marie came out to join him, giving him a massive hug on national TV.

On that week's Monday show, Richard found himself sobbing uncontrollably when Douglas, in one of the "this is your life" moments he enjoyed springing on his guest hosts, brought out surprise guest Miss Juliette Whittaker. Richard wept as she recalled the shy young teenager who looked to be no older than nine, showing up at Peroria's Carver Community Center asking if he could be in a play.

Later in that same broadcast, Richard, perhaps giddy from his emotional reunion with Miss Whittaker, began to snicker as guest Milton Berle attempted to tell a maudlin, heart-wrenching story from his just-published memoir about how he'd agonized over taking his girlfriend — an actress who, he hinted, later married a powerful producer — to Tijuana for an abortion in 1931. Not only did Pryor crack up over the story, he apparently blurted out a pretty good guess as to the woman's identity, judging from the look on Berle's face. "I'm sorry, man," Richard stammered, still laughing, "but I just — I just did it."

"I wish, Richard," Berle lectured him, "that I could have laughed at that time when I was your age the way you just laughed now, but I just couldn't." Richard, trying to make amends, offered to relight Milton's cigar. "No, thank you, I don't smoke that stuff," Berle huffed. He attempted to resume his story with a little background on how his domineering mother, who invariably attempted to thwart any romance that lasted more than two or three dates, instructed him to marry the girl just long enough to give the child a name and then divorce her. This only provoked more ill-suppressed laugher from Richard. "I'm sorry, man, it's just the story . . . it's funny." Berle refused to continue, saying he'd come back and tell the story some other time. "I told you this nine years ago and I'm going to tell you on the air in front of millions of people: Pick your spots, baby." Richard came back with a faux Humphrey Bogart, "All right, schweetheart." Berle gazed up into the studio lights, as though following the up-wafting smoke from his cigar and repeated the warning. "Pick your spots."

As the show's credits rolled, Berle howled as Richard, for the second time in his career, went down in defeat against the show's final guest, a wrestling bear.

That same autumn of 1974, Penelope Spheeris had a visit from her friend Lorne Michaels. He sat on the sofa in her Topanga Beach home and made his pitch, hoping to persuade her to come to New York and work on a new project of his. She never seriously considered the offer. Her longtime boyfriend, Bobby Schoeller, the father of their five-year-old daughter, had only a few months before died of a heroin overdose. The idea of uprooting her daughter and moving across the country was just too much. Besides, Lorne's idea sounded a bit flighty. He wanted to bring live skit comedy back to TV, the way Sid Caesar and Imogene Coca had done it back in the 1950s, except hip and edgy and bold, for the 1970s.

These, she recalls, were his exact words: "I want to do a live show, from New York, on Saturday nights."

When its time came, Richard would do for that show what he had done for Mitzi Shore and the Comedy Store, only nationwide.

PART **FOUR**

"I SEE THAT MAN IN MY MIND AND GO WITH HIM"

A joke went around in the early seventies that the continental United States had tilted slightly to the southwest and everything loose started rolling toward L.A. After watching so many of his top comics pick up and go west, Budd Friedman, owner of the New York Improvisation decided in 1975 that the time had come to get in on the action.

For Mitzi Shore, the opening of the L.A. Improv in West Hollywood was a declaration of war. Comics who played the Improv, she decreed, were no longer welcome at the Store. (She allowed a few exceptions, one of them being Jay Leno. He saw no reason to deny himself the prestige and exposure the Improv could offer, and he was too valuable for Shore to shut him out.) The L.A. Improv was just one among a rash of new comedy clubs to spring up within a mile radius of the Store. As well, existing clubs had begun adding comedy to their musical lineups. Against this onslaught, Mitzi had one weapon no other club could match: Richard Pryor.

The Comedy Store became the workshop where Richard would develop material for his heaviest LPs, from 1974's *That Nigger's Crazy* through 1978's *Wanted: Richard Pryor Live in Concert.* Anytime Richard wanted to woodshed new material, all he had to do was let Mitzi know and she would clear the decks for as many nights or weeks as he wanted. His name on the marquee guaranteed sold-out shows every night, and his appearances, William Knoedelseder writes, "had the frenzied feel of a heavyweight title fight in Vegas, with lines stretching around the block."

When Richard held court, other comics, of necessity, had to relinquish their time slots, but when he was in the house, nothing else mattered. "They recognized that Pryor was the closest thing their peculiar profession had to a genius on the scale of a Beethoven or a Van Gogh," says Knoedelseder. "Nearly every local comic who wasn't on stage somewhere else was on hand to watch and learn. What were a few lost time slots compared to the chance of studying the master at work?"

For those who weren't there to witness it firsthand, Richard Lewis says, it's impossible to convey the charisma of Richard in the mid-1970s. "To see him walk through a club, the way people responded . . . For a young comedian, it was like seeing God. You watched him and you thought, 'This man was born to be a comedian.' He was the most organic comedian I ever saw. It was like he grew up out of the ground." Franklyn Ajaye attests that Richard quickly became every comic's idol. "It was clear to everybody that Pryor was the best guy around."

———————

Every night over the course of a single week in the winter of 1975 Ajaye watched from the floor of the Comedy Store as Richard gave birth to Mudbone, his most enduring and recognizable character. "When I was a young comedian I liked to go back and see what other comics repeated from one show to the next, what they changed. It demystified the process." Seeing Richard Pryor spin his masterwork out of thin air did little to demystify anything. Just the opposite.

Mudbone showed up one night as a nameless old man in the middle of Richard's set. "One of those things that pop up in your subconscious that you don't even know are in there," Ajaye says. That first night, Mudbone spoke only a line or two at most, but Richard would bring the character out again every night and work on it. "That let me know that he was thinking about it during the day, building on what he'd done the night before. Each night he'd add a little bit more to it. That made me realize he was a lot more technical than I had thought. That's why his routines are great routines. They're very refined." By week's end, that nameless old man had become the crusty, wizened raconteur who commandeered more than a third of Richard's next Warner Bros. LP . . . *Is It Something I Said?*, recorded in May at the Latin Casino in Cherry Hill, New Jersey. Before Mudbone, Richard had always brought his characters into a specific situation to interact with each other while he, as storyteller, stepped in and out of the scene. Here Richard gives Mudbone a formal introduction before turning the stage — and his audience — over solely to him. It's telling, too, that Richard introduces Mudbone by speaking as himself but in Mudbone's voice.

RICHARD (*MUDBONE VOICE*): I was born in Pee-oh-rah, Illinois.

GUY IN AUDIENCE: What's that?

RICHARD: That's a city, nigger. You probably wouldn't know nothin' about that, see? Ol' country-ass boy.

And when I was little there was a old man, his name was Mudbone and he'd dip snuff and he'd sit in front of the barbecue pit and he'd spit, see? That was his job. I'm pretty sure that was his job, 'cause that's all he did. But he'd tell stories. Fascinatin' stories, see? And I loved him . . . He made me very happy. 'Cause I'd stay with him and listen to him. 'Cause you learn stuff listenin' to old people. They ain't all fools, you know. You don't get to be old bein' no fool. Lot of young wise men, they deader than a motherfucker, ain't they?

A few moments later, Richard quietly retreats, leaving Mudbone to stand on his own and speak for himself. It's a touching gesture, with Richard acting as caregiver, making sure this rickety old man is steady on his feet before he tiptoes away.

In what is essentially a one-man theatrical piece, Mudbone tells how he drove a tractor to Peoria, Illinois, from Tupelo, Mississippi, after revenging the physical and verbal assaults he'd suffered at the hands of his bossman's 465-pound mail-order bride.

I went in the toolshed and got me one of them Kreg jigsaws and I sawed the bottom out of the outhouse and I hid in the bushes and waited for this big collard-green-eatin' bitch to go to the bathroom. Well, long about eight thirty she commenced to going to the bathroom. I'm in the bushes lookin' at her. She wobbled out to the outhouse, opened the door, went in, shut the door. I heard a big splash. That's when I got on the tractor and drove up here. I wasn't mad no more, either.

Continuing on the album's B side, Mudbone, now an established resident of Peoria, next tells how he took his friend Toodlum to visit a conjure woman known as Miss Rudolph in hopes that she can cure a hex cast on Toodlum by a lady friend from Louisiana. Mudbone tells Miss Rudolf right away that they have no money. That's fine, she says. In lieu of cash, they can bring her a goose or a turkey at Thanksgiving time.

I said, well, shit, that's fine with me 'cause it was June then. If I don't never see this bitch no more in life it's alright with me, see? And just about that time a big motherfuckin' tarantula this big crawled up my arm, around my neck — I almost shit on myself, man — went down this arm, under my hand . . . I tried to mash him. When I lift my hand up, he was gone! That's when I put my hand on my knife. Because I figured if somebody get hurt in here, I ain't gonna be the last one, see?

I said, "Miss Rudolph, please tell me what happened to the tarantula." She said, "That ain't none of your goddamn business. But if you don't bring me that turkey, you will see him again."

As a youngster performing with his father and uncle at the Apollo Theater in the 1930s, Sammy Davis Jr. recalled that the best jokes were always told backstage. "We didn't call them jokes at the time, we called them lies. 'That nigger sure can lie' was a common phrase at the time." Mudbone said the same of his friend Toodlum. "He could lie his ass off. Oh, that nigger could tell *lies*! That's how we became friends, see? He'd tell a lie, I'd tell a lie. And we'd complement each other's lies. He'd make me laugh all day long, bless his soul. He told me this lie one time, he told me about the niggers with the big dicks."*

> These niggers had the biggest dicks in the world, and they were trying to find a place where they could have their contest, see? And they wasn't no freaks, didn't want everybody lookin'. They was walking around lookin' for a secret place. So they walked across the Golden Gate Bridge and the nigger seen that water and make him want to piss, see. Boy say, "Man, I got to take a leak." He pulled out his thing and was pissing. The other nigger pulled his out, took a piss. The one nigger say, "Goddamn! This water cold!"
>
> The other nigger say, "Yeah, and it's deep, too."
>
> Boy could lie his ass off. He say, "Yeah, and it's deep, too." Goddamn his soul . . .

Mudbone's folk wisdom and deft storytelling skills immediately drew comparisons to Mark Twain. ("Dark Twain" was but one honorific bestowed upon Richard by his peers.) The genius embodied in Mudbone prompted Bob Newhart in 1998 to effuse that it was entirely right and proper that Richard should receive the first-ever Kennedy Center Mark Twain Prize for American Humor because "he and Twain did the same

---

*Show business legends and privately circulated photographs attest that Milton Berle and Forrest Tucker were both endowed with penises of equine proportions. One afternoon Jackie Gleason saw them both in the locker room at Hollywood's Hillcrest Country Club and declared it was time to settle the matter once and for all. "We've got the East Coast champ and the West Coast champ," Gleason said, according to Berle. "My money's on Milton. I'll put up two hundred dollars even money." Berle tried to beg off. "I said, 'Jackie, enough.' And he looked at me and said, 'Milton, just take out enough to win.' It was maybe the funniest spontaneous line I ever heard," Berle said. Except it wasn't. Tales of dick contests, measured by length, girth, or weight, are abundant in African American folklore. Typical is the one in which a man comes home bearing wads of cash. His wife doesn't believe his claim that he won it in a dick contest. "You mean you done won all this money by showing your dick?" He assures her that he only needed to show half of it.

thing. Mark Twain wrote about life on the frontier, what it was like growing up on the Mississippi River, and Richard Pryor [told] what it was
like growing up in the inner city. Even without the raw and colorful language, his concepts are still rich." Richard, through his characters, provided entry into a side of life that seemed — that *was*, in fact — closed
off to most of middle America. And it was a side we wanted to know. It
was where all the best music and the biggest laughs came from.

Kathy McKee had no idea who Richard Pryor was in 1973 when he came
backstage at the Tropicana in Vegas to pay his respects to her boss and
boyfriend, Sammy Davis Jr.

The aspiring actress, a native of Detroit, had at that time played the
title role in Deluxe Movie Ventures' slavery-era feature *Quadroon*, appeared on *The Bill Cosby Show*, and in two episodes of *Sanford and Son*.
She may well have been the first black dancer to work a line in Vegas
by passing for white. If anyone asked, she said she was part Jewish,
part Italian. At that time she served as the "mistress of ceremonies" for
Davis's stage show. McKee had first met Sammy Davis when she was
eleven years old. Davis had stayed at the home of one of her classmates
when he came to Detroit for Martin Luther King's June 1963 Freedom
March. Davis recalled the meeting with only minimal prompting in 1970
when the seventeen-year-old McKee, dressed in full showgirl regalia,
approached his table at a Vegas club. When Davis later married his longtime girlfriend and mistress of ceremonies, Altovise Gore, McKee took
over both of Gore's former roles.

"I'm Sammy's woman," she told Richard when he started hitting on
her backstage that night, "and he knows what you're doing, so just stop."
But Richard wouldn't quit. He kept after her when the party moved upstairs to Sammy's suite, and then off and on for the next several years.
As he flirted with her that first night in 1973, chatting her up about her
career, they discovered that Richard (along with Paul Mooney) had
written both episodes of *Sanford and Son* she had been in. "When I got

those scripts, the names Richard Pryor and Paul Mooney meant nothing to me." After she and Sammy and Altovise returned to L.A., Richard wore her down with notes and gifts and phone calls, and she began seeing him on the sly. Then came the whirlwind of *That Nigger's Crazy,* followed by . . . *Is It Something I Said?,* and the next thing she knew she was seated next to him on a plane headed for New York where he would host the seventh installment of *NBC's Saturday Night.**

—————

Up until the mid-1970s, the networks had little interest in Saturday late-night shows. After the eleven o'clock news, the airwaves were a bone-yard for local affiliates, the final resting place for schlock movies from the 1950s and '60s. NBC stations had the option of rerunning recent episodes of *The Tonight Show* to predictably tepid ratings, which did not please either the affiliates or Johnny Carson. When Carson pulled the weekend reruns, preferring to repackage them as "best of" programs to air on weeknights so that he could enjoy some time off, NBC president Herbert Schlosser and vice president of late night programming Dick Ebersol tapped Lorne Michaels, a veteran of *Rowan and Martin's Laugh-In,* to create something edgy and new.

Johnny Carson dismissed *Saturday Night* as crude and sophomoric. He was right. That he considered the jibe a debilitating argument against the show only underscores how out of step "the lonesome hero of middle America" (as a 1970 *Life* magazine cover proclaimed him) had

———

*An ABC comedy-variety show called *Saturday Night Live with Howard Cosell* had debuted at 8:00 p.m. just a few weeks earlier on September 20, 1975. It's gleefully remembered by some as one of the greatest flops in the history of television. The crew of skit performers featured on the Cosell show included future NBC *Saturday Night Live* regulars Bill Murray, his brother Brian Doyle-Murray, and Christopher Guest. They were collectively billed as the "Prime Time Players," prompting Herb Sargent to dub the NBC *Saturday Night* crew "Not Ready for Prime Time." When Cosell's show was laid to rest after eighteen episodes in January 1976, Lorne Michaels pounced on the title, rechristening his show *Saturday Night Live* at the start of the 1977 season.

become. Crude and sophomoric was exactly what *Saturday Night's* de-
mographic craved.

Conventional wisdom held that it would be ludicrous to expect the
show's target audience to sit at home watching TV at eleven thirty on
a Saturday night. Michaels knew different. The audience he was after
had grown up watching TV. Too much TV. It was their collective point
of reference, the communal campfire around which they all gathered in
the new global village. They lived and breathed TV with an ironic self-
awareness that Michaels and his team used to frame the jokes within the
Big Joke that would define the show and leave most Americans born
before 1948 muttering to themselves and scratching their heads.

NBC's *Saturday Night* was arguably the first television show about
television. Then, as now, the show was dominated by ironic takedowns
of commercials, newcasts, sitcoms, talk shows, PBS-styled cultural programming, punditry, and presidential debates. Even those skits that
ventured beyond television's domain would typically break through
the fourth wall to skewer — or at least wink at — the familiar conven-
tions of variety-show sketch comedy. Perhaps that's why Richard's turn
as guest host proved such a sensation. His stand-up bits were a bracing
blast of fresh air for a generation accustomed to peering out at the world
through a peephole the size of a TV screen and snickering at what they
saw. The characters Richard brought out during his solo spots that night
bore little resemblance to television's stock types. The decent guy who
turns into a violent drunk on weekends, the Hennessy-quaffing cat who
accepts a hit of acid at a party, the junkie-berating wino — all were ren-
egades who rode into the medium's gated community with news from
the outside world.

That's why Lorne Michaels had to have Richard Pryor. The show's
claims to hip edginess or even bare relevance would ring hollow without
him. It's no exaggeration to equate the back-to-back salvos of *That Nigger's Crazy* (back in print on Warner Bros.' Reprise label just a month

earlier) and . . . *Is it Something I Said?* (released late in July) with Bob Dylan's electric epiphanies of *Highway 61 Revisited* and *Blonde on Blonde.* Just as every folk singer circa 1966 scrambled to plug into that same arc welder, lower the dark glasses, and send off a wild mercurial spray of white sparks into the sky, now it seemed every club comic carried a ghetto-talking phrasebook in his back pocket, as if that were the secret to doing what Richard did. "That's the difference between Pryor and the pretenders who use profanity just to get laughs instead of making it a part of the characters and scenes they are trying to create," says David Brenner. "Pryor could take the same bits he did at the Comedy Store or the Improv, vacuum out all the shits and motherfuckers for TV, and be just as funny."

With Richard as host, sufficient numbers of the alienated youth Michaels sought could be counted on to eject Pink Floyd from their eight-tracks, switch off the strobe lights, carry their bongs up from the basement, or switch over from their local UHF station's ghoulish movie host just to see what Richard might do.

The trouble was, NBC flat-out refused to allow Richard Pryor anywhere near a live studio camera. Richard, everyone knew, was a wildly unpredictable, uncontrollable cokehead. (So was just about everyone else on the show, but Richard didn't bother to hide it.) What was to stop him from letting loose a string of *shits* and *motherfuckers* on live TV, as he would sometimes do during rehearsal, just to mess with them?

Michaels resigned in protest. "I said, 'I can't do a contemporary comedy show without Richard Pryor.' And so I walked off. There was a lot of me walking off in those days." NBC finally relented on the condition that the broadcast be put on a ten-second delay. Michaels knew that Richard would never agree to that. It was insulting. After all, they'd let George Carlin go out live, as they had every other host (all six thus far). Richard would go apeshit if he found out they were treating him any differently. (He did and he did but not until later.) Michaels went back and forth with the network, finally agreeing to a five-second delay, as if the duration of the time lag had anything to do with it. Director Dave

Wilson now says the show in fact *was* live. His crew couldn't figure out how to work the delay.

Meanwhile, Michaels found just as much aggravation in closing the other end of the deal. As his scheduled week drew near, Richard was still playing hard to get. In an effort to negotiate, the producers made a junket to Miami where Richard was performing at a jai-alai arena.

Richard insisted that they hire Paul Mooney as his writer. His ex-wife, Shelley, and his new girlfriend, Kathy McKee, both had to be on the show. And he wanted tickets. Lots and lots of tickets. Enough to pack the studio audience with friends and family. Associate producer Craig Kellem says, "Lorne loved Richard. He thought he was quote-unquote the funniest man on the planet." But it was tough going. "As wonderful and as adorable as he was, it was also very tense being around him. It took so much work and effort to go through this process of booking him that Lorne, in a moment of extreme stress, sort of candidly looked around and said, 'He better be funny.' "

Herb Sargent and Craig Kellem arrived at Richard's Park Avenue hotel room the week of the show and found him in a foul mood. He was pissed because the network people had subjected Mooney to a condescending "job interview" — more like a parole-board hearing — before they would agree to hire him on for the show, which, of course, everyone knew they were going to do anyway because that's what Richard wanted.

Richard had questions they couldn't answer. Things got tense. Richard wanted to see a script. But there was no script. The staff was still in recovery mode from the previous week's show. Richard threatened to walk, but Sargent beat him to it. Kellem watched speechless as Sargent hopped up and made for the door saying he'd just dash over to the office and get the script. He never came back.

———————

When they weren't working on the show, Richard and Kathy McKee enjoyed their time together in New York. They saw Aretha Franklin at the Apollo and visited Miles Davis in the hospital. (In his opening monologue, Richard dedicated the show to Miles.) But Richard never told Kathy that Shelley was going to be on the show, too. "I'm with Richard," she says. "I'm his girlfriend, I'm traveling with him. You might think, when we got on the plane to New York, he would look over at me and say, 'Oh, by the way, Kathy, Shelley's going to be there.' Nope. Not a word. I never found out until I got to rehearsal.

"Richard didn't know how to manage his women the way Sammy [Davis Jr.] did," McKee explains. "Sammy Davis was a master at bringing his women together. Richard didn't know how to do that. He couldn't swing. He couldn't bring Deboragh and me or Pam Grier together. It always ended up being trouble for him. So we were kept separate."

It may have been that Richard still had feelings for Shelley and wanted to give her acting career a boost. Penelope Spheeris suggests the more likely scenario of a quid pro quo arrangement to make some of his child-support issues go away. Introduced as Shelley Pryor, she performed one of her poems, an interracial allegory of two differently colored carousel horses that brave society's scorn when they fall in love.

————————

Chevy Chase kept dogging Mooney all week to write something for him and Richard to do together. Just as Michaels needed Richard to establish his show's bona fides, Chevy needed airtime with him. Everybody else had a skit with Richard. He and Jim Belushi faced off as samurai hotel clerks; Jane Curtain interviewed him as an author who lightened his skin to see what life is like for a white man; Laraine Newman, as the devil-possessed Regan in a take-off on *The Exorcist*, threw a bowl of pea soup in his face; Dan Aykroyd debriefed him as a special-ops major; Garrett Morris, claiming that he was acting on Richard's request, did Chevy's trademark pratfall to open the show; and Gilda Radner, in a running gag throughout the show, repeatedly picked him out of police lineups. But Chevy had nothing. He kept sending emissaries to Mooney asking, "Could you please write something for Chevy and Richard?"

Paul Mooney recalls the genesis of the skit that critics and viewers alike continue to rank among the best ever in the history of *Saturday Night Live:*

> Toward the end of the week, as the Saturday show time approaches, he starts following me around himself, like a lamb after Bo Peep. "Richard hates me, doesn't he?" Chevy asks me. "He doesn't hate you," I say, even though I know Richard does indeed despise Chevy.
>
> Soon enough he's back tugging on my sleeve. "Write something for us, will you?" he pleads. "I have to get some air time with Richard."
>
> Finally, in the early afternoon on Thursday, I hand Lorne a sheet of paper.
>
> "What's this?" "You've all been asking me to put Chevy and Richard together," I say. After all the bullshit I've been put through to get here, the fucking cross-examination Lorne subjects me to, I decide to do a job interview of my own. Chevy's the boss, interviewing Richard for a janitor's job. The white personnel interviewer suggests they do some word association, so he can test if the black man's fit to employ.

The first words are innocuous enough. Chase says "dog." Richard says "tree." Fast/slow, rain/snow, white/black, bean/pod, then:

> Negro.
> Whitey.
>
> Tarbaby.
> What'd you say?
>
> Tarbaby.
> Ofay.
>
> Colored.
> Redneck.

Junglebunny.
(*bringing it*) Peckerwood!

Burrhead.
Cracker.

Spearchucker.
White trash.

Junglebunny.
Honky.

Spade.
Honky honky!

Nigger!
Dead honky!

As they wait for the long wave of laugher and applause to subside, Richard's face begins to spasm, his nose twitching like a maniacal rabbit. His character gets the job at three times the offered salary, plus two weeks' vacation up front. "Just don't hurt me," Mooney has Chevy say.

"It's like an H-bomb that Richard and I toss into America's consciousness," Mooney wrote. "All that shit going on behind closed doors is now out in the open. There's no putting the genie back in the bottle. The N-word as a weapon, turned back against those who use it, has been born on national TV."

It was, Mooney says, the easiest bit he ever wrote. All he had done was spell out what had been going on beneath the surface of his "job interview" with Lorne Michaels and the NBC execs.

Just as Michaels had hoped, Richard's appearance lifted *Saturday Night* out of the programming ghetto and established it as a cultural phenomenon. Two weeks later, Chevy Chase made the cover of *New York Magazine*, which dubbed him "the funniest man in America" and quoted an unnamed network executive championing him as "the first real potential successor to Johnny Carson," and predicting he'd be guest-hosting *Tonight* within six months.

Carson, understandably, offered a less-than-glowing assessment of Chevy's skills. "He couldn't ad-lib a fart after a baked-bean dinner."

Released only a month after his triumphant turn as host of *Saturday Night,* the mostly forgettable film, *Adiós Amigo,* costarred Richard with his friend Fred Williamson, who wrote and directed it. Williamson considered *Blazing Saddles* a silly movie, what with the Gucci logos on the sheriff's saddlebags, a Yiddish-speaking Indian chief, and the frontier town's Howard Johnson ice-cream parlor offering only one flavor. Williamson, too, wanted to make a comedy western but "down and dirty," like the real West. "I wanted to be able to maintain my straight-man figure to Richard's con man, still be tough and do my fight scenes — but just have someone floating around me like a butterfly to provide the comedy."

Richard plays the classic trickster as a Wild West con man. His character (called Sam Spade, of all things) repeatedly thwarts Williamson's plans, squanders his looted cash, and leaves him in the lurch with his life in peril. Each time, Spade pulls off a wily reversal of fortune, securing Williamson's rescue and replenishing their coffers. The movie is frequently out of focus, padded with overlong shots of the heroes and their pursuers crossing the picturesque landscape on horseback. Shot in nine days, working from a twelve-page script, Williamson was counting on Richard to improvise the majority of the movie. "I wanted to give him an idea, a concept, and then just turn the light on him and let him do whatever he wanted. You know what they say about comedians — that you can just open the refrigerator door and the light comes on, the jokes roll on out. Well, Richard's light didn't come on."

He made an honest effort, and at times he touched on brilliance, but the patched-together story really gave him nothing to build on, nowhere to go.

Adiós Amigo effectively marked the end of Richard Pryor's participation in small, indy films. He'd had an eventful run, learned some hard lessons, and turned in some of the best — though largely ignored — performances of his life. With his star on the rise, he couldn't afford to be associated with slap-dash fare like *Adiós Amigo,* no matter how well intentioned.

"Tell the fans I'm sorry," he told a reporter. "Tell them I needed the money." (It couldn't have been much, unless he got it all.) "Tell them I promise not to do it again."

"THERE'S A PERSON HERE THAT'S POSSESSED"

By mid-1976, it was no longer possible for Richard to make surprise appearances at the Comedy Store. Word always got out and suddenly a lot of fly-looking people would start pouring in. Crowds formed out on the sidewalk watching for his car. Comics who usually hung backstage would come out and claim seats back by the bar and stalwarts like Redd Foxx might be seen peeking through the curtain. By the time Richard bounced out on stage, the place would be primed to explode. One night a twenty-two-year-old Freddie Prinze leaped from his barstool and went running through the room, whooping like a worshipper at a revival meeting, punching random people in the arms and yelling, "He's the goddamn best! Man, Pryor knows what's right; he's paid all the dues!"

Franklyn Ajaye would often come to observe. "Every comedian looked at him with awe for the brilliance he was bringing out." Yet Ajaye said he never felt any personal warmth for Richard as a person, ever since their first meeting in 1969 when Ajaye reported for work on *Uncle Tom's Fairy Tales* and found him screaming abuse at Shelley. "There was absolutely zero he could teach me about living," Ajaye says.

> I could learn from how he did his comedy, but I didn't see anything about how he lived his life that I wanted to emulate. Zero. He was very tempestuous. I didn't even like to be around him. I don't like being around volatile people. I have no interest in being around geniuses. Those tempestuous volatile geniuses the media likes to hold up. But I had the deepest admiration for his

artistry. As a stand-up, not as an actor. He was just a troubled man. He was heavy into the drugs, heavy into alcohol . . . Who's sane doing that? Nobody. Just look what happened to Belushi. Freddie Prinze . . . Robin Williams survived it, but he was headed down the same road.

So when Ajaye heard that Freddie Prinze had started hanging out with Richard he thought to himself, Well, that's a mistake.

He could understand *why* Freddie wanted to hang with Richard.

Richard was pretty much every comedian's idol. But I remember thinking very clearly at the time, Richard can't teach him anything about life. Freddie was young and impressionable. That's trouble. Richard was deep off into drugs, Freddie was deep off into drugs . . . Richard was doing a lot of cocaine and he had a troubled background from his upbringing. That's just a recipe for disaster. Anyone could see that. There's no earthly way out of that.

Around three o'clock one morning that summer, Kathy McKee got a call from her sister, Lonette, who was then dating Freddie Prinze. Lonette said, "Kathy, you've got to help me. Richard Pryor is holding me and Freddie hostage with a gun in his house in Beverly Hills and he won't let us go. He's going crazy. He's snorted up Peru and he won't let us leave. I'm terrified and he keeps saying 'Get your sister. Call Kathy and have her come.'"

"Where are you?" Kathy asked. She wasn't fully awake.

"Richard's house. Can you get over here? Please?"

"Okay." Kathy got dressed and drove over. Three thirty in the morning. Richard answered the door.

"Sure enough, Richard has them captive. He's got a gun and he's going crazy, threatening to kill himself. Then I walk in, and he lets them go. I always had this calming effect on Richard," she explains. "Like a therapist. I came up in the hood in Detroit and I don't put up with that. He said, 'Okay, baby, you stay with me now and talk with me and party with

me . . .' So I did. I stayed like three days with him and kept him company
and got high with him until he passed out. Then I went home."

Richard got his first real taste of the Deep South during location filming
for his second Motown production, *The Bingo Long Traveling All-Stars
and Motor Kings*, the story of a Depression-era barnstorming baseball
team based on the novel by William Brashler. Richard was reluctant to
take on yet another supporting role, but Berry Gordy, who'd given him
his break in *Lady Sings the Blues*, insisted that Richard was the only actor
who could play the part of Charlie Snow, the team's intrepid third base-
man who tries passing for Cuban, Native American, whatever it might
take to get out of the Negro leagues and into the majors. Richard turned
it down cold. Producer Rob Cohen made his case by appealing to
Richard's sense of racial pride and was able to convince him to at least
read the script. Richard was impressed by its earnest ambition to re-
create an important but little-known epoch in black history, and he saw
shades of himself in the conflicted character of Charlie Snow.

The mostly upbeat movie "captured a lot of fans," recalls costar
James Earl Jones, "but the critics were hard on us because they expected
a black cast to exude black rage. They wanted the tragedy of black
baseball players in the black baseball leagues, not the comedy we gave
them. They wanted political relevance and content and protest. They
couldn't accept that this was not a black film, but simply a film about
black people."

While the rest of the cast stayed at the Macon Hilton, Richard, as
had become his habit, kept himself apart from his costars, renting a
house near Mercer University ostensibly so that he could be with his
family — Grandma Marie, Aunt Dee (his uncle Dickie's ex-wife), and,
according to one reporter, "a lady friend of Greek extraction" whom he
routinely introduced, as had also become his habit, as his fiancée. He
kept mostly to himself on the set, although toward the end of the shoot
he invited the cast and crew over for a feast whipped up by Mama Marie

that included fried chicken, okra, oxtail stew with string beans (Richard's favorite dish), and peach cobbler.

———————

Billy Dee Williams and James Earl Jones may have been the film's marquee names, but to the rural folks who came to gawk, Richard was the star they were most excited to see. They knew him from his TV appearances, magazine articles, and record albums. Richard had never before experienced small-town life in the rural South. The complacent poverty and miserable living conditions upset him — the leaning shacks with tin roofs and bare red-clay floors were essentially unchanged since the 1930s, which is why those locations were chosen — but the people were a delight. "You look at them," Richard said, "some brothers and sisters who can't read, some who may have combs sticking in their heads, or a big fat black woman with her hair going every which way — but when you live with them and hear them talk, you know that they are some of the smartest people on the planet."

They kept their distance during the day, but once shooting had wrapped, Richard would go join them out in the street and deliver impromptu concerts that lasted long into the summer nights — going until four or five in the morning on one occasion — swapping stories and telling lies. Producer Rob Cohen recalls that the black dialect got so thick at times he couldn't make out a word they were saying. Richard would let loose with something completely indecipherable to Cohen's ears, and then "there would be this huge burst of laughter. It was a real joy to see."

———————

Rob Cohen bore witness to a similar outpouring when he next worked with Richard on *The Wiz,* not in rural Georgia but in midtown Manhattan. When Cohen went to pick him up at the Plaza Hotel for his first day of rehearsal, he found Richard in a "very, very bad mood" that showed no signs of improving during their car ride downtown. Rather than handing Richard over to director Sidney Lumet and the assemblage of suits awaiting his arrival at the St. George Hotel, Cohen thought it might be better to give him some time and some air. He casually suggested they stop by the midtown rehearsal space where the film's choreographer was working on the Emerald City dance sequence.

Richard, wearing a T-shirt and a baseball cap pulled down over his eyes, followed Cohen docilely into the enormous space where some four hundred dancers were going at it full tilt. "All of a sudden," Cohen remembers, "some of the dancers in the front row saw me and who was next to me, and they stopped dancing. And it spread. Another five would stop, then twenty, then fifty. And the whole place stopped. They were just staring at him. Then they broke into spontaneous applause."

Richard fought back tears, acknowledging the ovation by going into a monologue as his preacher character. When he stepped up and said, "We are . . . gathered heah to-deh. . . ," the place erupted. By the time he finished, dancers were falling on the floor, they were laughing so hard.

After that, Cohen reports, Pryor was fine, although *The Wiz* would turn out to be a thirty-million-dollar flop, providing ammunition to the industry's contention that all-black movies were incapable of pulling in mass audiences.

———

"I don't like movies when they don't have no niggers in them," Richard told his audience at West Hollywood's Roxy Theatre in July of 1976. "I went to see *Logan's Run*, right? A movie of the future? There ain't no niggers in it! I said, 'Well white folks ain't planning for us to be here!' That's why we got to make movies."

On July 7, barely a week before cameras rolled on *Bingo Long*, Richard signed a three-million-dollar contract to write and develop screenplays of his choosing exclusively for Universal, with the option (but no obligation) to appear in them, plus a healthy share of the profits if he played a starring role. The deal provided him with offices on the studio lot and further stipulated that the studio would buy the film rights to any literary properties he wished to acquire. Universal would also hire additional screenwriters to assist him with the work. And he was free to appear in non-Universal films.

Universal's young president, Thom Mount, publicly touted the agreement as proof of the studio's belief that movies starring black actors and made by black filmmakers would make money, to which Richard rejoined that a "whole lot of niggers gonna be in trouble" if his movies didn't.

———————

Richard appeared onscreen for all of eight minutes in Michael Schultz's *Car Wash*, an ensemble comedy from a day-in-the-life screenplay by Joel Schumacher. By the time the film was released in October of 1976, the distributors saw fit to market it as a Richard Pryor movie. His image dominated the promotional materials, like a deity in the sky looming large over the rest of the cast, which included Bill Duke as a militant black activist, Ivan Dixon as an ex-con, Richard Brestoff as the owner's Mao-quoting son, Professor Irwin Corey as a mad bomber terrorizing the neighborhood, George Carlin as cab driver, and Franklyn Ajaye sporting a bouncy afro the size of a large beach ball.

Richard plays Daddy Rich, founder of the Church of Divine Economic Spirituality, who is chauffeured onto the car wash premises for the purpose of having a single pigeon dropping removed from the hood of his gold limousine. In a sequence that functions mainly as a musical interlude, Daddy Rich's female entourage, played by the Pointer Sisters, perform "You Gotta Believe." Schultz says he had conceived of the movie as "a closet musical. We didn't tell people we were doing a musical, but that's exactly what *Car Wash* was." Schumacher had based the character on flamboyant television and radio evangelist Frederick Eikerenkoetter, better known as Reverend Ike, the "success and prosperity preacher" whose slogan was "You can't lose with the stuff I use!" Initially, Reverend Ike had agreed to play the role himself, but he ultimately decided self-parody might not be in his best interest.

Richard came out for the one-day shoot primarily as a favor to Schultz.

The two had previously worked on a never-realized project called "Timmons from Chicago," a comedy developed by the Godfather of Black Music, Clarence Avant, who wanted Schultz to direct and Richard to play the title role, a Chicago man who becomes the first black president of the United States.

Schultz, who came up as a theatrical director with the Negro Ensemble Company, made his Broadway debut in 1969 with *Does a Tiger Wear a Necktie?* starring Al Pacino, before establishing himself as a film director with 1975's *Cooley High*. He would direct Richard in his first two starring roles, *Greased Lightning* and *Which Way Is Up?*, both released in 1977.

But, for the time being, Richard battled frustration as he struggled to get past the sidekick and second-banana roles offered him, such as the petty thief who gets swept up in the madcap scramble of an innocent man suspected of murder in Arthur Hiller's comedy-thriller *Silver Streak.*

———————

Richard was leery that the role, as written, would only paint him deeper into that corner where he would be known as nothing more than a comedian who occasionally played bit parts in movies. What decided it for him was director Arthur Hiller, a twenty-year veteran with a string of recent successes that included *The Out-of-Towners, Love Story,* and *Plaza Suite.* He was certainly the caliber of director that Richard wanted to be working with, and his recent film, *The Man in the Glass Booth,* was one of Richard's favorites. He gushed to Hiller that he had seen it at least fifty times.

More than an hour of the 114-minute *Silver Streak* has unspooled before Richard's character shows up, but once he does, the film is all his. Author and Gannett movie critic Marshall Fine wrote that "the script, by Colin Higgins, owes a big debt to Alfred Hitchcock; but the mystery isn't all that mysterious and the comedy isn't all that hilarious — at least not until Richard Pryor shows up, which is at least halfway through the film. Things definitely pick up from there." As was often the case when Richard played supporting roles, his onscreen arrival underscored how plodding and lifeless the movie had been up until that point. "For about fifteen minutes," Pauline Kael wrote in her *New Yorker* review, "Pryor gives the picture some of his craziness. Not much of it, but some — enough to make you realize how lethargic it had been without him." Arthur Hiller realized it, too, and immediately ordered a rewrite of the script so as to keep Richard on for the duration of the picture. Hiller credits Richard with improvising some of the movie's best lines and for suggesting a simple change that turned a potentially embarrassing scene into one of the biggest laughs in the film. Hiller felt a nagging concern about the scene in a train station men's room where Wilder, concocting a disguise to sneak past police, blacks up with shoe polish, dons a floppy hat, and flails hopelessly off the beat with a portable radio pressed to his ear. A white man who comes into the restroom is completely fooled. Richard suggested that "instead of a white dude being fooled by the disguise, have a black dude come in who isn't fooled." It completely flipped the scene and made it work.

Silver Streak was the first — and the best — of four films Richard and Wilder would make together. In the ones that followed, they would share star billing, but for Richard there was something gratingly minstrel-like about the whole arrangement. Hadn't that all died out with vaudeville? It felt like he was Rochester to Gene Wilder's Jack Benny. Television could always be counted on to bring up the rear of social progress, but surely the movies had moved on, hadn't they? Even Humphrey Bogart's Rick and Dooley Wilson's Sam had a better understanding than that. (But then, it was *Casablanca*, and there was a war on.) Again, Pauline Kael observes that Richard's performance rings false only when the script asks him to show pure-hearted affection for Gene Wilder. Interracial brotherly love "is probably the one thing Richard Pryor should never be required to express." When he does, she wrote, "you have never seen such a bad actor."

————————

Richard finally won his first starring role playing Wendell Scott, America's first black stock-car racing champion in *Greased Lightning,* opposite Pam Grier and Beau Bridges. The project was developed by writer-director Melvin Van Peebles, best known at the time for *Watermelon Man* and the breakout blaxploitation classic *Sweet Sweetback's Baadasssss Song.* Filming came to a halt over creative disputes between Van Peebles and the film's producers. Van Peebles left the project, and Richard, faced with the wheels coming off his first star vehicle, called Michael Schultz and begged him to take over as director. Schultz felt conflicted. Rightfully, the film belonged to Van Peebles and he didn't want to step on his toes. At the same time, Schultz was busy developing another star project for Richard, one he anticipated would be the first movie to star Richard Pryor had Van Peebles not cut in ahead of him. Ultimately, Schultz agreed to finish *Greased Lightning,* reasoning that he could do a good job with it and he didn't want Richard coming out with a bomb before he secured financing for his own Pryor movie. And, he notes, Melvin Van Peebles could not have been more gracious. "He had a substantially black crew and was shooting in Georgia and they were all going to leave with him in protest against the producer — who really wound up being a pill — and Melvin said, 'No, no. Stay. I want you to support Michael and Richard and do the best you can and make this movie happen.'"

Richard had invited Kathy McKee to come with him for the location shooting in rural Georgia. She was reluctant at first. She knew that artists can be moody when they're working. "During filming is not the best time to be with someone." Especially Richard, especially in his first lead role. But she assumed Richard would rent some palatial suite for the two of them where she could have her privacy. Instead, as he often did, "he rented this little shack of a house out in no man's land where he could walk right outside the house and fish. That's all he wanted to do." Kathy hated it. She hated the South. She hated being out in the sun getting bit by mosquitoes. And the whole time Richard was having an affair with

Pam Grier. "He didn't think I knew that, but of course I knew that. I'm not stupid. But I didn't care. I just wanted to go home." After two weeks she did, which must have given Richard pause.

———

Richard's first project under his deal with Universal was *Which Way Is Up?*, an adaptation of *The Seduction of Mimi,* Lina Wertmüller's dark comedy about political struggles and sexual politics among grape growers in Italy's wine country. The film was to be directed by Michael Schultz, and Richard picked his Berkeley pal novelist Cecil Brown and *Jaws* co-screenwriter Carl Gottlieb to transplant the story to California's citrus groves and amp up the laughs.

We get a glimpse of Richard's workload — and the skewered rapport between him and Gene Wilder — in this dual promotional interview, ostensibly in support of *Silver Streak.* Interviewer Roger Ebert graciously stands aside as Wilder pursues his own line of questioning:

WILDER: What are you doing next?

RICHARD: It's a movie called *Which Way Is Up?* This Italian director, Lina Wertmüller . . .

WILDER: No! Oh, my God! I'll kill myself!

RICHARD: What you moaning about, man?

WILDER: You're going to work with Lina Wertmüller? She passed right by me and saw you and said, "I must have that young man?"

RICHARD: You didn't let me finish. She made this movie called *The Seduction of Mimi,* and this will be a remake, set among the grape pickers of California.

WILDER: I would have killed myself out of envy.

RICHARD: And then I'm in a remake of *Arsenic and Old Lace.*

WILDER: Oh, my God! My favorite play next to *Hamlet*. All black cast, I suppose, nothing for me.

RICHARD: And then I'm doing *Hamlet*.

Richard threw his whole heart into *Which Way Is Up?*, playing multiple roles: orange picker Leroy Brown who works his way up in the farm-workers' union, Leroy's gray-haired father for which he drew heavily upon Mudbone, and a philandering minister. When filming wrapped in April, Richard bought two full-page facing ads in *Variety* to thank nearly 120 crew members by name and invited them all to a extravagant wrap party. The film's still photographer, Marsha Reed, snapped more than twenty-five-hundred photos during production. Richard ordered an eight-by-ten-inch print of each one. "I'm going to save them for the rest of my life," he said. "This film is the most special thing I have ever done."

The film's producer Steve Krantz told an interviewer that Richard "is a wonderful man, but deeply troubled. He needs emotional help."

Which Way Is Up? did decent business at the box office but received mostly disappointing reviews when it was released in November 1977. By that time, Richard was so over his head with work that he barely noticed.

"LET'S GET HIM BEFORE SOMEBODY ELSE DOES"

Richard had sworn off appearing on talk shows six years earlier because, as he said, there would always come a point in the conversation when the host would turn to him and say, "Isn't America wonderful, Richard?" And he would have to say, Yes, Merv/Mike/Joey/whoever, it sure is. Then the host would say, "See, guys? He said it. What's the matter with the rest of you?"

On May 4, 1977, Richard and Chevy Chase both went on *The Tonight Show* to plug their respective TV specials, airing back to back on NBC the following night. Chase had left *Saturday Night* midway through its second season to pursue a solo career. Carson and Chevy had met for the first time the previous day. Although he was noticeably cool toward Chase, Carson could barely conceal his glee over Chase's painfully inept performance as the comic actor, visibly flustered, stumbled over even the simplest questions groping for witty replies but coming up with none.

Carson asked Chevy to demonstrate, for the benefit of folks at home who may not have seen it, the pratfall that made him famous on *Saturday Night*. Using a chair and a glass of water for props, Chase gives an overlong introduction, explaining what it is he's about to do, what makes it funny, then instructs the audience (growing noisy and restless) on the proper way to land when taking a fall. Finally he does it. Applause. As he steps up onto the riser, returning to his chair, he trips and falls again.

Chevy became less tongue-tied once Richard came out and took the guest chair next to Johnny. Being pushed out of the spotlight seemed to

187

energize Chevy. His comic style being better suited to the role of a side-line taunter than ball carrier, he kept leaning over from the couch into Richard's frame and repeatedly interrupting with ineffective wisecracks. After suffering a number of verbal smackdowns from Richard — with the audience clearly on Richard's side — Chevy attempted to make amends by saying that he had seen Richard's special and that it was "hi-larious. Not *quite* as funny as mine, but, really, it's quite good." Richard remained unmoved. When Johnny asked Richard if he'd seen Chevy's special, he answered, "I don't like Chevy."

Carson went to a station break. When they came back, he asked Richard if he ever went back to visit Peoria. As a matter of fact, he told Johnny, he was going back that very weekend to spend Mother's Day with his grandmother and to see his son perform in a talent show. When Johnny asked Richard what his son's talent was, Chevy interrupted yet again, saying, "He's a hooker." Richard turned on him.

RICHARD: Huh?

CHEVY: Nothing.

RICHARD: What was it you said?

CHEVY: (*raising his hands to protest his innocence*) Hey, I didn't say nothing, man. I didn't say nothing.

RICHARD: I was going to ask you, why didn't you tell Johnny you was going to take over his show?

(*oooohs from the audience*)

CHEVY: I knew you'd bring that up and Johnny and I, we've dis-cussed it and neither of us cares.

RICHARD: That monologue you were doing with the chair is a per-fect replacement for Johnny.

CHEVY: A lot of chair falls. My opening monologue will be a fall over a chair tonight, thank you very much.

CARSON: You guys better be big hits tomorrow night.

RICHARD: I've got mine. I love show business. That's the only reason *I'm* in.

(*more oooohs from the audience at the punch he'd just landed*)

It's informative — and fun — to see Carson's bemusement as he watches the two men spar. Carson had put in his time, honing his craft for more than a quarter century, starting out at a local radio station in Omaha, emceeing church dinners, hosting variety shows and quiz programs before getting his own sketch comedy show, *Carson's Cellar* at KNXT, the Los Angeles CBS affiliate, in 1951. He wrote for Red Skelton and hosted more game shows before finally achieving success with *Who Do You Trust?* on NBC in New York. He did that for six years before being tapped to host *The Tonight Show*. And now people at the network — important people — thought this clod had the chops to take over his job? Chevy Chase, the overnight sensation who'd been hired on as a writer for *Saturday Night*, then added to the cast at the last minute despite having so little experience beyond performing in a few improv comedy troupes and providing voice talent on the *National Lampoon Radio Hour*? They wouldn't think so after tonight.

———

The excitement over Richard and his special was palpable within NBC even before the show aired and the reviews and Nielsen ratings came pouring in. The network rushed to sign him to a weekly comedy-variety series for the coming fall season. "The terms of the contract were almost unprecedented in television," said network publicist Kathi Fearn-Banks, "and NBC was taking a real chance." Their attitude was, "Let's get him before somebody else does."

"They offer what he calls 'bad money,' " Mooney writes. "So much cash that he can't refuse it: $2 million a year. 'What am I going to do, Mr. Mooney?' I know him well enough to know he's not really asking. The answer is already clear. 'You're gonna take the fucking money and run,' I say."

The irony is that Richard — the child in Richard — still believed in the transforming power of television. "One hundred and twenty-seven million people watch television every night," he said at the time. "One week of truth on TV could just straighten out everything."

The framing device for the special has a clean-shaven, tuxedoed Richard striding through the hallways of NBC between sketches as various characters accost him with suggestions for the show. LaWanda Page, who he'd known since her fire dancing days on the Chitlin' Circuit, essentially revamped her Aunt Esther persona from *Sanford and Son* to play Sister Mabel Williams, his "sister's aunt's cousin on your father's side. I've known you since you were a baby." Richard doesn't remember her. "It's so good to see you having your own show. All my years of prayin' for you finally paid off." All she demands of him in return is that he give his holiness the Reverend James L. White a prime-time spot on his show.

Richard's Rev. White, a funkier, more media-savvy incarnation of his signature minister character, descends a grand spiral staircase in a gold-trimmed white jumpsuit and enormous afro as the choir sings "For the Love of Money." Behind him, church volunteers wait by the mostly silent phones for viewers to call in with their donations. The church's financial problems, White says, are due to not getting the "crossover bucks."

> Most of our money comes from the minorities around the world and, although there are a lot of them, they don't have as much as one rich white person. What we're looking for — we're looking for the Billy Graham dollar. We want the money honey. So we

offered a little message to the white folks not sending in money. We're not begging for the crippled children. And we're not begging for the orphans, the black orphans of Watts. We're not begging for them, no. And we're not begging for the black old-folks home either. This money is to go to the BTAM: The Back-to-Africa Movement.

Every phone instantly rings.

———————

Mooney cast poet Maya Angelou — formerly a singer, dancer, and actress* — as the long-suffering wife of Richard's wino character Willie who, after an extended sketch in a neighborhood bar, makes his way across the street to his house. He stands reeling for a moment before climbing the front steps. "Please God, don't let me be sick. Get me though this one and I'll get through the next one myself." Willie staggers past his wife and collapses facedown on the couch where he remains, dead to the world, as Angelou delivers a wrenching monologue recounting her life with Willie, what he once was and what he has become. Angelou wrote the monologue herself, and as Mooney says, "It gets to the soul of what goes on." After her first run-through in rehearsal, studio crew members were in tears.

Richard's concept that the show should give voice to those who are seldom heard is most poignantly expressed by his musical guests "And the Pips," minus front woman Gladys Knight. Richard brought her background singers Merald Knight, Edward Patten, and William Guest out of the shadows and gave them the spotlight to perform their backup harmonies and synchronized dance moves to "Heard It Through the

———————

*Eight years before *I Know Why the Caged Bird Sings,* Maya Angelou Make (then married to South African civil rights activist Vusumzi Make) won early acclaim off-Broadway for her portrayal of the queen in Jean Genet's *The Blacks: A Clown Show* at St. Mark's Playhouse.

Grapevine" and "Midnight Train to Georgia," while an unattended micro-phone marked the spot where Gladys normally commanded centerstage.

———————

Five days after his special aired, Richard signed an exclusive five-year personal services contract with NBC to do a weekly series of at least ten shows, star in two specials, and serve in a creative capacity on a third special that would function as a showcase for new talent. For this he would receive $750,000. After the first year, he had the option to cancel the deal or renegotiate for more money for the next four years.

That same month, lawyer David Franklin renegotiated his Universal contract for five more movies and more money. Richard signed to do Paul Schrader's *Blue Collar,* play the title role in *The Wiz,* and costar with Jackie Gleason in a proposed sequel to *The Sting,* a film that never came to be.

Franklin kept handing him more contracts to sign, more than he could possibly keep track of, even if he'd tried.

By midsummer, David Franklin brought Richard yet another multi-picture deal, this time with Warner Bros., calling for him to star in, at minimum, four movies over the next four years, with the understanding that the studio would share Richard's services with Universal on an alternating basis. The films were to be jointly produced by Warner Bros. in association with Richard Pryor Enterprises, with Franklin as executive producer, at a guaranteed one million dollars per film plus fifty percent of the profits.

David Franklin had been a godsend. (In actuality, it was singer Roberta Flack who sent him to Richard.) The Atlanta-based attorney straightened out Richard's finances, renegotiated contracts, made certain he was paid his various royalties on time, retired Richard's more than six hundred thousand dollars in outstanding debt, and settled his alimony and child-support obligations. Further, Franklin established Richard Pryor Enterprises as a corporation to ease his tax burden, and Black Rain, a production company named for Richard's youngest daughter. He also encouraged Richard to move out of his Hollywood Hills bungalow and buy himself a house. Which he did, a Spanish villa with two guest houses situated on an eight-acre estate in the Northridge section of the San Fernando Valley with the Santa Monica Mountains providing a natural fortification against Hollywood.

Franklin's associate, Michael Ashburne, recalls that Richard went to the bank one afternoon and withdrew a million dollars. He took the cashier's check down the street and deposited it in a different bank. When Ashburne asked him why he'd done such a thing, Richard said, "I wanted to see if the money was really mine."

Richard told an audience that if his father were alive and "I told him how much money I had, he'd say, 'Boy, you's a lyin' motherfucker! Joe Louis never made that much money.'"

———————

When he appeared on *The Tonight Show* to promote his special, Richard announced that he would be in Detroit later that month filming Paul Schrader's *Blue Collar,* a story about auto assembly-line workers. Then he issued an advisory to that city's police: "I'll be jogging in the morning, police, me and Rashon [Khan; Richard's bodyguard], two black men, we'll be jogging, we're not robbing anyone, do not shoot us accidentally as we're jogging in the streets of Detroit."

Johnny Carson hung his head and sighed.

"You have to announce these things," Richard told him.

———————

Blue Collar was Paul Schrader's first film as a director. Although he'd amassed considerable prestige — if not Hollywood clout — when Martin Scorsese directed his original screenplay *Taxi Driver, Blue Collar* was still a tough sell, to the leading actors as well as to Universal. Schrader ran into resistance from the studio when he told them the story was about three assembly-line workers, two black and one white. Surely he misspoke. He meant the other way around, right? But no. The movie would have been a disaster in 1977 if the sole black protagonist had been the betrayer or the one betrayed. Those burdens the two black guys had to share.

Schrader was roundly criticized for fomenting vicious rivalries between Richard and his costars in the film, Yaphet Kotto and Harvey Keitel. In convincing the three ambitious actors to sign onto the film, Schrader — unintentionally, he says — left each with the impression that they had the starring role. Once filming began, they each became embroiled in a three-way cock fight for the lead. Richard emerged as the apparent victor. The movie's poster featured not one but two images of Richard — and Richard alone — headlined with a blurb from Vincent Canby's review in the *New York Times*: "Richard Pryor has a role that makes use of the wit and fury that distinguishes his straight comedy routines."

The situation was especially galling for Keitel, a prominent player in most all of Scorsese's films to date and the star of the director's first full-length feature, *Who's That Knocking at My Door?* Keitel left the production more than once. "Left" as in he went to the airport and got on a plane.

There was one scene, shot on location in a cheaply paneled bar favored by autoworkers, in which Richard went off on a most outrageously brilliant rant. The longer Richard kept going, according to Schrader, the angrier Harvey got, which would have worked fine for the scene, had Keitel not picked up a filled ashtray and flung its contents into the camera's lens ruining the take. Seconds later, Richard and his bodyguard, Rashon, had Keitel pinned to the floor and were pummeling him with their fists.

Still, a good portion of his lines that made it into the final cut are pure Richard, Schrader attests. "I wasn't that good of a writer," he says.

Here is Zeke at home after a hard day watching *The Jeffersons* on TV. His wife, Caroline, is played by Chip Fields.

ZEKE: Now that shit is pitiful. I don't know how in the fuck a nigga like that gets some money anyway. This is the dumbest shit — look at this motherfucker. Look like a motherfuckin' ostrich. Look at that shit . . .

CAROLINE: If you hate it so much, why don't you just turn it off?

ZEKE: Turn it off? Are you kiddin' baby? Took me three years to pay for that motherfucker. We gonna watch everything they show on it. All the shit they show. Even the snow when the motherfucker go off, I'm gonna sit here and watch that.

Not counting his concert films, this is far and away Richard's finest performance as an actor and the purest Pryor to be found onscreen, in one of the most overlooked films of the seventies.

Over the three years of their on-again, off-again rocky relationship, Kathy McKee had never judged Richard, had never fought back. She'd seen it all before. She knew the dance steps and she enjoyed the ride. When her sister called in the middle of the night saying Richard was holding her and Freddie Prinze at gunpoint, she showed up and stayed to party.

She came, too, when he asked her to get Pam Grier out of his house.

After we broke up, Pam moved in. He called me up one night — me, again, to come be the intermediary — and asked could I please come get that "yoga-ass bitch" out of his house. "I don't want to be with her no more and she won't go home; could you please come get her out of my house?" So I said, "Okay, I'll come." Sounds like fun, right? So I went in and I found Pam on the bed doing yoga and meditating. I said, "Pam, Richard asked me to come and speak for him. He really wants you to get the fuck out of his house." We had words. I told her, "I'm just doing what Richard asked me to. Personally, if somebody didn't want me in their house, they wouldn't have to ask me more than one time. They wouldn't even have to ask. I'd kind of pick up on the hint." So we had a little argument, but she left.

Later Richard took Kathy out and bought her a piece of jewelry as a thank-you for getting Pam Grier out of his house.

"Most of the women Richard got involved with," says McKee, "had nothing going on of their own. No career. That's how it is with a lot of big stars. They have to be the center of attention, they can't have someone competing with that. Just imagine if Richard and Pam Grier were out together and a fan came up and asked *her* for an autograph. That would be trouble."

———————

The next time Richard called Kathy he wanted her to meet him for lunch at the Polo Lounge in the Beverly Hills Hotel.

"Hey," he said to her across the table while the waiter poured. "I want to marry you." (Not "Will you marry me?" but "I want to marry you.")

"You want to *marry* me? You mean, like, make plans and have a big — ?"

No, right now, he told her. He had a plane waiting to fly them to Vegas.

They spent the next three hours talking it over. She went out to the pay phone from time to time to call friends and ask their advice. ("Richard *Pryor* wants to marry you? What the heck? Go ahead. Marry Richard.") From the moment she said yes, he took charge over everything. He wouldn't even let her go home to pack. He took her to Giorgio's on Rodeo Drive to buy the clothes she'd need, then on to the airport.

They checked into a suite at Caesar's Palace, got dressed, and were making ready to go downstairs to gamble for a while before getting married at one of the walk-in chapels on the Strip. Then the phone rang. It was David Franklin. Richard's mood got real dark. He asked Kathy to go into the other room and he closed the door to take the call in private.

"He's in there about twenty minutes on the phone with David Franklin. He comes out very dark. The mood has completely changed from up and happy, and fabulous and drinking champagne, to really dark. David has told him in so many words that he cannot get married without a prenup. I can just hear what David said, 'Nigger, you are crazy. Don't you dare marry that woman, she could take you for everything...' talking real fast the way he did."

Kathy had no objection to a prenup. "Fine. Whatever. We stayed in Vegas a couple of days, gambled, partied, didn't get married, then back to L.A. to wait for David to show up with the prenup." Then she had to leave town to do a show and Richard went out on the road. After that, she was hired to cohost *Good Morning L.A.* Everything from around that period — the years between 1978 and '79 are a little foggy, she says, because she was doing so much stuff and running around with so many people. She and Richard got into a big huge massive fight at the house. "Well, not a fight," she hastens to say. "I never raise my voice. I'm smarter than that. If somebody gets mad, I just get my little stuff together and walk out the door."

The marriage never happened. "Actually, when I look back on it now, it was a good thing that it didn't happen. It would've been a mess."

Richard, apparently, wanted to marry Kathy that day or not at all. He would have done well to heed the advice of Mickey Rooney who always preferred getting married early in the morning. That way, he said, if it didn't work out, he would not have wasted the whole day.

SURRENDER, RICHARD

NBC hosted a mega press conference at the L.A. Improv to publicize its new fall lineup. Richard arrived, as requested, unsure exactly what he was supposed to do. NBC publicist Kathi Fearn-Banks told him, " 'Just get up there and talk to them, let them ask you questions about the series.' He said, 'I'm not doing a series. I'm doing some specials.' [Kathi] said, 'Well, no, Richard, you're doing a series.' " This was news to him. Perhaps he had confused or conflated the two contracts he'd signed with NBC; perhaps he hadn't been told what he was signing or simply hadn't paid attention. It mattered little where the communication had broken down, a pool of seventy-some TV critics from across the country were waiting to meet him. Richard was enough of a pro not to let the misunderstanding mar that day's session with the press. Rather than describe the series — he had not a clue, after all — he kept the crowd entertained by riffing on what the show would *not* be. There would be no explicit sex, he said, although he had auditioned some people. There would be no violence, although one person, he said, had been killed during taping of the first show. Asked how he was able to work on TV without using profanity, he explained that NBC piled a big stack of money in front of the camera. "When I don't curse, it gets bigger. When I do, it dwindles."

At the first opportunity, Richard turned the stage over to the cast of *CPO Sharkey* and then called David Franklin to find out what exactly he'd gotten himself into.

Indeed, he had signed a lucrative contract to deliver a minimum of ten weekly, hour-long comedy-variety shows that fall. Occasional specials once or twice a year he could handle, but writing, staging, rehearsing, and producing an hour's worth of prime-time material once a week every week was out of the question.

Both sides eventually agreed to four shows instead of the contracted ten. Richard convinced himself that with Mooney and writer-producer Rocco Urbisci covering his flanks, he could will himself through four weeks of the ordeal. The network, for its part, was betting that once the show was under way, a routine was established, and Richard got a taste of basking in the certain glory, he wouldn't want to stop.

Here's one thing pimps know — and maybe everyone else does, too, but doesn't want to say: men don't pay prostitutes for *sex;* they pay them to go away afterward. As production on *The Richard Pryor Show* got under way, Richard couldn't deny the parallels. He well knew where that led.

More than once he quit the show, then came back. Meanwhile, the paycheck-to-paycheck cast and crew were left cooling their heels, not knowing for sure if they had a job or not. Some of them chipped in and hired a plane to circle above his house with a banner that said SURRENDER, RICHARD. It only pissed him off more. (Rocco thinks executive producer Burt Sugarman hired the plane. Richard thought it had to be Rocco. He called Rocco up and said, "You need this job that bad, motherfucker?")

At that point in his life and career, Urbisci says, Richard couldn't allow his muse to be stifled or hemmed in by the restrictions of television's standards and practices.

No, Mooney counters, it was the drugs.

The show was brilliant. Everybody loved it. Richard simply couldn't face the prospect of getting up early and going to work every day. And he had no one else to hide behind or blame if it flopped. It was his show; that was his name in the title.

The money was good. The money was outrageous. But this time it felt less like getting paid than being bought.

Richard worried he'd lose connection with his true audience who liked their Pryor raw and profane. Whenever Richard achieved any degree of mainstream popularity, he took that to mean he was not keeping it real. Mooney told him, "The minute you hear white people applauding you, you get all pissed at yourself because you think you ain't being black enough."

———————

Richard and Rocco and Mooney agreed it was important for the opening of that first episode to make a clear statement of what he was giving up to do the show. He was giving up his artistry, his integrity. Mooney had the idea to open with a Frankenstein skit where Dr. Frankenstein switches brains between a white guy and Richard. Richard sits up and, speaking in a golly-gee-willikers white voice says, "Good evening, ladies and gentlemen, welcome to *The Richard Pryor Show*. Golly, am I glad to be here."

Then Rocco got a 2:00 a.m. phone call from Richard.

" 'Rocco? It's Richie.' " Urbisci re-creates the conversation with Richard speaking in a late-night whisper. "I could barely hear him. He said, 'I want to do the opening where I've got no dick and no balls.' I said, 'You want to do what?' He said, 'Can you get me a makeup guy? I'll tell you about it tomorrow.' "

Rocco had hired Rick Baker who'd done makeup on George Lucas's original *Star Wars* to create the alien costumes for the show's *"Star Wars* Bar" sketch, which had Richard playing it straight — he was always funniest when he wasn't playing for laughs — as a bartender dealing with the aggravations of serving a crowd of rowdy aliens. "Hey, watch where you're going!" he barks at a bug-eyed creature who has just knocked into him while carrying a tray of drinks. "You got the biggest eyes in the place."

Baker put Richard in a pair of jockey shorts and covered them over with flesh-tone makeup. It was a rush job. The slightest movement would cause the makeup to crumple and spoil the effect so Richard had to stand perfectly still. Director John Moffitt started off with a tight head-and-bare-shoulders shot as Richard delivered his opening lines.

> Good evening, ladies and gentlemen, and welcome to *The Richard Pryor Show*. My name is Richard Pryor. I'm so happy to have my own show I don't know what to do. I could jump up and down and sing "Yankee Doodle." I'm telling ya, it's gonna be a lot of fun. You know, there's been a lot of things written about me, people wondering am I gonna have a show, am I not gonna have a show — well I'm having a show! People say, "Well, how can you have a show? You'll have to compromise. You'll have to give up *everything*." Is that a joke or what? Well, look at me. I'm standing here naked. I've given up absolutely nothing.

The camera then pulled back to reveal Richard standing naked with no dick and no balls.

"So enjoy the show!"

———

The day the show was scheduled to air, Rocco got a call saying NBC was going to edit out the naked opening. Rocco called Richard. "Did you know about this?" "I haven't heard a damn thing about it," Richard said. That afternoon there was a press conference announcing that Richard had quit the show over artistic differences. "The irony is," says Urbisci, "that the naked opening was shown that night on every network newscast, including NBC. It got more exposure than if they'd left it alone." Richard clearly knew what he was doing. Perhaps NBC did, too. Urbisci wonders now if NBC didn't yank the opening for that very purpose, fully aware of how Richard would react and knowing what the result would be.

The first episode opened cold with the "*Star Wars* Bar" sketch instead.

———

The tales of Richard's angst and furious meltdowns belie how utterly brilliant and defiant the show is, especially for its time. Forget pushing the envelope; they tore the envelope to shreds and tossed it like confetti. Director John Moffitt favored cinematic camera moves that were highly unusual for shooting on videotape, and many of the sketches, especially those set in exotic locales, began with leisurely, atmospheric introductions. Even in direction and production values, *The Richard Pryor Show* didn't look or feel like anything else on TV.

In the first episode, Moffitt's camera snakes its way through a swampy bayou night before taking us inside a wild hoodoo service where moaning worshippers wait to be healed by the frenetic Cajun faith healer Bojaws, whose refrain is "Let Bojaws handle it!" The sketch was inspired, according to Urbisci, by the flamboyant TV evangelist and faith healer, Ernest Angley — a Liberace in a leisure suit waving a floppy Bible and knocking worshippers to the floor as he casts out demons and disease. The Bojaws sketch also featured the then-unknown Robin Williams — nine months before he first assayed the role of the alien Mork on *Happy Days* — who did a hilarious impersonation of Angley in his own stand-up act.

Viewers tuning in at the half hour of the show's second episode would be treated to four and a half minutes of African drumming and dance before the scene shifts to a village where Richard is the "Come from Man," a charlatan who sells tourists tribal artifacts and traces their roots.

As with his special, the transitions between sketches often found Richard walking through the NBC studios, interacting with visitors and staff. In "A Pet Head," a female staff member knocks on the door of Richard's dressing room when she hears various bird sounds — a finch, a whooping crane, a chicken — coming from within. She scolds him that "we are not allowed to have pets in our rooms, Mr. Pryor." After he gets rid of the staffer, a stressed-out Richard removes the cloth cover from a birdcage to reveal the living head of an adult man (Charles Fleischer, later known as Carvelli on *Welcome Back, Kotter* and the voice of Roger

Rabbit). The two bicker and scream at each other, accusing each other of neglect and inconsiderate behavior. The head is in a snit because Richard forgot his promise to take the head to Disneyland. "You think I'm going to take you to Disneyland?! Huh? And have you bouncing all around like you did at the dentist?" Richard, near his breaking point, says, "Let me tell you something, man. If the Muslims ever find out I got a white head in my dressing room, I'm in big trouble!" Then, self-loathing: "Only a nigger would keep a pet head." When Richard accidentally knocks the bottomless cage to the floor, the head freaks out. It can't bear to be out of its cage.

Our only clue into the attraction at work in this clandestine relationship comes when the head plays harmonica (on a rack, naturally). As the head begins blowing into the harmonica, Richard runs for cover, hiding behind a potted plant. Then he begins to dance, rigidly at first, as though succumbing against his will to the music's conjured spell.

"A Pet Head" is perhaps the strangest, most subversive thing ever aired on network TV. The sketch stubbornly adheres to its own surreal logic with no explanation. On its surface, it's as matter-of-factly unsettling as any Kafka nightmare. Make of it what you will.

––––––––

In the third episode, playwright and actress Kres Mersky (best known for her one-woman shows *The Life and Times of A. Einstein* and *Isadora Duncan: A Unique Recital*) delivered a monologue as a lonely rooming-house dweller who recounts conflicting versions of what may or may not have been a lesbian encounter with a neighbor in a park the night before. Viewers couldn't be sure.

When production of *The Richard Pryor Show* was first announced, Mersky sent Rocco Urbisci an audition tape that included a number of the dozen or so pieces she performed in her one-woman show *At the Codfish Ball,* which she was then performing on stage at the Holly-wood Center Theater. Rocco flipped when he saw her *Rashomon*-like telling of her character's lesbian encounter. "I loved the tape and showed it to Richard," says Rocco. "We decided to call the segment 'New Talent.' I wanted to frame it in something that maybe could be used as a weekly feature." The sketch begins and ends with Richard standing over a piano in a glittery glamorous costume and outrageous wig lip-synching Little Richard's "Good Golly Miss Molly." In a nod to Orson Welles's 1937 radio adaptation of H. G. Wells's *War of the Worlds* (Welles doing Wells in "the broadcast that panicked America"), the image of Richard as Little Richard flickers in and out, a static-filled snowy screen is replaced by the black-and-white video image of a barefoot, bathrobed woman seated in an upholstered chair in an otherwise scantly furnished apartment. The effect was of a pirate TV station breaking in on NBC's frequency.

"I've fallen in love again," she says. "She's a woman here in the rooming house." Her contradictory versions of their encounter veer from describing a mutually satisfying tryst, to her being the seducer, to having been assaulted by the woman, to it all being a lonely fantasy for a closeness that is unattainable to her. It ends with her saying, "I like being alone. It's better that way. At least then there's none of the pretense of closeness, none of the frustration of trying to be close and finding only walls." The screen goes staticky again and returns to Richard at the conclusion of "Good Golly Miss Molly."

The most likely reason the sketch didn't cause more of a stir at the time was that viewers might not have been entirely sure what they had just seen. Had that really been a part of *The Richard Pryor Show*? It sure didn't look like it. No way would NBC have given the okay for *this*. "When it went on the air back east," Rocco says, "I got a call from my sister. She was angry and outraged at NBC for screwing up her brother's show by interrupting Pryor's parody of Little Richard with some PBS tape of a lady talking crazy. When I told her we did it on purpose, then she laughed."

Whoever was in charge of vetting the show must've thrown up his hands upon seeing this. Richard had only one more show to do anyway, so why make a fuss?*

––––––––––––

After *The Richard Pryor Show,* Urbisci produced specials for Alan King, Lily Tomlin, Whoopi Goldberg, Carol Burnett, Rodney Dangerfield, and ten HBO specials for George Carlin over a span of twenty years. "My girlfriend said to me, 'Richard Pryor loved you because you were young and innocent, and George loved you because you weren't.' I think that's true. If the order had been reversed, we wouldn't be having this conversation."

What impressed Urbisci most about Richard was how quick he was, the way the man's mind worked. "We were standing in a hallway at NBC blocking a scene with LaWanda Page. Richard's facing me, and behind him, I see coming down the hallway Billy Barty." Billy Barty was one of the very first dwarfs, or little people, to break into Hollywood in the late 1920s. Back then they were called "midget actors." He got his start playing Mickey Rooney's little brother in a string of two-reelers and from then on he worked nonstop until he died in December 2000, appearing in more than two hundred films and TV shows. "So Billy was down the hall at NBC doing a pilot with Don Rickles," says Rocco. "I can see him coming, but Richard has his back turned. Billy comes up behind him and tugs on his jacket and says, 'Hey, Richie, how're you doing?'

––––––––––––

*Seven years after parting company with NBC, Richard returned to TV with *Pryor's Place,* a CBS Saturday morning kid show that premiered on September 15, 1984, and ran for ten weeks. The expected parties were outraged that Richard Pryor should in any way be presented as a role model for children. It was a thoroughly wholesome affair, following two young boys on their adventures in a *Sesame Street*–type neighborhood as they faced moral dilemmas and learned lessons from them. Richard somberly played himself as host and narrator but showed much more life playing neighborhood characters. Critics were kind, though few could resist pointing out that he'd come full circle and was back to doing Bill Cosby's act.

Richard turns around and says, 'Hey, Billy. Have you bumped into any good pussy lately?'

"That's how quick Richard was. He turns around, looks down, sees Billy, and comes up with the line, 'Have you *bumped into* any good pussy lately?'"

———

Producer Rob Cohen recalls visiting Richard's bungalow at the Beverly Hills Hotel shortly before the release of *Bingo Long*. Cohen was grousing about all the commercial hype surrounding the U.S. Bicentennial. Richard was unresponsive, in one of his moods, until Cohen said, "Jesus, the only product that hasn't jumped on the Bicentennial bandwagon is Tampax." Richard immediately came to life. "He jumped up," remembers Cohen, "assumed the voice of your typical unctuous, white-bread announcer, and said, 'Hi there, girls, have you tried Bicentennial Tampax? It's already white and blue, you can make it red!' And I thought to myself, Christ, in less than a second, he hooked up the red, white, and blue of the flag, and the fact that Tampax wrappings are white and blue, with blue lettering, and that menstrual flow is red. Red, white, and blue. He just tied the whole thing up instantly."

———

One night, on top of the world at Redd Foxx's club, Richard and Redd were snorting coke, telling lies, flirting with the cocktail waitresses. Even as he nodded off, barely able to keep himself awake, Richard went on snorting. "Why do I always want more?" he asked Foxx. "Because you're a junkie," Redd said. As flat-out cold as that.

"YOU HOLLYWOOD FAGGOTS
CAN KISS MY RICH HAPPY BLACK ASS"

At Lily Tomlin's request, Richard volunteered to take part in a star-studded benefit for gay rights at the Hollywood Bowl on Sunday, September 18. The "Star Spangled Night for Rights" (subtitled "A Celebration for Human Rights") was organized by the San Francisco–based Save Our Human Rights in response to an anti-gay campaign fronted by California senator John Biggs and former Miss America and orange-juice shill Anita Bryant. The capacity crowd of seventeen thousand Hollywood luminaries included Paul Newman, Cher, Alice Cooper, Norman Lear, Chevy Chase, John Travolta, and Truman Capote.

Richard arrived in good spirits and reportedly enjoyed the first half of the show, laughing and applauding from the wings while watching his friend Lily Tomlin, Christopher Lee, David Steinberg, a young dance troupe called the Lockers, the band War, and going on just head of him, two members of the Los Angeles Ballet Company.

Richard opened the second half of the show unprepared. (He was, after all, doing this for free, as were the others.) But he could riff on human rights for twenty minutes, easy.

He started off haltingly, feeling his way. "I came out here for human rights . . . and I found out what it's about . . . what it's really about is . . . is it's about not getting caught with a dick in your mouth."

The crowd went wild. Richard warmed to his topic.

"I've sucked dick, and it was beautiful . . . but I couldn't deal with it. I went home and didn't tell nobody."*

After several minutes of playing to the crowd, his mood changed. He stumbled over his words, seemingly talking to himself.

"Shit. This is really weird. What the fuck? I never seen this much traffic in my life . . . I seen cars all the way from where to what . . . coming to this motherfucker this evening . . . to give us some money . . . to suck a dick?"

The crowd got restless and he turned on them, dropping the word *faggot* as freely, if not as affectionately, as he did *nigger.* "I came here for human rights, but I'm seeing what it's really about. Fags are prejudiced. I see the four niggers you have dispersed. White folks are having good fun here tonight."

Here he was, a notorious pussy hound, an embodiment of hetero cool in the late 1970s — an era when most Americas couldn't even pick up on the signals telegraphed by the Village People when they sang about the delights of staying at the YMCA — with some nine million dollars in studio contracts, and he'd just come out and boasted to a crowd of seventeen thousand assembled in one of the most conspicuous places on earth not only that he'd sucked cock, but that he liked it. That it was beautiful. (He'd said as much before, in clubs, and in a performance filmed at the Improv in 1971, but that movie, *Live and Smokin',* had not yet seen the light of day.) Perhaps it was starting to sink in on him that he'd better walk that back, and do it fast.

---

*In 2002, we had the opportunity to read through Richard's first attempt at writing his memoirs. He had filled the unruled pages of two and a half leather-bound volumes before abandoning the project in the early 1980s. The volumes were unnumbered, undated. The first volume opened with the confession that he'd had sex with men maybe ten or twelve times and they had been among the most profound experiences of his life. "Does that make me a fag, a queer, a bisexual or what?" he had written. "The answer is none of the above. It just makes me, me. My sexual preference is for women, but what makes a man? His words? His actions? Am I a straight acting queer, or a queer who just happens to love pussy?"

This is an evening about human rights, and I'm a human being.
I just wanted to see where you was really at, and I wanted to test
you to your motherfucking *soul*. I'm doing this shit for nothing.
But I wanted to come here and tell you to kiss my ass with your
bullshit. You understand? When the niggers was burning down
Watts, you motherfuckers was doin' what you wanted to do down
on Hollywood Boulevard. Didn't give a shit about it.

Then he turned his back to the audience, hiked up the tail of his jacket,
thrust out his backside and said, "You Hollywood faggots can kiss my
rich happy black ass."

"I thought they would kill him," says composer Van Dyke Parks, in attendance that night with his wife, Sally. "Seriously. I was scared Richard
wouldn't get out of there alive."

An *L.A. Times* reviewer wrote that Richard's remarks "jolted the audience, confused them, in the end angered them . . . It was left to Tom
Waits to recover the audience and he tried nobly with songs including
the old Four Lads tune 'Standing on the Corner.' But his was an unen-
viable task — following Pryor and preceding Miss Midler. He finished
quickly."

Bette Midler knew what to do. She pranced out and reclaimed the
crowd with, "Who wants to kiss this rich happy *white* ass?"

Lily Tomlin, who had invited Richard to take part in the show, tried
to shrug it off, saying, in effect, that when you ask for Richard Pryor, you
get Richard Pryor.

"I don't know," she said years later, "maybe he was high." Then: "Duh!
What am I saying? Of course he was high."

———————

That was Sunday. Late Tuesday, Richard knocked on Rocco Urbisci's
office door to ask if it would be okay if he came in late the next morning.
Sure, Rocco said. It was his show. Rocco didn't ask the reason why, but
Richard volunteered, "I'm getting married." And then he sort of laughed.

Rocco congratulated Richard, wished him good night, then picked up the phone and ordered a cake.

Richard came in late the next day still sporting his white wedding tux. Everyone crowded around as he introduced his new bride, Deboragh. Urbisci had the presence of mind to grab up a bouquet of flowers and, pretending a jubilant gesture, plunged their stems into the decorated cake, rendering illegible the inscription congratulating Richard and Pam Grier.

"Are you sure that was Deboragh?" Rocco asked when we interviewed him for this book. "I didn't recognize her. She looked about seventeen. I figured she was just some girl he knocked up."

———————

Richard was wrung out from the nonstop ordeals of *Greased Lightning, Which Way Is Up?* (produced through the provisions of his Universal deal), doing the special and then butting heads with NBC over creative control of his weekly TV show in between the insanity of filming *Blue Collar* and facing fallout over the Hollywood Bowl kerfuffle. Plus, he had married again. As soon as they finished taping the final episode of his show on October 12, he and Deboragh took off for a brief and belated honeymoon in Hawaii. They were there just long enough for Richard to fall in love with the place and buy a parcel of land in the isolated community of Hana on the easternmost tip of Maui. From there, he was off to New York to finish filming *The Wiz,* then home to Peoria, and then he had a heart attack.

"DOES IT LOOK LIKE I'M SMILING TO YOU, MOTHERFUCKER?"

I was walking around in the front yard and something say, "Don't breathe!"

"Huh?"

Richard looks from side to side, like, who said that?

He twists his fist into his chest.

Said, "You heard me motherfucker, I said don't *breathe!*"

Richard's face contorts in pain.

"Okay, I won't breathe I won't breathe I won't breathe."

"Then shut the fuck *up!*"

"Okay, I'll shut up. Don't kill me don't kill me don't kill me . . ."

"Then get on one knee and *prove it!*"

Richard tightens his fist and drops to one knee on the stage.

"I'm on one knee, don't kill me don't kill me . . ."

"You thinkin' about dying now, ain't you?"

Another twist. Richard curls up in a fetal position on his back.

"Yeah, I'm thinkin' 'bout dyin' I'm thinkin' 'bout dyin' . . ."

"You didn't think about it when you was eatin' that *pork.*"

Funny as a heart attack.

Everyone marveled that here was a man who could turn a very real brush with death into an uproarious stand-up routine. It wouldn't be the last time.

The bit ended with Richard sitting up and saying, "I woke up in the ambulance, right? And there wasn't nothing but white people staring at me. I say, 'Ain't this a bitch? I done died and wound up in the wrong motherfuckin' heaven. Now I got to listen to Lawrence Welk for the rest of my days.' "

The bit was a perfect illustration, critic Mel Watkins wrote, of Richard taking an audience to the peak of emotion and then letting them off with a nice laugh.

In December, Louie Robinson of *Ebony* magazine visited the Northridge estate to write a cover story on newlyweds Richard and Deboragh, with full photo spread. The triumphs of 1977, he wrote, had made Richard "a folk hero to millions of Blacks (they mob him wherever he appears, tugging at him, wanting to touch him)" and "one of the wealthiest of the 'new breed' of actors in Hollywood."

His marriage to Deboragh was his third "on paper," Richard said, but insisted it was his first real marriage, the first time he'd married for love.

Sometime in the first hours of New Year's Day, 1978, things went awry at the Northridge house. Paul Mooney and his wife, Yvonne, had been there earlier but left when he saw the pentagram begin to glow on Richard's forehead. "There's going to be some shit happening here," he told his wife.

"Richard never lays a hand on a woman when I am around," Mooney writes. "It's like he is afraid of my judgment. Then again, when I see the werewolf in Richard about to come out, I know enough to get gone. So I'm never present to witness him turn violent. But I see evidence enough that he abuses his wives and girlfriends horribly."

The fuse was lit, according to actor D'Urville Martin, when Richard became convinced that Deboragh had been more than just friends with one of the women at the party. Richard got his .357 Magnum, then told Deboragh and her two friends, Beverly Clayborn and Edna Solomon, they had five seconds to get out of his house.

Richard fired in the air, shattering a ten-thousand-dollar Tiffany chandelier as he herded them out. The three women took shelter in Clayborn's Buick. Richard rammed the Buick repeatedly with his Mercedes. When the women took off on foot, Richard walked over to the abandoned car and shot out its tires and windshield, executioner-style.

On January 19, Beverly Clayborn, wearing a neck brace, filed a personal suit against Richard in Los Angeles Superior Court for seventeen million dollars. "If she gets it," he quipped, "I'll marry her."

When Deboragh filed for divorce on February 3, the January issue of *Ebony* was still on newsstands with the cuddling newlyweds smiling out from the cover.

It took Richard a long time to come to terms with what he had done — how quickly he'd managed to ruin the marriage he swore would last. The sad part (yes, there's a sad part to this story) is that Richard and Deboragh were still in love, they said, still wanted to make their marriage work, but vile and hateful things had been said that night that could not be unsaid or swept aside. Such things fester, lurk in the house like dozing demons, liable at any time to awaken in fury.

In November, Richard pleaded no contest to a misdemeanor charge of malicious mischief, was fined five hundred dollars, and ordered to seek psychiatric help. By that time, he was opening his sold-out concerts with a reenactment of the incident, though amending certain details. "It seemed fair to kill my car to me, right? Because my wife was going to leave my ass. I say, 'Not in this motherfucker, you ain't. Uh-uh. No, Lawd. If you leave me you be driving those Hush Puppies you got on, 'cause I'm gonna kill this motherfucker here."

More frequently on stage, Richard was giving voice and personality to all manner of animals, body parts, bodily functions, and inanimate objects. Here he is shooting out the tires: "I shot it. 'Fooo-whoom!' Tire say, 'Aahhhh-aaaahh.' It got good to me, I shot another one. 'Bwooom!' ... Aahhhh-aaaahh.' And the vodka I was drinking said, 'Go ahead, shoot something else.' I shot the motor, motor fell out the motherfucker, right? The motor say, 'Fuck it!'"

As Mel Watkins notes, the device "enriched his performances with a resonance that transcended race . . . Routines in which dogs, monkeys, pipes, or automobiles spoke in black voices called forth images of antebellum animal tales and the oral techniques of black storytellers or 'liars.'"

It wasn't just the voices. Richard had developed an almost eerie ability to transform himself physically to mimic physical characteristics, body types, and facial expressions. One of the most moving segments of his 1978 concert program comes when Richard describes walking in his backyard, grieving the accidental deaths of his pet spider monkeys,* when a neighbor's usually ferocious German shepherd jumps the fence to console him. Richard's face takes on not just the attitude of a German shepherd, but one feeling confusion and pity.

David Brenner has said that "Pryor's routines were really more like plays; one-man theater where he plays all the parts." And, we would add, he plays the props and the scenery, too.

The tour was cut short when Richard got the news that his grandmother Marie had suffered a stroke. Richard rushed to her bedside at his house in Northridge where she had been staying.

He had to face the fact that it was time to take her home to Peoria.

––––––––––

Marie died some weeks later, in mid-December, at Methodist Medical Center. Richard fell apart. Relatives struggled to pry his hand loose from hers as he cried and shook "like a rag doll." When they had succeeded in dragging him out of her hospital room, he broke loose and ran back, crying, "Everything I've had and everything I've got is gone."

---

*In the routine, Richard claims the monkeys died while he was out of town. He'd left them in the care of a friend. The curious monkeys turned the knob on a gas stove but, having no matches to light it, asphyxiated and died. "He said *what?*" Penelope Spheeris said when we told her about this routine. "No! He fucking starved those monkeys to death! They forgot to feed them."

Mama Marie had been the one person he could always turn to. Even after he got to be a big star, she always called bullshit on him. She never tried to flatter him or win favor. But neither did she ever relinquish her role as his "mama."

Richard unnerved his young daughters, Elizabeth and Rain, on the trip back to Los Angeles. "I just don't see how I can go on," he told them. "Nothing means shit no more." (Probably not the best thing to tell one's nine- and eleven-year-old daughters, Rain allows, "but I guess he needed to tell someone and we were handy.")

It took him years, according to friends, to come to grips with Mama Marie's death. Rain is not certain he ever got over the loss.

Yet it could not have been more than a week or two after she died that Richard, at the Terrace Theater in Long Beach, California, on December 28, 1978, gave what is considered the greatest performance of his life. Or, if you accept the judgment of critic Pauline Kael, the greatest performance of anyone's life.

———————

Cameras were rolling as people milled in the aisles and chatted in the lobby during the intermission that followed Patti LaBelle's opening act. Without introduction and the house lights still up, Richard bounded out across the stage and, with a great leap, seized the microphone from its stand as he landed on both feet with a loud thump that sounds, on film, to our ears, like the signal rim shot that opens "Like a Rolling Stone."

Richard performed the act he had honed to perfection on tour the previous autumn. He began by goofing with those in the audience as they scurried back to their seats, and he never let up or even settled into anything that felt like a practiced routine. The one time he paused to catch his breath, Richard asked that the house lights be turned up so that he could introduce an old friend in the audience. "Ladies and gentlemen," he said, "Mr. Huey P. Newton." Maddeningly, the camera did not pivot to capture the moment when Huey half stood and waved to the crowd, in the unlikely event he actually did.

For an hour and fifteen minutes Richard riffed on his troubles with the law, his recent heart attack, and how his machismo was undone by the mysteries of the female orgasm. Richard relied on none of his seasoned characters — there was no Oilwell or Big Bertha, no sermons from Reverend Du Rite or Mudbone monologues to fall back on — just pure, uncut Richard Pryor. Working entirely without props, gimmicks, or excuses," *Chicago Reader* film critic Jonathan Rosenbaum wrote, "he creates a world so intensely realized and richly detailed that it puts most million-dollar blockbusters to shame." When the resulting movie, *Richard Pryor: Live in Concert,* was released to theatres just one month later, David Handelman, writing in the *New York Times Magazine,* called it his "indisputable moment of glory." Not only is *Richard Pryor: Live in Concert* the crown jewel of stand-up comedy movies, it was also the first. Never before had a feature-length stand-up concert film received a theatrical release. Which seems fitting, in the same way that Henry Aaron, the last major leaguer to have played in the Negro Leagues, remains the first player listed in the alphabetical *Encyclopedia of Baseball.*

New Yorker film critic Pauline Kael wrote that it was "a consummation of his years as an entertainer" and "probably the greatest of all recorded performance films. Pryor had characters and voices bursting out of him . . . Watching this mysteriously original physical comedian you can't account for his gift and everything he does seems to be for the first time." In sum, she deemed it the greatest performance she'd ever seen or ever hoped to see.

"WHEN YOU GET OFF THAT STAGE,
THERE'S A LONELINESS THAT COMES OVER YOU"

Comedian Thea Vidale continues: "It's like all the love is gone. So you can see why comics have demons. You're trying to fill that void until the next stage time you get where you'll find your love."

Back home in Northridge, with the concert tour completed, the movie in theaters, and the companion double-LP *Wanted* in record stores, Richard had time to feel the full weight of the reality that the woman who raised him, had always been his rock and his anchor, was gone for good. In the wake of Mama's death, Richard's drug consumption only escalated, the violence got worse, and his behavior grew increasingly bizarre.

Richard's daughter Elizabeth Stordeur Pryor, now a professor of nineteenth-century U.S. history and race at Smith College, believes it was a source of torment for her father that he often told painful truths about other people in his stand-up.

> He always told the truth in a childlike way, without calculation or guile. He simply didn't know any other way to be. But I don't think he liked the aftermath of telling that truth — of feeling exposed, and feeling inside out, and maybe having hurt people. I don't think he liked that, but he couldn't help doing it any other way. I think he just spewed out his truth, and he did it beautifully onstage, and then he'd feel horrible. Maybe alcohol helped that feeling go away. And I think the crazy people helped it go away, too. That may have been an alternate addiction. He liked being around people who

told him the truth. Now, the truth was that he was brilliant and kind. But the ones who told him he was a fucking asshole, those were the ones he believed because that's how he felt about himself. He tended to surround himself with dark and devious people.

Jennifer Lee had been Richard's live-in girlfriend for nearly a year, moving in soon after Deboragh left. Her devastating diary-cum-memoir, *Tarnished Angel*, published in 1991, chronicles being beaten to a pulpy mess on a nearly daily basis, either by Richard's hands or emptied champagne, vodka, and Courvoisier bottles. No matter how bruised or lacerated her face became, all it ever took, by her own account, was a call from Richard — an "I love you," or a "baby, I need you" — and her heart would melt. Page after page, chapter after chapter, she forgives him with renewed hopes and swollen smiles. Rain Pryor, in her 2006 memoir *Jokes My Father Never Taught Me*, archly recalls that her dad must have really loved Jennifer "because he would beat the shit out of her, and she must have really loved him — because she always took it."

What was that advice his father had given him? When you hit a woman, one of two things will happen. She will either pack up and leave or she's yours for life.

If that's the love Richard wanted, he had found it.

———————

In February 1979 Jennifer wrote that even though producer Ray Stark had been sending scripts to the house on an almost-daily basis, Richard didn't have much interest in anything but cocaine. What follows is a not-unusual entry from her diary at the time:

> Richard is doing a benefit with Muhammad Ali, which entails staging a fight. He dreads it and drinks many glasses of vodka before he even gets dressed. When I suggest that he "cool it," I become the object of his rage. All hell breaks loose. He grabs my diary and my phone book and chucks them into the living room fire. Then he runs into my closets and slashes all my clothes. Not satisfied

with murdering my wardrobe, he rips the watch off my wrist and smashes it. Then he comes after my diamond studs, trying to tear them out of my ears. Just as suddenly, he calms down and leaves. I inspect the gashes and rips in my Armanis, Basiles, and my thousand-dollar, worn-once, Cracked Ice pants.

Hours later, Jennifer got a call from her old friend Waylon Jennings who happened to be performing at the same benefit. Richard, he told her, had "just been raving about how much he loves you. Damn, I should've known he was with someone like you. He's lookin' good. You're takin' real good care of him, Jen."

"Music to my bloody ears," she writes.

Odd, that after so much insanity, it took Richard shaving off half of his mustache while taking a bubble bath to convince him that he needed professional help. He was on his way to visit a female coke dealer he'd been spending more and more time with when Jennifer stopped him at the door and told him to just look at himself. He was wearing a red Adidas jogging suit, silver Nikes, a top hat, and half a mustache.

Richard checked himself into a hospital under the care of psychiatrist Dr. J. Alfred Cannon, an active champion for advancing mental health care in minority communities who had been instrumental in establishing the Drew Medical School in south-central Los Angeles.

Submitting to a hospital stay and daily sessions with a psychiatrist was difficult for Richard. Talking about his life was too personal, too painful. Doing it onstage was one thing, but one-on-one with someone trained to see into the workings of the human psyche was something else. Dr. Cannon asked him why he liked cocaine. He recounts their conversation in *Pryor Convictions*.

> "Do you see how it removes you from reality? Mentally as well as physically? You spend days and even weeks isolated in your house alone in your bedroom, getting high."
> "Yeah, but that's okay."
> "Why's that? Why's it okay?"

"I don't see any need to be in reality because I've seen how ugly the world is."

He didn't buy that shit. Not for an instant. Wanted to know how I was so confident of the world's ugliness when I wouldn't venture into it to check things out.

Dr. Cannon suggested that he make a trip back home.

But now that Mama was gone, he had no home to go back to.

No. He meant *home* home. Everyone's home. Africa.

Richard has decided to drive himself and a girlfriend from the city of Nairobi out across the sprawling bush to a safari resort seventy miles to the south. Already he has been shaken by the autonomy and casual dignity of the Kenyans in the capital city, the specter of black people truly occupying every position of a society. In truth, he hardly notices their blackness; its every variant is so vividly on display that it ceases to signify anything in particular, much less demark the limits of anyone's opportunity.

Racing across the scorched plain, Richard feels electrified by the possibility of being truly liberated, of owning his soul in a way that he never has; of fully growing into his skin and loving it; of living beyond it.

The wide dirt road narrows abruptly and dips into a valley; and where a small stand of trees throws shade across the path of the now slow-moving car, six grown lions lay dozing in the hot afternoon.

Richard slams on the brakes, and out of the crunch of gravel and stirred dust, one of lions stands and stretches, squaring off with the grill of the car.

Richard grips the wheel in a stunned silence, feeling elated, oddly free of fear and in alliance with the lioness, who lowers her head, seems less sleepy and more guarded as the moments pass.

"I'm an African," Richard says under his breath and as he begins to climb from the car. "These are my lions."

"Jesus Christ, Richard!" his girlfriend begs, sinking lower in her seat — "get back in the fucking car! Fuck — RICHARD!"

"These are my lions," Richard says again, meeting the lion's reproachful eye.

As Richard takes a single step from behind the open car door, the lioness follows a yawn with a deep groan that rouses the other five, who have now all come to their feet.

"My lions," Richard repeats, even as he slams the door and dives head-first through the open window and back into his seat, quickly finding reverse.

Richard and Jennifer began their three-week trip on Easter Sunday, flying to Nairobi where they made a connecting flight to Mombasa. For the first few days, Richard sulked. Jennifer writes:

> I ask him to please stop whatever it is he's doing and just let us love each other. Says Richard, "I don't love you. I love Deboragh."
> "Do you mean it?"
> "With all my heart!"

Two paragraphs later:

> I start packing my suitcase. Every time I put something in it, he dumps it on the floor. This mean slapstick routine continues until I figure out that all I really need is my pocketbook. As I'm walking out the door, he rips the bag off my shoulder and empties it onto the floor. We both dive for it and end up wrestling over the contents. He gets hold of my passport and starts ripping it page by page while I futilely try and rescue it. I go into my full-tilt stubborn mode. "Fuck it! I'll go to the U.S. Embassy and get a new one!"
>
> As I start out the door, Richard flings himself at my feet and grabs my ankles holding on for dear life. "Please, don't leave me, I love you so much."
>
> When I look down at him my heart melts. I'm his once again, and all else is forgotten

And so on.

For the next several days, Richard was sullen and moody. Most days he slept while Jennifer wandered the open-air markets and drank in the scenery.

Richard had read Richard Leakey's *Origins* in preparation for the trip. When they returned to Nairobi, Jennifer dragged him to the National Museum. It was an amazing visit, Jennifer reports. It wasn't until later that afternoon, as Richard sat in the lobby of the Nairobi Hilton, that it really hit him.

> I was sitting in the hotel and a voice said to me, "Look around. What do you see?" And I said I see all colors of people doing everything." And the voice said, "Do you see any niggers?" I said, "No." It said, "You know why? Because there aren't any."
>
> And it hit me like a shot, man. I started crying and shit, you know, sitting there. I said, "I've been here three weeks. I haven't even said it. I haven't even *thought* it." And it made me say, "Oh, my God, I've been wrong. I've been wrong. I got to regroup my shit." I said, "I ain't never going to call another black man 'nigger.'"

Although many fans applauded his disavowal of the N-word, Richard was stunned by the reactions of those who viewed it as a sellout, that he'd gone soft, turned his back on the community, the movement. In Richard's mind, his epiphany had been on the order — if not the magnitude — of Malcolm X's awakening in Mecca, where he saw Hajj pilgrims of all colors and understood that white people were not devils, that white is a state of mind.

"But I wasn't Malcolm or Martin, or anybody else," Richard wrote in his memoir. "I was a drug-addicted, paranoid, frightened, lonely, sad, and frustrated comedian who had gotten too big for his britches."

The doorman lifts his head but averts his gaze when they enter the lobby, the party upstairs is already raucous and troublesome enough without more leather-clad hipsters packing the place, their shaded eyes already dim and drifting ahead of nightfall. Richard and his date glide into the elevator that rises some fifteen floors and opens on to loud music, a rumble of talk and deep laughter. The couple push inside to hoots of recognition and snake their way through to the bar. Within moments, Richard is quietly steered into a back bedroom, the door closing behind him.

Cocaine is scarcely a secret indulgence on the scene, but something in here certainly is. Richard wants the good shit — jokes that it costs him six hundred dollars a day just to get his dick hard, the full freeze long gone.

"Well, what — you ain't read Pilgrim's Progress? *You have to stay current, my brother, got to go higher up the mountain if you wanna talk to God."*

The skinny man produces a small rock and a glass pipe, sparks his lighter, and offers it to Richard who for laughs drops to his knees as if at a communion rail.

"Easy now, Rich, take it easy — like sucking a chick's dick," the man coos, and then Richard is in; off; gone.

Hours do not become less than hours but feel as if they are all running concurrently — the whole expanse of the evening viewed in a single frame, its scale abstracted and made disproportionate as if something close at hand were viewed through a long and cracked telescope.

Richard's girlfriend, having gone to look for him, slips into the back room where Rich and a small circle have remained sequestered and peers through the same lens. She passes out on the floor but in time is brought weakly to the surface by the weight of a man's body, moving over and then within her.

"No, Richard . . . no, stop — not here," she mutters, trying to work her way from beneath the man who only pushes himself deeper in between her thighs.

There is a whirring sound, then laughter, as the woman finally finds Richard's eyes within her fleeting focus; but the grinning familiar face floats past her, circling, and she realizes it is not attached to the body of the man now having sex with her.

"Smile, bitch," says Richard as he snaps Polaroid pictures of her assault. "Smile!"

The whirring sound continues, as gray-and-white squares slide from the camera and fall to the floor, the girl's astonished face not yet developed enough to recognize.

"MY MIND'S THINKING ABOUT SHIT
I DON'T WANT TO BE THINKIN' ABOUT"

Richard, for all his fearless, self-revelatory truth-telling, consistently lied about one thing, and that was cocaine. In every interview, performance, or personal encounter, he cheerfully reported that he was off drugs for real this time.

Early in 1980, David Brenner had finished doing an afternoon talk show at CBS and was on his way out to his car when he saw Richard in the parking lot wearing a baseball cap. They greeted and hugged. Brenner asked him how he was doing.

> He says, "Oh, I'm great, man. I got the shit out of me. I'm done with all the shit." He says, "I'm straight and I'm cool and I've got it together and I know what's what and I know where I'm going and I'm cool."
>
> I said, "I'm glad to hear that," because you know you were always afraid with him that there was going to be a disaster, like with Freddie Prinze, who was a good friend of mine — that there would be that kind of an ending. So it was always with great trepidation when you saw him because you thought, "God, I hope he doesn't go home and kill himself." And a few times, we know, he almost did.
>
> And he says, "Come on over, we'll sit around, we'll bullshit, we'll have some fun . . ."
>
> I said, "I'd love to do it, Richie, but I've got another TV show. I've got to go." I said, "We'll hang again." I gave him a big hug and

he takes off his cap and he has his hair tied up in well over one hundred tiny little bows of different-colored cloth. I just said, "Hey, Richie, I am really happy that you're off the shit and you've got it together," and he said, "Thanks, man," and walked away. And I thought, "Oh my God, is he fucked up." It was hysterical. It would've made a great routine of two guys meeting and that happening. Of one guy trying to convince the other that he's off the drugs and he's straight? It was wonderful. Wonderful.

During their long drive up to Berkeley in the spring of 1971, between the Motown tunes and swigs of Courvoisier, Richard confided to Paul Mooney that sometimes he saw devils. Actual ones. "I'm in a meeting in motherfucking Hollywood, Mr. Mooney, and I ain't kidding, all I see is horns and tails! Really! All these folks around me got cloven feet and forked tongues!"

When freebase first swept through Hollywood, Richard insisted it was a line he would never cross. Then he casually mentioned to David Franklin one day that, when you stop and think about it, freebase is actually a purer form of cocaine, free of contaminants. Franklin had warned Richard from the very start of their association that he didn't represent drug addicts. He recognized the rationalizing voice of a junkie when he heard one. He realized, with alarm, that he was hearing one now.

Richard began freebasing in November 1979 and did little else during the next seven months, except costar with Gene Wilder in *Stir Crazy*.

A popular YouTube video (an earlier audio version had circulated for years on a bootleg cassette of celebrity meltdowns) captures Richard giving a coked-out interview on the set. He simultaneously boasts about and mocks the amount of money he has been paid for his role in the film. "Two million dollars! My grandmother never saw that much money in her whole life," he tells someone standing to his right, just out of view, "and she was a better woman than you are a man . . . you know how much a million dollars is? I can't even count to a million. You'd need an accountant — a Jew!"

And on it goes, for more than thirteen minutes.

The movie sucks. I don't care 'cause I got paid . . . Gene Wilder is a fag . . . All I want is to leave Tucson alive . . . I didn't get caught yesterday buying seven pounds of cocaine in front of eight policemen. They can't catch me! I'm a lucky, black, *greasy* motherfucker . . . I'm happy because Sidney Poitier is directing a ten-million-dollar movie and it don't mean shit. They spent *four billion* dollars on the Americans who went to Iran, and they crashed. Eight people died and they was all black.

Even when he seems on the verge of giving the desired answer to a question, he renders the take unusable by slouching in his chair and throttling his cupped hand above his crotch, miming jacking off. There is plenty of laughter on camera and off. Even though the day is wasted, everyone is having a jolly time. Even Richard, although his eyes say he is dying inside.

Jennifer Lee accompanied him to Tucson for location filming at the Arizona State Prison. As usual, he rented a private house several miles away from the rest of the cast and crew. At this point, he prized any and every opportunity to be off by himself so he could smoke.

Jennifer read aloud to him from the Alcoholics Anonymous "Big Book" while he refilled his pipe and kept a wary eye on the demons that prowled the room where they slept. It freaked her out the way he would point to them, show her where they were, and describe in such calm and precise detail exactly what they looked like and what they were doing. She watched with growing alarm as his bloodshot eyes followed their movements around the room. Soon enough, because she was sharing his pipe, she began seeing them, too. And they were exactly as he had described them.

Richard and his friend Charles Weldon, who was also in *Stir Crazy*, kept the party going once they got back to L.A. After an especially debauched night with perhaps a half-dozen hookers — including a pair of twins who couldn't keep up with them, Weldon remembers — they decided to give AA a try. They sat through part of a meeting, listening to people weep and talk about the degrading things they'd done in exchange for drugs or drug money. One woman told of stealing her parents' television. Richard had a routine about that. At one point they just looked at each other and said, in effect, "Shit, we ain't got no problem. Not compared to these people." They got up and left, went out and scored.

———

One night at the Northridge house, Jennifer looked out the window and saw all these caped dwarves and goblins — a whole army of them — moving through the bushes, coming after her. She became so terrified, she called the police and frantically led the bemused officers on a search of the area outside the house. Jennifer actually grabbed the flashlight away from one of them and shined it underneath the bushes to show them where the goblins were. "But my dark creatures have disappeared," she writes, "and so, obviously, has my mind."

Weeks later, she and Richard were clutching each other as they made their way through the house in a paranoid delirium. They saw — they *both* saw — the orange face of the devil glowing in the dark at the top of the stairs outside Richard's office looking down at them.

In what would become an almost-nightly ritual, Richard swore off smoking, smashed his glass pipe, then went out the next morning to buy a bigger and better one.

———

By springtime, Richard was unable to go five minutes without freebasing. He tried. He set down his pipe, looked at the clock, and told himself, "I'm not doing anymore freebase for the next five minutes." But he couldn't do it. He couldn't wait that long. If he couldn't go five minutes without freebase, what *could* he do? What was left? He'd come to the end of something he couldn't see past.

On June 7, Richard confided to Jennifer that he'd seen himself as the devil. An orange-colored skeletal creature came walking through the wall like a ghost. It looked just like him. Richard spoke to it. He asked the apparition if it really was his own self he was seeing. "Yes, I'm you," the devil said to him, then walked back through the wall.

Late in the day of June 9, 1980, after weeks of nonstop freebasing, Richard doused himself with 150-proof rum and flicked his Bic lighter, resulting in third-degree burns over more than half his body. Put bluntly, after he'd smoked every bit of cocaine he could find, he smoked himself.

Friends were called to the house throughout the earlier part of that day to come do something — anything — to help him. Jim Brown, Paul Mooney, and Jennifer Lee all found him cowering in his bedroom like the Kafka character Gregor Samsa, scurrying from the light they let in, racing for the dark places, and hissing at them to get the fuck out and leave him alone.

Kathy McKee doesn't remember who called her to come over that day. Probably Rashon, or maybe his housekeeper, Mercy, or Richard's aunt Dee. They were all there.

Kathy always had a calming effect on Richard, but on this day he was too far gone. She walked into his room and there he sat "with that damn base pipe glued to his hand. He was completely one hundred percent out of his mind. It was terrible. You couldn't communicate with him anymore. You know that if he doesn't put that base pipe down and go to the hospital and get some help, there's no way he's coming out of this. You have to understand," she says, "freebase isn't like doing cocaine. You can't think of it that way. Everybody at that time was doing coke. Sammy Davis did coke. Johnny *Carson* did coke. Dean Martin, Frank Sinatra, everybody did. But once he got on that damn base pipe" — the anger still rises in her voice some thirty-five years later — "that was it. There's no coming back from that. Like AIDS in the gay community, base took people down. People died."

Kathy described for us how Richard used a cotton swab on the end of a wooden stick — like the throat swabs they use at the doctor's office — and he would dip that into 151 rum or 200-proof grain alcohol and light that with a lighter.

> He would light the swab and use that as a flame torch to light the pipe. I really don't know the reason behind that, but I would imagine it's because it wasn't toxic to light the pipe with rum like it would be with lighter fluid. You'd be inhaling lighter fluid. Richard was dipping that cotton flame torch into the rum bottle — 151-proof rum! Plus he's high, he's out of his mind. And, you know, after three days on a binge, or whatever it was, that's a pretty risky thing to do, because if that torch is hot, or still lit by mistake, and you dip it down in that bottle, you've now got a molotov cocktail.
>
> "I told him — the last thing I said to him was, "Richard, at least pour that rum in a cup."

Richard, in his book, describes descending into serious dementia, a surreal darkness of hallucinations and voices — people from his past outside his window, on the other side of his door, taunting him, mocking his weakness. When he ran out of dope, he debated his options, then reached for a bottle of rum and doused himself. It seemed like a good idea. He wasn't scared. Neither did he feel inner peace. "I was in a place called There."

It took three tries for his Bic to catch — just as his cousin opened the door to look in on him. Richard says he tried to wrap himself in a comforter to put out the flames, but he couldn't pick it up. It wouldn't move. "I must have gone into shock," he writes, "because I didn't feel anything."

His aunt Dee came in and yelled at his cousin to "Smother him!" In his delirium, Richard thought she meant "Suffocate him" as in "Put the sorry motherfucker out of his misery."

He could have rolled on the floor, says Kathy McKee. The shower was right there off the bedroom. But there was also a window. He crashed through it and headed toward the street.

———

Officers Richard Zielinski and Carl Helm, responding to a call just after 8:00 p.m., saw Richard running along Parthenia Street, trailing smoke. The identity of the burning man had been confirmed.

Officer Zielinski jumped out of the patrol car and began jogging alongside him. He noted that the weave of his polyester shirt had melted into his raw flesh.

"Richard, we've got to get you to a hospital."

"I'm *going* to the hospital. Just show me where it is."

"Why don't you just stop and wait for — "

"I can't stop. If I stop, I'll die."

Zielinski didn't argue the point. He simply assured Richard that help was on the way and that he would stay with him until the ambulance arrived.

"I really fucked up, man. Please, God, give me another chance. I know I did wrong, but there's a lot of good in me. Haven't I brought happiness to anyone in this world?"

"Sure you have," Zielinski told him. "We all love your stuff."

Richard paused briefly in front of the San Fernando Valley Christian School, nearly a mile from his house, then took off again, turning the corner and heading south on Hayvenhurst Avenue where, some time later, an ambulance caught up to him.

———

Richard gave multiple accounts of how the fire started, most of them attempts to vouch for the well-meaning explanations put out by his friends and management — covering for those who were covering for him.

In one, Richard admitted that he *had* been freebasing the day before but had run out of base. (Think we'll be freebasing tonight? We're not? Well, what the heck.) So he and an unidentified "partner" — perhaps Rashon, perhaps some phantasmal character, the product of a hallucination — were drinking the highly volatile rum he generally used to fire up the base. He went to light a cigarette and — POOF!

Tony DiDominico, chief of the Los Angeles Fire Department, confirmed that overproof rum, properly atomized, with a very hot ignition force, would indeed ignite. "But a violent explosion? A flash fire? I don't think so."

In the version Rashon told, he and Richard were in the living room, in a haze, drinking the high-octane rum and watching something on TV about the Vietnam War. A monk sat down in a public square, doused himself with gasoline, and set himself ablaze.

Said Rashon to Richard, "You have to have a lot of courage to light that shit." To which Pryor replied, "You have to have more courage not to flinch when you light it!"

Rashon laughed. He got up, went to the kitchen, then heard a scream. "I opened the door and out comes this ball of fire. And I sidestepped it, because I seen a knife in his hand, and I know when you're in that state, there's nothing I could do. But he did pour the shit on himself, and he did light it. It was no accident."

Late that night, the waiting area in the Grossman Burn Center at Sherman Oaks Hospital was overfilled with Richard's children, aunts, uncles, and an assemblage of ex-wives and girlfriends, all of whom rose in unison when a hospital rep came out and called for "Mrs. Pryor."

Jennifer Lee was shut out. Richard refused to see her and she found herself ostracized by his family members camped in the waiting area because she told the doctors that Richard had been freebasing earlier in the day. That information, one doctor told her, according to her own account, saved his life.

No charges were filed. Someone had gone into Richard's house and cleared out any drug paraphernalia before investigators arrived. The only apparent evidence of what had taken place in that room consisted of a singed bedspread and a patch of scorched paint on one of the walls.

Richard's "accident" prompted an article on the dangerous new drug craze in the June 30 issue of *People,* written without byline by Peter Lester, a friend of Jennifer Lee's who telephoned her days after the fire, quizzing her on the basic mechanics of freebasing and Richard's consumption habits. He failed to inform her until the end of their conversation that he had been taping it. Freebasing — or baseballing as the article claims it was also known — derives from the process of using ether to "free" the alkaloid cocaine (or "base") from the additives and impurities typically found in drugs sold on the street. Powdered cocaine is dissolved in ether to separate extraneous matter, leaving a rock-hard piece of pure coke. Users then apply a flame to the pure coke and inhale the vapors.

A hit of freebase delivers a thirty-second rush followed by a minute or two of what is described as unimaginable euphoria. The high ends with a crash and an insatiable desire to get it back. The high is frequently followed by depression. The urge to have more grows stronger and stronger the more one smokes.

"Freebase gets into the brain and produces a maximal high, and that is what's so compelling about it," said Dr. Sidney Cohen, a clinical professor of psychiatry at UCLA. After repeated use, freebase can cause critical changes in consciousness such as paranoia or schizophrenic psychosis. "Some people think they're more creative when they freebase," Dr. Cohen said. "Certainly they get ideas in their heads that they normally wouldn't." Chronic users often become delusional. UCLA research psychopharmacologist Ronald Siegel said he had witnessed a delirious freebaser clawing the skin off his own arms in the belief that they were host to a nest of slithering white snakes.

Siegel estimated that some users freebased up to thirty grams of cocaine in a single day — with a then-street-value of approximately $2,500 — and it wasn't unusual for some to spend $250,000 a year. One other thing: while alcohol, pot, even snorted coke tend to be casually shared in convivial settings, freebase, Dr. Seigel warned, is a loner's drug.

———————

Doctors Richard Grossman and Jack Grossman, resident plastic surgeons and burn specialists at Sherman Oaks, initially gave Richard a one-in-three chance of survival. His entire upper body, including his torso, back, chest, arms, neck, and parts of his face, had been severely burned.

As soon as the risk of infection had subsided enough to allow visitors, Mooney went to Richard's room and found his friend lying unbandaged so as to allow his oozing third-degree burns sufficient time to air out in preparation for the coming skin grafts.

"We managed to save his face," Dr. Jack Grossman told Vernon Scott of United Press International, "but the burns on his ears are so extensive the cartilage is visible."

Said his brother Dr. Richard Grossman, "There is virtually no skin on his torso. You can see the raw muscle tissue, fat tissue . . . If you saw our patient without his dressings, you would faint. Most people would."

Paul Mooney did not.

He had his own theory about the fire, which was this: Richard's money and success made him feel so white that he had tried to burn himself black. One might just as reasonably argue that he had tried to dispense with the skin issue altogether. Either way, it was a bust.

Mooney put on his bravest face and his most solemn German accent.

"Dr. Frankenstein," he said, "the operation did not succeed."

It hurt to laugh, but when did it not?

After all of it — the spent shell of self-loathing, the match and fire, the smoldering streak from Parthenia Street to Hayvenhurst Avenue, the months of denial and therapy and recuperation — Richard returns to his home in Northridge. It's like he's a ghost returning to a place he is vaguely certain used to be his. His friends and family, having given him up for gone, have looted the place of everything they could carry: stereos, television sets, jewelry, furniture, family pictures, lamps, and rugs. "Motherfuckers had a fire sale," is what it looks like.

The hollow rooms, airless and hot, echo his footsteps. Dust bunnies stir in his wake as he tosses aside a pile of rumpled sheets, steps over an abandoned extension cord. He goes to the back room, into the rear closet. Its ill-fit molding gives way at the floor and he pries up a short corner board with his boot, as easy as a kid's thick puzzle piece to reveal his secret, secret stash, still there. He closes his eyes and offers up a prayer . . . Of thanksgiving? For deliverance? He makes himself comfortable on the floor and begins one step at a time. Pipe. Rock. Rum. Lighter. Light.

PART FIVE

"THE PART OF ME THAT WANTED TO DIE DID"

> For me, the three geniuses of comedy are Jonathan Winters,
> Woody Allen, and Richard Pryor before the fire.
> — Franklyn Ajaye

Several times a day doctors and staff at the Grossman Burn Center in Los Angeles lowered Richard into a whirlpool bath where hot water and antiseptics washed over his body. Next they painted his torso with a silver sulfa cream to fight infection. Twice a day, for up to two hours at a time, they slid him into a cylindrical hyperbaric chamber that tripled the normal atmospheric pressure, thereby forcing pure oxygen into his body to speed the healing process.

Despite the excruciating treatments, Mooney reported that Richard was happier at Sherman Oaks than he had been in quite a long while. Having (presumably) no access to vodka or cocaine, his demons were malnourished, had grown too weak to intervene.

After six weeks of skin grafts, plastic surgery, and physical therapy, Richard was released on July 24 and taken directly to do an interview with Barbara Walters for ABC's *Good Morning America*. Sitting there, nearly bald, his skin patchy and discolored with fresh scar tissue, he repeated the ridiculous story that he and his partner — did no one ever ask who? — were in his bedroom, talking bullshit, talking about life, drinking overproof rum. It spilled. His partner got up to get a towel from the bathroom to wipe it up. Richard lit a cigarette, igniting the spilled rum and himself along with it.

"Were you on drugs?"

"No. I do drugs. I've done drugs, you know that. I've talked about it, but I wasn't on drugs then."

"People think that you were freebasing co — "

"Yeah, but you can't blow up yourself freebasing."

Not until their follow-up interview in 1986 did he admit that he had been lying to her, that the fire had been the culmination of a weeks-long freebasing binge, and that, no, it had not been an accident. He admitted, too, that within three weeks of leaving Sherman Oaks he was back freebasing again.

Walters leaned forward with a furrowed brow like a scolding mother. "Richard! Why?"

He needed it, he said. Starting a new life was scary.

––––––––––

The cover of *Ebony*'s October 1980 issue shows Richard perched on the hood of a Rolls Royce in a baggy white sweat suit with a pink towel around his neck, his arms raised in a flaccid pose as though flexing his muscles but not really. His smile is empty, his eyes are blank. The headline "I've Been Tried by Fire — Now I'm a New Man" recalls his line (and variations attributed to both George Carlin and W. C. Fields) "Cocaine made a new man out of me. And he wanted some, too."

The photos accompanying the interview by managing editor Charles L. Sanders show Richard with bandaged hands and a cigarette dangling as he leafs through a pile of get-well cards sent in by fans, shares a light lunch with his aunt Dee, and plays chess with David Banks. The article trumpets his newfound love of life. He has straightened up, he says, and is starting fresh, cleaning house, getting rid of the people who pulled him down.

Richard was furious. Furious with his weak-ass self for what he had done. Disgusted with the people he thought he could trust, who said they loved him and then came in and looted his house. Took everything. Things Mama gave him. The crinkly old hundred-dollar bills her people carried upriver when they got run out of New Orleans that she never would spend so she would never be broke. Those were gone, too. He felt like crying.

He had given up jokes, and now he was *one. Dudes would strike a match, bob it up and down, and say, "Check this. You know what this is? Richard Pryor running down the street." (Okay, that was pretty good. He might use that one.) But all the supermarket tabloids and* People *magazines with their inflammatory, pun-happy headlines about how he was the hottest thing in show business. Even* Film *fucking* Comment. *Jonathan Rosenbaum wrote a deep, moving piece about him and they had to go and change the title to "The Man in the Great Flammable Suit." Motherfuckers. They call themselves educated. Didn't they know fire was the only way he could save himself? The only thing that could purify his soul? Didn't they teach the basics anymore?*

It's everybody's favorite story: Somebody dies and comes back to life. Jesus did it best, returning for a few hours, perhaps — no more than a day judging by scriptural chronology — then ascending forthwith to glory. But what kind of hero plays the fool by returning from the dead and then lingering around for another twenty-five years, a pitiable imitation of his former self?

In F. Scott Fitzgerald's time, there were no second acts in American life. Now, it seems, the second act is all. The years of hard work and achievement that bring fame or stardom merely count as the qualifying round, a setup for the crash and burn. That's the show everybody wants to see.

In this, too, Richard Pryor was a pioneer.

After the fire, Richard perversely turned the myth of the hero on its head. When offered a way out of his devil's bargain, he took it. He exercised the escape clause and never looked back.

Richard Pryor the revolutionary, game-changing artist was pretty much finished. But Richard Pryor the celebrity movie star was just getting started. When Richard walked out onstage as a presenter at the 1981 Academy Awards ceremony, he was greeted with a standing ovation.

Today, Richard's rightful legacy as the world's most brilliant stand-up comedian — even as he kicked to pieces the very notion of what stand-up comedy could be — has been largely overshadowed by the string of mostly mediocre movies he churned out in the 1980s. This is a travesty of the same magnitude as the fact that Frank Sinatra is now identified with "My Way," the most un-Sinatra song in his catalog. There's no drinking to forget, no blues in the night, no angel eyes, no ring-a-ding-ding. Or like Louis Armstrong, who, after setting the skies ablaze in an outpouring of work that almost single-handedly defined the shape of jazz, has come to be known for a straightforward cover of a middling show tune ("Hello, Dolly") and a sappy ballad ("Wonderful World") on which he doesn't even play his horn. So Richard now is best known as Gene Wilder's sidekick and for such atrocities as *The Toy*.

Richard Donner's queasy remake of the French film *Le Jouet* (1976, starring Pierre Richard), *The Toy*, writes Julian Upton, is "a witless and degrading farrago that casts Pryor as an expensive plaything for a spoiled little white boy. *The Toy* could have had allegorical potential, not just regarding Pryor's career but for all those ethnic actors in Hollywood, but it fell far short of any such insight, and existed solely to show Pryor freaking out and looking scared."

One such scene early on in *The Toy* has Pryor caterwauling in bulging-eyed fright as he goes rolling head over heels down a department-store toy aisle in an inflatable Wonder Wheel. (This comes approximately eighteen minutes into the movie, which is as much as anyone enamored of Richard Pryor's genius can comfortably watch in a single sitting.)

"It's a horrible, post-pro-slavery movie," says Richard's daughter Elizabeth Stordeur Pryor. "There are people who come up to me and say their favorite movie is *The Toy*, and I feel like saying, 'Well, you're racist.' It's very disturbing. I have not let my children watch that movie."

Elizabeth had been there on the set when her father and Jackie Gleason were filming *The Toy*. Richard always brought the family, says Elizabeth.

Family was important to him. He made it a priority. He brought his children with him to things. We were on the set; we went to premieres and plays. It astounds me in retrospect, that he was able to do as much as he did, knowing what kinds of drugs he was using and the amount of alcohol.

My father was such a sweetheart, but he could be horrible and he was attracted to horrible people, he really was attracted to some dark people, and I don't just mean that in a drug-addicty sense. I never knew who was doing drugs and who wasn't. My sister [Rain] is so different from me. She always understood what was going on around her. She would say to me, years later, things about "all the whores Daddy had around him," and I was like, "What!" I was like, "You mean his friends that he would have over named Tiger and ...?" My brain doesn't work like that. I just thought my father had a lot of different girlfriends. Some of the nicer people were prostitutes that he had around him, but some of the people he brought into his life were just truly terrible people.

————————

A little more than a year after the fire and four years into their brutal on-again, off-again relationship, Richard and Jennifer Lee were married August 16, 1981, in Hawaii, in an intimate ceremony attended by a few friends, including Richard's lawyer Skip Brittenham, who greeted Jennifer with a pen and a prenup. Alone in their room that night, Jennifer slipped into her wedding nightgown. Richard rolled over, turned out the light and told her good night. "Richard? Why the hell are you giving me the freeze on this night of all nights?" A glass Richard grabbed up from the nightstand barely missed her head, shattering against the wall with such force, a triangle-shaped shard lodged in the wood. "I can't believe you just did that!"

Richard leaped out of bed, grabbed her by the neck, slammed her head against the wall, and threw her on the floor. "Believe this, bitch. I'll fucking kill you." Jennifer ran outside and fell sobbing into the wet grass. She ripped her nightgown to shreds, stuffed it in the trash, put on a T-shirt, and cried herself to sleep on the living room couch. The next morning, she awoke to hear Richard on the phone in the next room asking Skip Brittenham if he could have the marriage annulled.

"We patch things up," Jennifer writes, "but the first blood has been spilled on our clean slate of matrimony."

The marriage continued in much the same vein for the next four months. In January 1982, once filming for *Live on the Sunset Strip* had been completed, the couple chartered a fully staffed hundred-foot-yacht for a belated two-week honeymoon cruise in the Caribbean. We'll spare you the details. They are more of the same: glassware hurled, faces lacerated, deaths threatened, heads pummeled, hearts melted. Suffice it to say, the honeymoon brought their marriage to a swift end. "I've never met a man who needed love so badly and resisted it so much," Jennifer writes.

Not to say that Richard Pryor wasn't loved; he simply could not trust anyone who said so. Those who knew him up close saw a man who felt undeserving of love, undeserving of most everything good that came his way. Richard at times mocked, abused, and pushed away those who loved him most. It's as though he put them through hell as a test: You say you love me? Then here, take this. Let's see if you love me *now*, motherfucker.

———————

Live on the Sunset Strip was filmed over two nights in December of 1981. The first night was disastrous. There were problems with the sound system and the lights were set overly bright to accommodate cinematographer Haskell Wexler and his crew. Richard relied on Paul Mooney for cues — and reassurance — but couldn't locate him in the audience. (An easy solution would have been to let Mooney wear the Day-Glo red tuxedo a friend of Jennifer's had designed especially for Richard. Even Jennifer conceded that it made him look like "a monkey on acid.")

Richard walked onstage the first night and right away began talking about the fire and his freebasing, which cast a pall over the eager audience, packed with invited friends and well-wishers. Richard started shaky and never really found his groove. Less than halfway through his planned performance, Richard put himself and the audience out of their collective misery. He stopped midsentence. "I don't know what I'm doing here," he told them. "I'm not funny anymore. It's better if I leave." He set the mic down on the stool and walked off.

Friends from the audience followed him out to his dressing-room trailer where they all held hands while the Reverend Jesse Jackson led them in a prayer for Richard in his hour of need. Richard, standing among them, looked shell-shocked and embarrassed.

The experience left Richard badly shaken.

He'd tried to come back too soon after the "accident," everyone agreed in retrospect. Still, the producers had a movie to make. They talked him into giving the concert another try. It went much smoother the second night. Meticulous editing helped pick up the pace and eliminated the missteps and false starts that had marred the concert itself.

Richard's reenactment of the weeks-long freebase binge that led up to the fire contains some of his most fearless and personally revealing material ever. He turns his freebase pipe into a character that offers him refuge and assurance: "Time to get up, Rich, time for some smoke. Come on, now, we're not gonna do anything today. Fuck your appointments — me and you are just gonna hang out in this room together." Soon enough, the pipe gets the upper hand in the relationship. "You let me get a little low last night. I don't like that."

"Only gradually," Roger Ebert wrote in his review, "do we realize that the pipe is speaking in the voice of Richard Nixon."

He stops short of outright admitting that he'd deliberately set himself on fire, although he danced around other explanations, dropping coy rhetorical hints that it may not have been entirely accidental.

"Have you ever heard of a motherfucker burning up freebasing other than me? If nobody else burned up freebasing, why do you think it happened to me? I did not burn up freebasing. I burned up because I *quit* freebasing."

> Now here's how I really burned up. My friends really know how it happened, okay? Usually before I go to bed, I have a little milk and cookies. One night I had that low-fat milk and that pasteurized shit, and I dipped my cookie in it and the shit blew up.

That was a joke. A gag writer brought it to him and Richard Pryor paid for it.

Live on the Sunset Strip was released on March 12, 1982, one week to the day after John Belushi was found in his bungalow at the Chateau Marmont dead of an overdose — too soon to assign any intentional meaning to the shot of the iconic West Hollywood hotel that appears in the film's opening sequence.

IS COMEDY STAND-UP POETRY?

Comedians and jazz musicians have been more comforting
and enlightening to me than preachers or politicians or philosophers
or poets or painters or novelists of my time. Historians in the future,
in my opinion, will congratulate us on very little other than
our clowning and our jazz.
— Kurt Vonnegut

Self-proclaimed comediologist and professor of English at New Mexico Highlands University, Eddie Tafoya makes a case that *Live on the Sunset Strip* is a modern American answer to Dante's *Inferno.* "Just as Dante did for the world at the beginning of the Renaissance, Pryor provides for twentieth-century America a literary and spiritual assessment of the times. "In his immensely entertaining *The Legacy of the Wisecrack: Stand-Up Comedy as the Great American Literary Form,* Tafoya breaks Richard's filmed performance down into twenty-eight separate bits, which he then roughly equates to the *Inferno's* thirty-four cantos, and arrives at the conclusion that Richard is perhaps "the only person of the last century able to venture into the depths of this particular Hell."

Live on the Sunset Strip "belongs to the world of classical literature," Tafoya writes.

When taken as a single unit, the twenty-eight bits included in the performance tell a story with a classic mythological structure, one that begins with a rebirth and ends with a dual baptism by fire and water, a story that follows closely the initiation-separation-return hero cycle Joseph Campbell describes in his seminal book *The Hero with a Thousand Faces.*

As with Dante, the venture into the Dark Wood is initiated by the loss of female love. Just as Beatrice's love is lost with her death and then returns with the message from Virgil, Mama Bryant's love is lost and then resurrected in the person of Jennifer.

Tafoya offers no evidence that Richard had any particular knowledge of or interest in Dante's fourteenth-century epic. For this, we hold him blameless. The all-embracing scholar Guy Davenport published an essay that laid out in meticulous detail how Eudora Welty had transmuted the symbolism and imagery of the Greek myth of Persephone, queen of the underworld, in her novel *Delta Wedding*. When they later had occasion to meet, Welty chided Davenport in her playful way that it was news to her that *Delta Wedding* had anything to do with Persephone. That made no difference at all, Davenport insisted. The story, he said, had known it for her. Stories can do that. Just as Richard's characters were wiser and more clear-eyed in their understanding of the world than he ever managed to be in navigating in his own life. But when he was all alone in command of a bare stage with no obstacles, he could go with them anywhere and not stumble.

———————

Is stand-up comedy literature? It is if you accept Ezra Pound's contention that literature is "news that stays news." The oldest, mustiest, and most venerated literature we have managed to flourish for centuries as popular entertainment, delivered by performers equipped with nothing but breath, gesture, facial expression, and memory.

Is it poetry? Our answer comes, fittingly enough, from Pound's life-long friend and sometime tormentor, the physician and poet William Carlos Williams, who, when he wasn't treating jaundiced factory workers or delivering babies, wrote stanzas such as this, often on the backs of prescription pads while pulled over in his car on the side of a road in Rutherford, New Jersey. "It is difficult to get news from poetry," he wrote, "yet men die miserably every day for lack of what is found there."

"I GUESS THAT'S A SMILE.
I HOPE THAT'S HIS FACE"

"Richard's black and doesn't have the same career opportunities," said Paul Schrader. "This is a racist society: people aren't offering him the Oliver Sacks role that Robin Williams got in *Awakenings*." The only role he ever got that had not been specifically written for a black actor was Corporal Eddie Keller, a returning Vietnam vet in an adaptation of James Kirkwood's novel *Some Kind of Hero*.

Eddie is released from a POW camp and comes home to find that his wife has borne him a daughter and fallen in love with another man. His mother has suffered a stroke and is now in a nursing home costing twelve hundred dollars a month, but his wife and her boyfriend lost all his savings in a business venture and the army is withholding his back pay because, in exchange for medical help for a dying buddy, he had signed a statement presented by his captors admitting that the United States was conducting the war illegally.

Once Paramount had signed Richard Pryor, they decided the movie ought to be a comedy. Some moments in the film are genuinely funny, but the jokes are jarringly off-key in what began as the earnest story of a man overwhelmed by absurdity as he tries to reassess his life. (Example: Eddie uses a water pistol to rob a bank, but the ruse gives way when — wait for it — the pistol starts to leak. Why on earth would he — a corporal in the 101st Airborne — fill the thing with water in the first place?)

The brutal opening scenes, set in a POW camp, are by far the best part of the film. For those first twenty minutes, Richard gives one of the best dramatic performances of his career. After that promising start, *Some Kind of Hero* goes wobbly. The movie works as well as it does only because Richard plays it straight. Vincent Canby, reviewing in the *New York Times,* wrote, "The performance, if not the script, is a series of revelations of the singular Pryor talent as the actor inhabits a particular character," and he declares it Richard's "most complete, most honest characterization to date in a fiction film."

Costar Margot Kidder detected a recurring pitfall in that "most directors didn't direct him, they just let him go, thinking suddenly he could turn in a brilliant performance just by — I don't know what they thought. They were a little intimidated by him." Kidder admits that she "fell in love with him in two seconds flat."

Shooting a love scene, they nervously got in bed together.

> Then he looked up, and it was very genuine, and he went, "(*Gasps*) Richard Pryor's in bed with Lois Lane!' He was really adorable. He was a wonderful, wonderful, wonderful man. Much underrated as a human being. I mean, he was really generous and kind and thoughtful, and I think the best actor I'd worked with, in the sense of when you were in a scene with him, it was like doing a dance. He didn't miss an eyelash-flicker. He was so in the present. And I remember saying to him, "God, you're really a good actor. Why does everybody insist you be funny all the time?"

A few months later Richard asked for and received the unheard of sum of four million dollars for his role in *Superman III* — a million more than Christopher Reeve got for reprising the title role. The Superman franchise seemed exhausted and director Richard Lester was counting on Richard to carry the film, which he did. Again, once they had Richard, they weren't sure what to do with him. The filmmakers never decided for certain whether they wanted it to be a Richard Pryor movie or a Superman movie with Richard Pryor in it. There are a few moments of inspired comedy, clearly put in for no other reason than to capitalize on Richard doing what he did best, as they had nothing to do with the story. The movie essentially had to stop and wait while they let Richard do his thing.

It did not escape Richard's notice that the more he screwed up, the worse his movies were, the more money the studios threw at him. Billy Wilder made the droll observation in 1982 that studio executives looking for a hit movie "approach it very scientifically — computer projections, marketing research, audience profiles — and they always come up with the same answer: Get Richard Pryor."

Following the box-office bonanza of *Live on the Sunset Strip,* Columbia Pictures offered a five-year, forty-millon-dollar deal giving Richard full creative control over four films to be produced by his own Indigo Productions, presided over by his friend and former NFL star Jim Brown. Rather than make Indigo an exclusive showcase for Richard Pryor films, Brown wanted to diversify, using as his template Desilu Productions, a co-venture between husband and wife Desi Arnaz and Lucille Ball. Desilu quickly moved beyond their own *I Love Lucy* series to produce a diverse slate of shows that came to include *Star Trek, My Three Sons, Mission Impossible, The Andy Griffith Show, I Spy,* and *Hogan's Heroes.* That's what Jim Brown wanted, for Indigo to be an umbrella for African American writers, actors, producers, and directors to realize their dreams. They had forty million dollars to spend on whatever they wanted to do. At the press conference announcing the company's launch, Richard said no one was excluded. They wanted to make quality films. They were open to anything. The only film Indigo made before Richard unceremoniously relieved Brown of his duties was *Richard Pryor: Here and Now.*

"Richard wasn't a filmmaker," Penelope Spheeris says, thinking back to their work together on *Uncle Tom's Fairy Tales.* "Richard was a comedian and a brilliant one. And a good actor. But I don't think filmmaking was a priority for him. And it's hard to have anything else as your first priority when you have cocaine and Courvoisier in battle for number one."

———————

Although *Live on the Sunset Strip* had been a shaky, uncertain effort — three of four filmed performances spliced and patched together, actually — it ultimately delivered twenty riveting minutes of pure devastation. *Richard Pryor: Here and Now,* filmed at the Saenger Theatre in New Orleans in 1983, finds him off his stride and out of his depth, low on energy and retreating at times to old material. He never really takes off or gives the impression that he could. The junkie routine that ends the film affirms that this is indeed a man once possessed by genius.

A young woman leaving the cinema at Briarwood Mall in Ann Arbor on the film's opening weekend spoke for many when she said, "He was funnier when he was on drugs."

———————

It's worth remembering that, for all he gave up, Richard did, in fact, make some good movies. He played Billie Holiday's strung-out piano player, an auto assembly-line worker who robs his union and sells out his friends, champion race-car driver Wendell Scott, a petty thief who seizes an opportunity for adventure, a shipyard welder who teams up with an FBI agent to avenge his wife's murder, a pimp's enforcer, and a Vietnam vet who comes home to find what's left of his life in shambles. Then he played an unemployed actor falsely — and utterly implausibly — convicted of a bank robbery in a comedy that started out promisingly enough, then promptly ran off the rails. That movie, though, made him a bona fide movie star. His lifelong dream. That done, he settled into making Richard Pryor movies, and thereafter, Richard Pryor was the only character he played.

Not that he never again had the opportunity to play meatier roles. Superstar producer Robert Evans — a failed actor who, without ever having produced a movie, was named Paramount Pictures' head of production at age thirty-five and oversaw films such as *The Godfather,*

Chinatown, The Odd Couple, Love Story, Rosemary's Baby, and *Marathon Man,* to name a few — relentlessly courted Richard for the role of Sandman Williams in what Evans believed would be the jewel in his crown, Francis Ford Coppola's *The Cotton Club.* Based on a Jim Haskins book of the same name, *The Cotton Club* re-created the verve, elegance, and violence of the white gangsters and black entertainers who populated Harlem's most famous nightspot of the 1930s. "Gangsters, music, and pussy," Evans reasoned. "How could I lose?"

Evans invited Richard to dinner to discuss the part, but all through the meal, Richard broke down in tears talking about Jennifer. The next day, Evans sent a limo for her and spent five hours trying to charm her into having dinner with Richard. She agreed finally to a double date that included Evans and his ex-wife Ali McGraw. Every day of the week leading up to the dinner, Richard called Evans to ask his advice on what he should wear, what he should say. At the last minute, Richard canceled the date, telling Evans he just wasn't ready. Still, he was so grateful for all Evans had done that he agreed to *The Cotton Club.*

Evans was elated. "In 1982," he writes in his memoir, "there wasn't a hotter box-office star than Richard Pryor."[*]

Then he got a call from one of Richard's lawyers saying that his client wanted four million dollars — far more, he knew, than Evans could afford. "I was advised it would be a disaster and the best thing to do would be to get out of it," Richard later explained. "And the best way to get out of something is to ask for money, and that's what I did."

Instead, the role of Sandman Williams launched the film career of Gregory Hines. Richard's next movie was *Brewster's Millions* — a "wicked

---

[*]Evans recalls that his eleven-year-old son overheard him discussing *The Cotton Club* with Barry Diller, Michael Eisner, Don Simpson, and other power brokers during a Saturday meeting at their home. His son kept pestering him to come out onto the patio, saying he had something urgent to tell him. Exasperated, Evans finally excused himself and demanded to know what was so important that it couldn't wait. To his surprise, his son earnestly wanted to know if *The Cotton Club* was really as important as Evans seemed to believe. "Don't use Richard Pryor then," his son said. "If you do, it'll just be another Richard Pryor movie."

waste," Vincent Canby called it in his *New York Times* review: "Watching Richard Pryor as he forces himself to cavort with simulated abandon in *Brewster's Millions* is like watching the extremely busy shadow of someone who has disappeared. The contours of the shadow are familiar but the substance is elsewhere. *Brewster's Millions* is another in the series of earnest attempts to tame — to make genteel — one of the most original, most provocative, most unpredictably comic personalities to come onto the American scene in the last 20 years."

It was, Richard said, the first movie he ever did completely sober, and he could never bring himself to watch it.

———————

Richard preemptively dismissed his films and his roles in them before anyone else could: "Tell the fans I'm sorry," he would say. "I got greedy. I did it for the money."

In 1976, he apologized for *Silver Streak,* his first teaming with Gene Wilder. "It was a career move, and I'm sorry I did it. But I'll be glad when the movie is out and over with." After *Stir Crazy* broke the hundred-million-dollar mark, making it the highest-grossing comedy to date, Richard told a nightclub crowd that he and costar Gene Wilder "appreciate that y'all went to see it, we really do — but I saw the motherfucker and I don't get it."

He did it to his own *Jo Jo Dancer, Your Life Is Calling,* a film depicting the events of his own life that he directed, starred in, and cowrote with two of his best friends. He wasn't saying he did it for the money but that his sincere effort had failed. "I don't know what happened," he told Thom Mount in the March 1986 cover story for Andy Warhol's *Interview* a month before *Jo Jo*'s release. "I like the script and I'd do it again today. To see what I did with it makes me somewhat sad. I asked myself a thousand times, 'How could I have fucked up?'"

———————

The project started with promise. In 1985, Rocco Urbisci was going through a difficult time. He had separated from his wife and was living apart from his two children in an apartment on the beach near the Ventura County line, miles away from everything else. He needed time to figure things out. Then the phone rang.

"Rocco, it's Richie. What are you doing?"

"You want to know the truth? I'm taking a dump."

Richard didn't miss a beat. "Well, after you wipe your ass, come meet me at Columbia Studios."

Richard had decided to do a movie based on his own life and he wanted Rocco to help write it.

"Why me?" Rocco still asks. Richard Pryor could've hired the best — David Mamet, William Goldman, Paul Schrader, Robert Towne . . . anybody. He wanted Rocco Urbisci. He needed him to be there. Rocco had earned his trust. Richard could tell him anything, and did. Horrific stuff about his life. Some of it Rocco still refuses to divulge and says he never will. It refused to be written as the comedy the studio was hoping for. It ended up being more like an inventory of events in his life. It was therapy, he said, "more like basket-weaving."

The studio, predictably, wanted more of Richard's stand-up material. That was the Richard everyone loved. Richard and Rocco didn't know how they could shoehorn that into what they had written, so they brought Paul Mooney on board. He knew where the stand-up bits would fit, but it changed the tenor of the whole thing. The sequences are jarring, like a montage copied and pasted from one of those rise-to-the-top celebrity biopics where the star is seen triumphing on a variety of stages while calendar pages flip past, and newspaper headlines spin.

———————

The story is told from the disembodied vantage point of Jo Jo in the aftermath of the freebase incident that nearly kills him. While lying bandaged in a hospital bed, his spirit leaves his charred body and journeys out to retrace the steps of his life, paying ghostly visits to his younger selves at key junctures along the way.

The scenes from Jo Jo's early life were filmed on location in Peoria (in the movie, they say it's Ohio), in the actual house where Richard grew up. It took real courage, Rocco says, for him to confront his demons and the pain of his childhood, reenacting actual scenes from his life in his grandmother's house, directing his younger self to peek over the same transom into the same room where his mother turned tricks.

Jo Jo's father humiliates him using the same words Richard's father had: "This boy ain't shit and his mama ain't shit, either." In other ways, he cheated the story. One of his wives — representing Shelley — slaps him and he doesn't hit back. He sulks. The worst transgression is a scene at the bus station as he is leaving town to chase his dreams. He earnestly begs his first wife to come with him.

When the corporeal Jo Jo invites his alter ego back into his body ("I thought you'd never ask") at the end of the film, a restored Jo Jo returns to the concert stage, using the voice of Richard's old-time preacher to eulogize the burned-up corpse of his former self.

> The boy was a mess. He run through life like shit run through a goose. And now he rests here with a smile on his face. I guess that's a smile. I hope that's his face. You sure that isn't his ass? It look like his ass! Some people lead with their chin. Life kind of forces you to do that — to lead with your chin. But this man here, he led with his nuts. If his nuts wasn't in a vise, he wasn't happy.

The trouble was, Richard tried to make a heartfelt drama from the same material he had, for so many years, been spinning into wild and irreverent comedy gold. Richard knew it would be a hard sell for his fans. "They want laughs — lots of laughs, which it hasn't got. It could be moving and good, but people may say, 'Why are you telling us this? We don't want to know this.'"

Writes Pauline Kael:

> Pryor doesn't have the skills to tell his story in this form. As a standup entertainer, he sees the crazy side of his sorrows; he transforms pain and chaos into comedy. As a moviemaker, he's a novice presenting us with clumps of unformed experience. It isn't even raw; the juice has been drained away. He was himself — demons,

genius, and all — in *Richard Pryor — Live in Concert* and, though to a lesser extent, in *Richard Pryor — Live on the Sunset Strip.* Here, trying to be sincere, he's less than himself.

"Perhaps the worst thing about *Jo Jo Dancer*," Julian Upton writes in *Bright Lights Film Journal*, "is Pryor himself."

In what should have been a primal scream of a performance, a fusion of the electrifying power of his best stand-up with the howling demons that dogged him off-screen and offstage, the actor instead gives an awkward, largely poker-faced turn, occasionally hitting the high notes but generally looking lost in his own movie . . . The disturbing truth of *Jo Jo Dancer* is that it confirms that Pryor's excitable greatness had vanished. All we see is the laundered Pryor of 1986 trying to imitate the wild, wired, and reckless Pryor of a decade earlier — and as in *Here and Now*, it's an act he could no longer pull off.

Approximately two-thirds of the way through the movie, we are treated to a progressive montage of Jo Jo, sporting an increasingly voluminous natural, performing snatches of Richard's now-classic stand-up routines under the sound-track recording of Marvin Gaye's "What's Going On." Working with some of the greatest stand-up material ever conceived (his own), there is no spark, no volatile clash with audiences that had never before encountered comedy such as this. It's all perfunctory, performed by rote in front of an accepting audience. Inevitably it falls flat, merely set down for the record, as it might be performed by a Richard Pryor impersonator. Jo Jo's renditions are stillborn, like museum pieces, empty of the struggle, the chaos, the sloppiness of discovery at the moment of conception in an uncertain encounter with a live audience. Richard knew what he was talking about when he told Mooney that no one could steal his material. As this sequence makes excruciatingly clear, no one but Richard Pryor knew what to do with it. Not even Jo Jo Dancer.

———————

An alarmingly frail and emaciated Richard went on *The Tonight Show* in October 1986 in part to squelch rumors that he had AIDS. He'd lost twenty pounds in preparation for a film role, he said, but then his weight kept dropping.

"I was getting really scared. I was losing weight and my pants were falling down. I said there's something wrong. I was worried about those diseases around. I thought 'Richard, it's finally caught up with you.' I thought I had one of them and I was going to die. I was very calm about it. I went and got the blood checked. The doctor said I was fine, but the next day my eye went out. My right eye is blind," he told Carson. "You could hit me on this side and I wouldn't see it coming."

Richard knew what the trouble was, in name, at least. A few months earlier, Deboragh had flown with him to the Mayo Clinic.

The diagnosis was multiple sclerosis. He didn't know what that was. After listening to the doctor's explanation, he was convinced no one else did, either.

He understood what he was in for, that the incurable, degenerative disease would likely take away his motor skills, balance, and control of his bodily functions. He was determined not to give anything up before the disease took it away. The very next day after that *Tonight Show* appearance, he got married for the fifth time, to a twenty-three-year-old actress named Flynn Belaine. (They separated after two months of marriage and were divorced in January but would remarry following the birth of their son in 1990.)

"I'M FINDING IT HARD IMITATING RICHARD PRYOR"

"Listen, you spoke the truth. They have to make you
famous now. That's how Hollywood deals with the truth . . . They
make you so famous that nobody'll take you serious anymore."
— Cecil Brown, *Days without Weather*

Not counting *Jo Jo Dancer*, Richard Pryor — or someone calling himself
that — appeared in the following films, almost always in the starring
role.

Critical Condition (1987)

Moving (1988)

See No Evil, Hear No Evil (1989)

Harlem Nights (1989)

Another You (1991)

The Three Muscatels (1991)

Mad Dog Time (1996)

Full confession: we haven't seen any of these movies, not all the way
through, anyway. But we've seen enough. They are unbearable. We never
believed that Paul McCartney died in a 1966 car wreck or that Elvis staged
his own death in 1977 to live a life of obscurity in northern Michigan, but
we can say with fair certainty that the hapless actor passing himself off as
Richard Pryor in these movies was an impostor.

Richard — the real Richard — well knew of this doppelganger's existence and spoke of him often. The terrible irony is that in his prime the
genuine Richard believed *himself* to be the impostor. (*Who Me? I'm Not
Him* is the title of a 1977 LP of older material issued on the Laff label.)
He often said that Richard Pryor the movie star and famous comedian
was someone else, living and breathing and walking around out there
in the world somewhere while he spent Richard Pryor's money, slept
with his women, lived in his house, and cashed his checks, fearing all
the while that one day the real Richard Pryor would show up and kick
his ass. He knew he could do it, too.

While in the hospital recovering from the fire, he told his friend, the
producer Thom Mount, "I got *real* scared. I was this person that I had
inherited in life. And *I* was a person that nobody knew. *Nobody knew
me.* All I could keep doing was act like this person, this Richard Pryor,
because I was afraid. I was afraid they'd kill me if they found out I wasn't
Richard Pryor."

Kathy McKee saw him two or three times in the years following the
fire and she confirms: "He was not the same person."

If this usurped Richard Pryor can be said to have a spiritual forebear, it is
Shakespeare's Sir John Falstaff — the lusty, besotted, conniving, whore-
mongering, nose-tweaking, purse-snatching rapscallion and corrupter
of the crown who strides the boards in *Henry IV, Part 1* and *Part 2,* and
again in *Henry V.* But now observe: this swaggering colossus is reduced
to a kowtowing, repentant, subservient tool in *The Merry Wives of
Windsor,* a work Shakespeare dashed off at the behest of Queen Elizabeth who wanted to see her favorite character fall in love. Harold Bloom
calls his *Merry Wives* incarnation the "pseudo-Falstaff," a nameless impostor masquerading as Shakespeare's most sublime creature. Shake-
spearean scholar A. C. Bradley catalogs the indignities. The Falstaff of
Merry Wives, he writes, "is baffled, duped, treated like dirty linen, beaten,
burnt, pricked, mocked, insulted." Worst of all, he repents and begs pardon. "It is horrible."

As with the pseudo-Falstaff, the impostor Pryor is, in Bloom's words, "uncomfortable with what he is doing and wishes to get it over with as rapidly as possible." He "loathes not only the occasion but himself for having yielded to it."

The spectacle would make us "lament a lost glory" if we did not "know him to be a rank impostor" masquerading as the great man.

Richard's friend, bodyguard, trainer, and sometime spiritual adviser Rashon Khan confronted him point-blank and asked him why he was doing a "crazy movie" like *The Toy*. Why, when even his costar Jackie Gleason said it was bullshit. "Richard said, 'The money. I get paid for this one.'"

Richard could no more turn down Hollywood's millions than Shakespeare could refuse his queen.

Like Elvis Presley before him, Richard reached heights of absolute genius when commanding a stage with a microphone in his hand, then squandered his energy and talent on a string of forgettable movies. Greil Marcus could have been speaking of Richard Pryor's entire postfire output when he wrote this response to Bob Dylan's *Self Portrait*: "I once said I'd buy an album of Dylan breathing heavily. I still would. But not an album of Dylan breathing softly."

Writer Andy Breckman (cohost of WFMU's long-running comedy program *Seven Second Delay*) recalls a full-cast read-through of a screenplay he wrote starring Richard Pryor.

What was it called? It doesn't matter. It wasn't *Stir Crazy*, okay?* It was one of the shitty ones he made later, after he started to shrivel up, when nobody could bear watching him.

---

*It was *Moving*, directed in 1988 by Alan Metter, costarring Beverly Todd, Stacey Dash, and Randy Quaid.

There was a scene where one of the characters — a senile old lady — takes a crap in the backyard. Shamelessly, in broad daylight. Like a dog. Mr. Pryor felt that scene didn't work. I respectfully disagreed. We went back and forth. He wanted it out. I thought it should stay.

Finally, the director turned to Pryor and said, "Richard, is this something you feel strongly about?" And this is what Pryor did: he reached into his jacket and pulled out a gun! A real gun. A Derringer — with two short barrels. I'd never seen one before but I could tell it was definitely real. I was so scared I almost blacked out.

Pryor put the Derringer on the table — thunk — and stared at me, sort of defiantly. It was like a saloon scene in a bad western. Everyone gasped and laughed nervously. Nobody said anything for about five seconds. Then I playfully ripped the page out of the script, indicating "Heh, heh, okay Richard, you win!" Everyone tittered nervously some more. Finally, Mr. Pryor put the gun away and the read-through continued. We never saw the gun again. Although, as I recall, everyone laughed at Mr. Pryor's lines a little louder from that point on.

There was one movie Richard made that apparently no one has seen. Called *The Three Muscatels,* we can only say that it was ostensibly based on the Alexander Dumas novel of the Musketeers and that it starred and was cowritten by Flynn Belaine Pryor, Richard's fifth (and sixth) wife.

Richard's physical condition deteriorated considerably after he and Flynn divorced for the second time in 1991. Deboragh returned and took on the duties of a twenty-four-hour caregiver. Richard managed to make a few more TV appearances and received an Emmy nomination for his role as a cranky MS patient — with Rain playing his daughter — on the CBS drama, *Chicago Hope.* And he turned up in an offbeat part as a garage owner in David Lynch's movie, *Lost Highway.*

Roger Ebert was gracious enough to overlook Richard's role as "Jimmy the grave digger" in his final movie, *Mad Dog Time,* a film he described as being no more or less engaging than looking at a blank screen for the same amount of time. "Oh, I've seen bad movies before. But they usually made me care about how bad they were. Watching *Mad Dog Time* is like waiting for the bus in a city where you're not sure they have a bus line . . . I don't have any idea what this movie is about — and yet, curiously, I don't think I missed anything."

Directed by Larry Bishop (son of Rat Packer Joey Bishop), *Mad Dog Time* stars Richard Dreyfuss, Diane Lane, Jeff Goldblum, and Ellen Barkin, with Gabriel Byrne, Kyle MacLachlan, Gregory Hines, Burt Reynolds, and Billy Idol. Thus, Richard ended his film career exactly as he began it, playing a supporting role in a star-bloated gangster comedy. Only this time no one singled him out as the movie's promising bright spot. Instead, they looked away.

THE LAST TEMPTATION OF RICHARD

"Richard," writes Mooney, "is a junkie first, a genius second. Always." Yet "he never bleeds, he never rots out his nostrils like a lot of coke hounds do. He's got a cast-iron septum."

Richard didn't deny it. He gleefully admitted that he loved cocaine, and in copious quantities — but always as though his usage were a thing of the past. He persistently declared himself free of the drug. On his 1975 LP . . . *Is It Something I Said?*, he says, "I snorted cocaine for about fifteen years — my dumb ass. I must've snorted up Peru. I could have *bought* Peru, all the shit I snorted." The truth is, he never stopped or even slowed down since taking his first snort in 1965.

Even the "fifteen year" boast was a lie. (Oh, he could tell *lies!*) The chronology never quite tallied. When he filmed *Here and Now* in October of 1983, he told the audience at the Saenger Theatre in New Orleans that he'd had no liquor or drugs in seven months.

Richard claimed he had never smoked pot or even been drunk before he turned twenty-two. For all the whoring and payoffs and knife fights and whatnot he witnessed going on all around him, he adhered to a strict upbringing. The change came when he went out on the road.

> You're lonely and you feel rejected, so you take a walk or get in your car and drive around looking for someone to talk to . . . to love you. You run into some man or some lady and they say, "Here, take this. Go ahead. Try some." So you try it and you fantasize that you're feeling better, that you've found good friends . . . And later

you go back and look for that same person, or you look for the person he or she represents — anybody who can make you think you're happy and not being rejected. And it builds and builds.

You create a new you . . . a much-loved, very happy you. Then you find that you have to start competing with that person you've created . . . that image you want to think you are . . . that hip motherfucker who knows everything about life and people and getting high. But, man, I didn't know shit about it. I didn't know a damn thing, but I went ahead and did it.

Lots of people battle demons, but few are called to account for them in such a public manner.

"I've never seen anyone more messed up over success than Richard Pryor," says Mooney. "For him, it's a constant battle between success in the white world and keeping it real for his black self . . . He can't fight his way out of this bind. He loves the money, he loves the approval and women and celebrity, but it costs him his soul."

"Richard was not able to live his own life as a man," says Kathy McKee.

His personal skills, his relationship skills just for living his life as a human being, they weren't there. He was a strange person and he had a very dark side. When you were alone in the room with Richard in bed at night, there was no laughing, there were no jokes. He was a completely different person. A very dead personality. If you asked him a question, he would answer yes or no. Not at all a fun person, not a great conversationalist, not somebody you can laugh and talk with. Not at all. When you were alone with Richard, it was very, very, very, very, very, very, very boring, to be honest with you. The only thing that kept you there with Richard was the fact that you knew he was a genius. One live performance with Richard when you were in the wings or in the audience could carry you for a month. The jolt of electricity that you got from

being around him when he was *on* was magnificent. And you also
had this feeling that you knew you were part of a legend. There was
something about this man that was beyond anybody else.

"If a man is touched by genius, he is not an ordinary person," Dame
Joan Plowright once said, speaking of her late husband Sir Laurence
Olivier. "He doesn't lead an ordinary life. He has extremes of behaviour
which you understand and you just find a way not to be swept overboard
by his demons."

"Richard was a genius," McKee sums up. "You're not going to have a
normal relationship with someone like him. You're just not."

———————

Richard undertook a final stand-up tour in the fall of 1992. He knew as
well as anyone that it would be his last.

David Banks called Kathy McKee and invited her to the Detroit show
at the State Theatre.

Then he said, "Here, Richard wants to talk to you." He put Richard
on the phone and the first thing he said was, "You got any coke?"
and "Bring the bitches." He's in a wheelchair, right? He's looking
for drugs and he's looking for bitches. I said, "I don't know about
any of that, Richard. I don't have any bitches and I don't have any
drugs, but I will be there." He said, "Well never mind, then, bitch!"
But I went anyway. It was embarrassing. Richard struggled to
read his material off of cue cards that were spread out on the floor
in front of him. It was a full house. Everybody and their mama
showed up to see Richard in Detroit. I was completely humiliated
and ashamed for him. Richard should have never been out on that
stage."

———————

In August of 1993 Richard received the Apollo Hall of Fame award at
the Apollo Theater where the man who answered when Richard came

knocking at the stage door some thirty years earlier told him he'd have better luck down in the Village. The hallowed Apollo where Chick Webb, Duke Ellington, Ella Fitzgerald, Count Basie, Dusty Fletcher, James Brown, Shooby Taylor — far too many to name — had trod the boards setting the crowds a-frenzy or finding themselves hooted off the stage. Robert De Niro read his tribute off cue cards: "Richard always exposed himself so we wouldn't have to and, in doing so, made us more aware of who we are." And concluding with, "Richard, I continue to respect you for the work you've done in the past and I look forward to seeing more in the future."

Richard could barely hold himself upright in his chair.

Then Bill Cosby came out and struck the perfect note, striding across the stage without so much as a pause to acknowledge that an audience was present and, descending the five steps to where Richard was seated on the aisle in the second row, handed him his plaque with all the pomp of a classmate returning a borrowed pencil.

"Richard, here's your award, man. They told me to give you this. I have no idea why you're getting it."

"Bill . . ."

Richard began to choke up.

"Stop it. Stop it. We're going down to the Village and play our old room again."

———

When Richard received the American Comedy Awards' Lifetime Achievement Award, Bob Newhart asked George Schlatter, ACA founder and executive producer of their annual show, if he could present Richard with the award. Richard was already confined to a wheelchair so he could not come up to accept it. Newhart narrated a film of Richard's career highlights and they went to a station break. When they returned, he was standing in the audience next to Richard with the award. Richard looked up at him and said, "I stole your album." "What?" "I stole your album. In Peoria. I was in a record shop and I put it in my jacket." "You know, Richard, I used to get twenty-five cents a copy for that album." Richard turned to the people seated around him. "Somebody give me a quarter!"

Brooklyn multimedia artist Larry Nathanson was at the Comedy Store in May of 1995 on the night Richard gave his last stand-up performance ever. "Eddie Murphy introduced him. He was very disoriented and un-sure of himself. It was like he started a thought and couldn't carry it through. He started off sitting down, then stood up. He began to waver physically. Everybody gave him plenty of time. Nobody rushed him. People called out encouragement. 'It's okay, Richard.' 'Go, Richard!' Under no circumstances should he have been up on that stage. He never made it through a single joke. Eddie Murphy and some other guy came and took him off. He got a big ovation."

Before Richard Pryor, few comics, or solo performers, ever took on characters of their own invention without benefit of sets or supporting players. Lily Tomlin, Bob Newhart, Kres Mersky, Red Skelton, Jackie Gleason, Pigmeat Markham, Moms Mabley, Dusty Fletcher, Ruth Draper, Bert Williams all did, but none of these attempted it without either costume, props, scenery, or blackface. And, even then, they as-sayed but one character at a time.

Richard might populate his stages with upward of eight or ten charac-ters who he permitted to flirt with, mock, con, love, hate, enchant, beat, and begat each other. Like those plate-spinning vaudeville jugglers who passed through Peoria — and perhaps took refreshment at his grand-mother's establishment — who would be waiting in the wings ahead of him on *The Ed Sullivan Show,* playing out their final days by racing about the stage in time with Ray Bloch's swirling circus music, sweat glistening their brows as they dashed from pole to pole, giving each, in passing, a frantic twirl to set its wobbling plate spinning aright just before it crashed. For Richard it seemed as natural as breathing.

———————

Rocco Urbisci was sitting in a car with George Carlin on location in New Jersey waiting to shoot an opening sequence for one of his specials. Out of nowhere, Carlin said, "Rocco. What the hell would we have done without HBO?" If the Richard Pryor of the late seventies had survived into the era of HBO, Rocco says, "he could have done thirty specials without any compromise." *That* Richard could have done anything. Onstage. "Richard had such courage. If stand-up is your art, you can go make your movie, go do your sitcom, but you're going to come back to standup because that's Where. You. Have. Your. Roots. They can take away your movie, they can cancel your sitcom, but they can't take away what you created, what you did on stage, what you believed in. They can't take that away from you."

On March 1, 2008, Rocco directed George Carlin's final special, their tenth together. The stage was decorated with rugs and heavy furniture to look like a cluttered and cozy home office: stuffed chairs, bookshelves, lamps, a dictionary stand, a desk, an old Mac Classic, and a picture of Richard Pryor.

"George paid a price," Rocco says. "Richard paid it. Somebody always has to pay the price. Lenny paid it for George and Richard. There's no way to rank Lenny Bruce, George Carlin, and Richard Pryor. It's just a matter of personal preference who you'd rank second or third."

———————

We asked Elizabeth Stordeur Pryor if she recalled the moment she first realized just how significant and earth shattering her father was. When did she have that epiphany?

"Still haven't had it," she said. "This is one of the weirdest things for me about being my father's child. I don't know if I can even put this into words. It's normalized for me in some ways, in some ways it's totally surreal. It's fun to be watching *Modern Family* with my kids and hearing a joke about the father being 'the Richard Pryor of real estate.' But it doesn't make sense to me." She was floored when a student came into her class carrying a copy of the Mel Watkins book, *On the Real Side: Laughing, Lying, and Signifying — The Underground Tradition of African-American Humor That Transformed American Culture, from Slavery to Richard Pryor.* A book that draws a direct line from African American traditions in slavery times to her father? Transforming American culture? She could not equate such things with the man as she knew him up close. "My mother basically raised me as a Jewish girl from the San Fernando Valley. Nobody ever sat me down and said to me, 'Why don't you listen to your father's stuff?' There's still a lot I haven't heard. So it's funny. I don't think I, still, fully realize who he is.

"I've told my children, 'I know you think your grandfather was like a former celebrity, but there's going to come a time where you realize that he was completely groundbreaking and it's going to blow your mind.'"

———

Dr. Cornel West declares, "Richard Pryor is the freest black man America has ever had. He is not just a genius, he exercises *parrhesia*. He exercises the most plain, frank, honest, unintimidated speech we had in the sixties, even more than Martin and Malcolm."

———

"The subject of blackness has taken a strange and unsatisfying journey through American thought," wrote Hilton Als, in his 1999 *New Yorker* profile, "A Pryor Love."

First, because blackness has almost always had to explain itself to a largely white audience in order to be heard, and second, because it has generally been assumed to have only one story to tell — a story of oppression that plays on liberal guilt.

Richard Pryor was the first black American spoken-word artist to avoid this. Although he reprised the history of black American comedy — picking what he wanted from the work of great storytellers like Bert Williams, Redd Foxx, Moms Mabley, Nipsey Russell, LaWanda Page, and Flip Wilson — he also pushed everything one step further. Instead of adapting to the white perspective, he forced white audiences to follow him into his own experiences.

Even Richard's most triumphant LPs deliver but a slice of Richard's genius as a stand-up comic. So much of his performance is physical — his facial expressions, contortions, his mimicry/mimetic movements. If not for *Richard Pryor: Live in Concert,* the full glory of a Richard Pryor performing at the height of his powers and firing on all cylinders would have been lost to posterity, the stuff of legend. But the movie exists. It is proof that on the night of December 28, 1978, in Long Beach, California, at least, no one could touch him.

But what of the countless unrecorded and vaguely recalled routines Richard conjured up in clubs, on the road — settings where his genius most reliably took wing — that lived only in the space of a moment, never to be seen or heard again? Like other true artists — Bob Dylan, for example — even on his major tours when he performed the same bits night after night, he never did them the same way twice.

We sometimes come across tantalizing scraps of recollected performances, such as the one sociologist and jazz enthusiast Joan Thornell saw at the Cellar Door in Washington, D.C. Richard did a series of one-man skits, concluding with his portrayal of Richard Nixon as the devil. "The transformation visually was something, and he was right on it . . . The lights went red, and he got into it as an actor would get into a role. He out-Laurenced Olivier." Thornell attended the show with a psychiatrist friend who declined the opportunity to meet Richard after the show. "That man is so disturbed that he frightens me," was his diagnosis. "I fear for him. I fear for his safety. He doesn't have any personal defenses. These have left him. He's very interesting, but very frightening."

———————

Fortunately, David Brenner was at the Improv in New York the night Richard did this bit about a nine-year-old kid on the roof of a tenement building, stoned, and threatening to jump off and kill himself. Here's Brenner's re-creation of the scene:

> So a crowd gathers. There's the white priest and the black minister and the white cops and the gang members and the people scream-ing for him to jump . . . I think he even put the mayor in there somewhere. And of course Richie played all those parts, plus the nine-year-old kid. It was one of the funniest things I've ever seen or heard in my life. He was such a great actor. When he became these people, he *was* those people. When he became the white cop who goes up and tried to talk him out of it, he *was* this white cop. You know how Richie could do those great white voices: "Well, uh, what are you doing, son? Do you really want to jump?" And when he became that nine-year-old boy, he was a nine-year-old boy on the precipice of a roof in Harlem ready to jump. And the kid was hysterically funny. The lines he came up with for this kid . . . The routine went on for fifteen minutes . . . twenty minutes, whatever it was. And then Richie stops talking. He stares down like he's up on top of this roof at the edge of the stage. And he jumps.
>
> He *jumps.*
>
> It ends with the nine-year-old boy, stoned, leaping off the roof and killing himself. He lands hard with both feet on the floor and then walks off down the aisle, through the audience, in dead si-lence. Richie took an audience where there were people wiping their faces with tears from laughing so hard, to people actually cry-ing, all in a millisecond. It's still the most devastating thing I've ever seen a comedian do.

A late-afternoon sun pushes in through the drawn Venetian blinds. The room is crowded with a hospital bed, vital function monitors, and a rolling table scattered with prescription bottles. Richard wears a plush dressing gown open at the neck revealing savage scars from extensive third-degree burns, scars that have grown hard and leatherlike. A large console television occupies the opposite wall, and the fizzy revelry of a game show seems to mock the convalescent gloom of the waning day.

Richard squints his eyes against a harsh light, peering out through the blinds. His hands are unsteady as he fumbles for a cigarette and a plastic butane lighter that repeatedly sparks but fails to ignite. He finds a match.

Richard nods, half dozing through a TV newscast, the cigarette smoldering between twitching fingers, as a news anchor interrupts with breaking news and announces the death of comedian Richard Pryor.

It takes a few moments to fully grasp what's being said. Richard tries to call out, but is unable to speak. He frantically pushes the Call button on the controls next to his bed, but there is no immediate response.

Richard fumbles in his nightstand, scattering pill bottles and overturning a water glass. He lifts a Magnum pistol from the drawer. It wobbles, heavy in his shaking hands, as he aims it in the direction of the TV.

The first shot is wild, missing the screen but splintering the corner of the cabinetry. Using both hands to steady his aim, Richard fires again, this time blasting out the TV screen, shattering the image of Eddie Murphy, standing at the gate outside his home in Beverly Hills, having begun a spontaneous eulogy.

Rocco Urbisci recalls that Richard was in a panic while preparing for *Live on the Sunset Strip*. He had an hour and a half to fill and he didn't know if he could do it. He had the married-to-a-honky-ass-bitch routine, the trip to Africa with the gazelles and the lions, the funky-smelling hack driver, his realization that there are no niggers, and his whole freebase-inferno thing, but the pressure was on and he was still coming up short. Everybody was rooting for him, but he knew they would be secretly delighted if he fell on his ass.

He had this one other bit, too, about the one time he'd truly been brave. He pulled a gun — a starter's pistol, really — on Mafioso club owners in Youngstown, Ohio (Dean Martin's cousins, probably, from over in Stubenville), when he was touring the Chitlin' Circuit with Satin Doll and the man said they weren't going to get paid. He had the accent down, but he didn't know any Italian words. He called Rocco.

Ring, ring, ring . . .

"Rocco? It's Richie."

"Hey, Richie. What's up?"

"What's the funniest word for a kind of food in Italian?"

That's easy. *"Scungilli."*

Perfect.

"It means squid."

Richard didn't give a fuck what it meant. It was funny.

He went out there and made up four or five words just riffing on the word *scungilli.* "Hey, Carmichael, give him a plate of sunninio, some fugazi, sprinkle a little scuggi on it, some guzolli . . ."

"If George Carlin had asked me about *scungilli*," says Rocco, "he would have done three minutes on the etymology of the word and done it exactly the same way every night. And both bits would have been genius."

———————

And then there was the afternoon Richard called Rocco up, speaking in a whisper, all conspiratorial-like, the way he always did when mischief was afoot.

"Rocco," he said. "It's Richie."

"Oh. Hey, Richie. What's up?"

"Come over to the house for dinner, but don't bring your wife."

"Okay. I won't bring my wife."

"I'm not being disrespectful, it's just guys."

Richard could have called anybody, but this was for Rocco. He knew Rocco would love this, and he needed a witness.

"I'm sitting there at his table," Rocco told us. "I'm the only white guy. Across from me is Miles Davis. At the other end of the table is Oscar Peterson. I don't say a thing. There's nothing for me to say. Then Miles Davis says, 'Rich, who's the cracker?'

"Richard told him who I was. We went in his den and Oscar Peterson played for an hour.

"Now," he said, his voice catching with emotion, "you tell me how much that's worth."

People we've spoken with in the course of writing this book have, one after another, expressed regret that they had not gone to visit Richard in the confinement of his final years. One who did visit him often was Robert Townsend. He sprang from his chair at Joe's kitchen table one December morning and enacted for us a scene he had witnessed in Richard's living room. A highly animated Hispanic caregiver was giving a tour of the house to a newly hired employee. She pointed to the framed photos of Richard posed with his famous pals, attempting in vain to impress upon her the magnitude of the man it was now her job to attend. There was a glazy-eyed Richard posing with a glazy-eyed Robin Williams. Richard with Jack Nicholson, Dave Letterman, Mitzi Shore, Eddie Murphy . . .

"*Sí, sí.*" Townsend nodded, in character as Richard's new caregiver, then smiled and said, in practiced English, "Nice family."

In 2002, Pryor and Jennifer Lee married for a second time, a bond they entered into primarily for the purpose of granting Jennifer the authority to oversee his care and manage his affairs. She dug in and fended off all comers, especially children and ex-wives. Their visits — those she allowed to visit — were strictly limited and closely monitored. Even at Richard's funeral, Jennifer's guest list was strictly enforced. Deboragh Pryor and Janis Gaye, wife of Marvin and Richard's dear friend of more than thirty years, were turned away.

———————

On a Christmas getaway to Hawaii with his children in 1983, Richard experienced what he described as a moment of clarity. It was December 20. His daughters begged him to come with them to the beach, but he stayed back at the house by himself so he could smoke his base.

"I looked at myself. I was alone in the house. I said, 'Richard, how did you end up back here? Alone.' It was like myself going, 'You schmuck, what are you doing?'" He had smashed or thrown pipes away so many times before. "This time was different because I wanted it *so* bad. I dropped it all in the garbage. And I went to the beach and I found my kids."

An avid fisherman who never learned to swim, he allowed Rain to lead him into the water. It was, says Rain, "an expression of trust, almost unheard of for him."

She cradled his body, keeping him buoyed on his back in the supportive salt water out beyond the breaking waves. It was beautiful.

"I'll tell you," he wrote. "It was that instant, man, something happened to me. Something really big . . . It was like in the hospital when I started feeling grateful that I was alive."

He opened his eyes and understood he was alone. Rain had let go. It was just him and him alone, floating on the surface. That sound of the ocean's water lapping at his ears may have been his children, back on shore, clapping.

EPILOGUE: GOING TO MEET THE MAN

Our final meeting with Richard Pryor took place on Monday, September 9, 2002, the day after our grandmother, Edna Haltiwanger Derrick, died at age ninety-three.

Jennifer Lee Pryor threw open the door before we even rang the bell. With a cigarette poised aloft in one hand, she greeted us each with hugs. She was asking us a question. Maybe something about if we had any trouble finding the place, but our attention was fixed on the slumped figure with his back to us parked in a wheelchair in the center of the room.

His caregiver, a motherly Hispanic woman with an easy smile, stood by at her post with a plastic tub of supplies: soft washcloths and medical-looking devices of uncertain purpose. Jennifer placed her hand on Richard's shoulder, her voice going up half an octave and a few decibels whenever she spoke to him. "These are the guys who are writing about you," she reminded him. The project we had come to discuss that day was a screenplay based on his life.

His hands were flopping in his lap. The ravages of multiple sclerosis. He summoned up the effort to suck back some drool and said a simple hello.

We told Richard about our grandmother, about how she had taught her Ladies' Bible Class at Thrift United Methodist Church in Paw Creek, North Carolina, just the previous Sunday, as she had done most every week for the past half century or so. He, having no choice, listened with rapt attention.

We got a laugh from Richard when Joe — we forget how the sub-ject came up — quoted what our mother had said to him as he was ap-proaching his fortieth birthday. "You know that midlife crisis you're supposed to have?" she had said to him. "Well, I have some advice for you — skip it."

Richard Pryor laughed. A sharp, guttural bark but clearly a laugh.

"Midlife crises . . ." Jennifer repeated. "We know all about those, don't we, Richard?" and she gave his head a playful rub. When she took her hand away, Richard's caregiver, ever on duty to wipe away his drool, leaned down and pressed her face in his thinned gray hair and bestowed upon the crown of his head a kiss.

He was tired. His grunted replies were growing softer, the spark in his eyes dimming. We said our good-byes with a squeezing of hands amid talk of big plans and assurances of good things ahead. Neither of us saw him again save once, in a vision, through a glass darkly, on his way out.

JOE'S POSTSCRIPT

In early December of 2005, only a few short months after Hurricane Katrina made landfall on the Gulf Coast and raised the water levels around New Orleans high enough to breach its faulty levees and swallow much of that beloved city whole, British singer/songwriter Elvis Costello and Allen Toussaint — pianist, songwriter, producer, arranger and patriarch of Crescent City musicians — were holed up in a recording studio on Piety Street in the neighborhood of Bywater, just on the bowl's rim of the city's lower Ninth Ward.

The Piety Street studio is housed in a late-nineteenth-century building that had once been a post office and, as such, is a heavy slab fortress, standing flat and gray on a quiet corner. On December 10 of that wicked 2005 season, it was a rare building being occupied along that stretch of the ward, and one of the few that had electricity and running water (though it was still without phone service). The floodwaters had stopped a mere block away from the building's front door, and when one stepped outside of its bunkerlike confines after dark, the surrounding row houses and storefronts were darker than the night sky, and lifeless by comparison.

Late on this Saturday night, Elvis, Allen, myself (being their producer), our engineer, and a small band of musicians were working doggedly to finish the project we'd begun eleven days earlier in Los Angeles, everyone exhausted, raw and emotional, charged and anxious, as we hurried to add a few last flourishes to some sixteen songs before the curtain came down in earnest, and all of us would scatter either home or back out on the road, far from this seemingly godforsaken war zone.

All in attendance were bleary and stooped. The horn players, natives of New Orleans, had, to a man, all lost their homes. Allen Toussaint moved through the room with an elegant buoyancy that defied not only his own losses (friends, a home, a lifetime's worth of possessions), but the weight of seeing his beloved hometown washed away to a ruin that was as heartbreaking as it was preventable.

Pushing on toward midnight, Allen stood in a dark, glass-walled isolation booth, layering a deft backing vocal to one of his own songs cut earlier that afternoon. He was lit dimly from below by a single small bulb clamped to his music stand. The lights of the control room, though few, were enough to reflect the room's own image back from the glass, rendering Allen barely visible on the other side of it, and then only as a faint, floating, ghostly presence . . . his gray afro and thick mustache catching shards of light as he nodded and grooved along to the music he heard through headphones.

As tape was being spooled back to the beginning of a verse, I peered hard at Allen's face as it continued to bob and weave in the silence between takes, and I offered, without much forethought, "Allen, you know, in this light, you look just like Richard Pryor — had he taken better care of himself, of course. You look like his ghost moving in that room."

Allen said not a word to me in response to this but met my gaze intently, smiled broadly, and nodded, affirming his own understanding of how he might appear to me in that moment.

Toward the end of that same hour, my cell phone rang loudly from the back of the control room. Everyone turned to look, since none of us present had ever been able to find coverage within the cold, thick walls of the old building.

Scrambling down the hall and out onto the frigid, pitch black street, hoping not to lose the call, I said, "Hello?" and at first mistook the noise on the other end for pure static, only to realize that far from this decimation, in Southern California my wife stood joyfully crowded in a theater full of revelers for our son's winter holiday concert. She didn't speak but simply held the phone high above her head as people sang and cheered and the high school jazz band lurched into a raucous swing number. And then the call faded.

I stood teary and alone now on the corner of Piety and Dauphine streets and noticed something I hadn't a moment before: a half block away, a single strand of Christmas lights threaded around a wrought-iron stair rail . . . blinking on and off from the stoop of a seemingly abandoned and powerless townhouse. The joy and music of the quick call had disappeared in my hand, but the phone still showed a signal and blinked with a new message waiting — received, oddly, in unison with the call that had just sneaked through somehow.

"Hey, Joe? Joey . . . hello. I'm sure you've had dozens of calls already, but I just wanted to say, you know . . . that I am really sorry. I just heard."

Richard was dead.

Just nine days following his sixty-fifth birthday, Richard Pryor, whom I had come to know and who had so intensely occupied my thoughts and work for so long now, had finally loosed those spidery fingers and let himself rise like smoke, up and out of his frail, useless, earthly frame to which he'd been tethered for years, unable to speak — but not unable to hear and brood.

Drifting, I concluded, on his way to making one last haunting stop in Peoria, Richard seemed now to have materialized in front of me for a fleeting moment of farewell in the frightened, fighting city of New Orleans that, like himself, had for so long wildly — scandalously, anomalously — flowered up in glorious defiance of all that surrounded it; a strange specter of beauty laid at the threshold of an otherwise dispirited country never far from the throes of violent transformation.

But he had always been drifting: an unknown to all including himself. His slippery countenance — with the duality of the naive genius, the righteous hustler; the fluid sexuality; the laugh masking tears — made Richard so strangely and persuasively *other* that most everyone can recognize some part of their secret selves in his reflection, because we all believe ourselves, ultimately, to be strangers. This may account for the subversive sprawl and endurance of his influence: that his brokenness left him so vulnerable to the times that he absorbed them all. It left little room for anything else; and when the storm of his zenith years passed, Richard was left teetering and hollow like a once-flooded house, whose high waterline, nonetheless, confounds as it provokes awe.

That Richard, while exiting, might take pause in the person of Allen Toussaint — a man whose music is as deep as silence, his silences as telling as a compass blade — shouldn't have surprised me, and didn't. Richard, as we know, was always charged like a vibrating wire ... standing like a reed and giving buzzy voice to every wind blowing through; riffing with a tumble of words driven as much by tough rhythm as conscious thought; sounding always as if at any moment his cry or laugh might stem and flower, becoming fully — finally and forever — *song.*

ACKNOWLEDGMENTS

The seeds of this book first took root more than a decade ago when we imagined we could tell Richard Pryor's story within the confines of a three-act screenplay for a feature film. An evening's entertainment. The universe knew better. What we at first believed to be a triumphant arrival turned out to be a mere resting place. Once we'd caught our breath, the view from there was daunting. We could see that we had barely begun our ascent of Mount Richard. What we must write, we decided, was this book.

On that first leg of our journey, we were assisted and encouraged by T Bone Burnett, Bruce Heller, and Jennifer Lee Pryor, who gave us rare access to volumes of Richard's unpublished writings.

We are indebted not only to a number of cultural historians but to the generosity of many eyewitnesses — these friends, family, and cohorts of Richard Pryor's — whose unguarded reflections brought the past vividly forward and called flesh and blood out of abstraction. We offer our sincere thanks to:

Franklyn Ajaye	Richard Lewis
Michael Ashburne	Phil Luciano
Harry Belafonte	Stuart Margolin
Sandra Bernhard	Kathy McKee
Jimmy Binkley	Kres Mersky
Kathleen Brennan	Elizabeth Stordeur Pryor
David Brenner	Daryl Mooney
Cynthia Dagnal-Myron	Penelope Spheeris
Cabral Franklin	Lily Tomlin
Janis Gaye	Robert Townsend
Angie Gordon	Rocco Urbisci
Brian Hyland	Fred Weintraub
Tom Jones	Charles Weldon

For their early encouragement and good advice, we offer special thanks to Sue McNally, Eve Bridburg, and Amy Cherry. We feel a deep and abiding appreciation for the staff of Wild and Woolly Video and the Louisville Free Public Library, particularly those associated with the Western branch.

We are forever beholden to Bob Miller, former group publisher at Workman Publishing, both for his initial interest and ongoing support. Our champions at Algonquin Books — Kelly Bowen, Emma Boyer, Jamie Chambliss, Brunson Hoole, Debra Linn, Lauren Moseley, Craig Popelars, and publisher Elisabeth Scharlatt — invigorated us with their infectious enthusiasm and cajoled us with their kind patience. We were most fortunate to have as our copy editor the ever-vigilant Jude Grant. Finally, our venerable editor, Chuck Adams, wholeheartedly embraced our project from the get-go, giving shape and discipline to our often-times rambling narrative. He deftly and with good humor guided us back onto the main road whenever we pulled over to browse some yard sale or flea market, convinced we could find the ideal spot to display every curio or shiny bauble that caught our eye. (We come by it honestly.) Our book's defects and shortcomings are entirely our own and stand here despite his better judgment.

SOURCES

Books/Articles

Abrahams, Roger D. *Deep Down in the Jungle: Negro Narrative Folklore from the Streets of Philadelphia.* Rev. ed. Chicago: Aldine, 1970.

———. *Positively Black.* Englewood Cliffs, NJ: Prentice-Hall, 1970.

Ajaye, Franklyn. *Comic Insights: The Art of Stand-Up Comedy.* Los Angeles: Silman-James Press, 2002.

Als, Hilton. "A Pryor Love." *New Yorker,* September 13, 1999, 68–81.

Asim, Jabari. *The N Word: Who Can Say It, Who Shouldn't, and Why.* New York: Houghton Mifflin, 2007.

Berger, Phil. *The Last Laugh: The World of Stand-Up Comics.* Updated ed. New York: Cooper Square Press, 2000.

Biskind, Peter. *Easy Riders, Raging Bulls: How the Sex-Drugs-and Rock 'n' Roll Generation Saved Hollywood.* New York: Simon & Schuster, 1998.

Bloom, Harold. *Shakespeare: The Invention of the Human.* New York: Riverhead Books, 1998.

Bogel, Donald. "Black Humor — Full Circle from Slave Quarters to Richard Pryor." *Ebony,* August 1975, 123–28.

Bowman, Rob. *Soulsville U.S.A.: The Story of Stax Records.* New York: Schirmer Trade Books, 2003.

Boyd, Todd. *The Notorious Ph.D.'s Guide to the Super Fly '70s: A Connoisseur's Journey through the Fabulous Flix, Hip Sounds, and Cool Vibes That Defined a Decade.* New York: Harlem Moon, 2007.

Brashler, William. "Berserk Angel." *Playboy,* December 1979, 242–43, 248, 292–96.

Breckman, Andy. "Nobody Move! It's Richard Pryor!" WFMU, 1997, http://wfmu.org/LCD/20/pryor.html.

Brown, Cecil. *Days without Weather.* New York: Farrar, Straus & Giroux, 1983.

Brown, H. Rap. *Die Nigger Die!* New York: Dial, 1969.

Bruce, Lenny. *The Essential Lenny Bruce.* Compiled and edited by John Cohen. New York: Ballantine Books, 1967.

————. *How to Talk Dirty and Influence People.* New York: Fireside. 1992.

Bullock, Ken. "'Mrs. Pat's House' at La Peña Cultural Center." *Berkeley Daily Planet,* November 6, 2008, http://www.berkeleydailyplanet.com/issue /2008-11-06/article/31549?headline=-Mrs.-Pat-s-House-at-La-Pe-a-Cultural -Center.

Cleaver, Eldridge. *Post-Prison Writings and Speeches.* Edited with an introduction by Robert Scheer. New York: Vintage Books, 1969.

————. *Soul on Ice.* New York: Dell, 1968.

Cohen, Scott. "Interview: Richard Pryor." *High Times,* December 1977, 56–61.

Cross, Paulette. "Jokes and Black Consciousness: A Collection with Interviews." *Folklore Forum* 2, no. 6 (November 1969): 140–61.

Daly, Michael. "The Making of The Cotton Club: A True Tale of Hollywood." *New York Magazine,* May 7, 1984, 41–62.

DeGroot, Gerard J. *The Sixties Unplugged: A Kaleidoscopic History of a Disorderly Decade.* Cambridge, MA: Harvard University Press, 2008.

DeLeon, Robert A. "Richard Pryor Looks to '75." *Jet* 47, no. 16 (January 9, 1975), 56–61.

De Remigis, Peter. "A Canadian's View of Harold's Club in Peoria, Illinois." http://www.scribd.com/doc/47719511/A-Canadian-s-View-Of-Harold-s -Club-in-Peoria-Illinois.

————. "Toronto's Secret." http://peterderemigis.net/.

Driver, Justin. "The Mirth of a Nation: Black Comedy's Reactionary Hipness." *New Republic,* June 11, 2001, 29–33.

Duberman, Martin Bauml. *Paul Robeson.* New York: Alfred A. Knopf, 1988.

Dumont, Frank. *The Witmark Amateur Minstrel Guide and Burnt Cork Encyclopedia.* New York: M. Witmark & Sons, 1905.

Dundes, Alan, ed. *Mother Wit from the Laughing Barrel: Readings in the Interpretation of Afro-American Folklore.* Englewood Cliffs, NJ: Prentice-Hall, 1972.

Dylan, Bob. *Chronicles: Volume One.* New York: Simon & Schuster, 2004.

Ebert, Roger. "Hanging out with Wilder and Pryor." *Chicago Sun-Times,* December 23, 1976, http://rogerebert.suntimes.com/apps/pbcs.dll/article?AID =/19761223/PEOPLE/612230302.

————. "Mad Dog Time." *Chicago Sun-Times,* November 29, 1996, http:// rogerebert.suntimes.com/apps/pbcs.dll/article?AID=/19961129/ REVIEWS/611290303/1023.

Ellison, Ralph. "An Extravagance of Laughter." In *Going to the Territory,* 145–97. New York: Random House, 1986.

————. *Invisible Man.* New York: The Modern Library, 1994.

Evans, Robert. *The Kid Stays in the Picture*. New York: Hyperion, 1994.

Falkenburg, Claudia and Solt, Andrew (editors), Leonard, John. *A Really Big Show: A Visual History of the Ed Sullivan Show*. Edited by Claudia Falkenburg and Andrew Solt. New York: Sarah Lazin Books, 1992.

Felton, David. "Einstein's Brain." In booklet included with *Richard Pryor — Evolution Revolution: The Early Years (1966–1974)*. Rhino (R2 78490), 2005.

———. "(Portrait of the Godhead as a Young Dog) Richard Pryor's Life in Concert." *Rolling Stone*, May 3, 1979, 22–26.

———. "Pryor's Inferno." *Rolling Stone*, July 24, 1980, 11–16.

———. "Richard Pryor: This Can't Be Happening to Me." *Rolling Stone*, October 10, 1974, 40–41.

Forbes, Camille F. *Introducing Bert Williams: Burnt Cork, Broadway, and the Story of America's First Black Star*. New York: Basic Civitas, 2008.

Foxx, Redd, and Norma Miller. *The Redd Foxx Encyclopedia of Black Humor*. Los Angeles: W. Ritchie Press, 1977.

Gates, Henry Louis, Jr. *The Signifying Monkey: A Theory of African-American Literary Criticism*. New York: Oxford University Press, 1988.

Gaut, Berys. "Just Joking: The Ethics and Aesthetics of Humor." *Philosophy and Literature* 22, no. 1 (1998): 51–68.

Goldman, Albert, with Lawrence Schiller. *Ladies and Gentlemen — Lenny Bruce!!* New York: Random House, 1974.

Gottschild, Brenda Dixon. *Waltzing in the Dark: African American Vaudeville and Race Politics in the Swing Era*. New York: St. Martin's Press, 2000.

Goudsouzian, Aram. *Sidney Poitier: Man, Actor, Icon*. Chapel Hill: University of North Carolina Press, 2004.

Gregory, Dick. *Dick Gregory's Political Primer*. Edited by James R. McGraw. New York: Harper & Row, 1972.

———. *From the back of the bus*. New York: Dutton, 1962.

Gregory, Dick, with Robert Lipstyle. *Nigger: An Autobiography*. New York: Washington Square Press, 1964.

Grier, Pam, with Andrea Cagan. *Foxy: My Life in Three Acts*. New York: Springboard Press, 2010.

Grier, William H., and Price M. Cobbs. *Black Rage*. New York: Basic Books, 1968.

Haggins, Bambi. *Laughing Mad: The Black Comic Persona in Post-Soul America*. New Brunswick, NJ: Rutgers University Press, 2007.

Handelman, David. "The Last Time We Saw Richard." *Premiere* 5, no. 5 (January 1992): 78–90.

Haskins, Jim. *Richard Pryor: A Man and His Madness; A Biography.* New York: Beaufort Books, 1984.

Havens, Richie, with Steve Davidowitz. *They Can't Hide Us Anymore.* New York: Avon Books, 1999.

Headlam, Bruce. "Dick Gregory." "For Him, the Political Has Always Been Comical." *New York Times,* March 14, 2009, http://topics.nytimes.com/topics /reference/timestopics/people/g/dick_gregory/index.html. Accessed 6/24/2011.

"Healthy and No Longer 'Ba-ad,' Richard Pryor is 'Bustin' Loose.' " *People Weekly,* June 29, 1981, 74–78.

Henry, William A., III. *The Great One: The Life and Legend of Jackie Gleason.* New York: Doubleday, 1992.

Hinckley, David. "Not Just Black & White: The Curious Case of Vaudeville Comic Johnny Hudgins." *New York Daily News,* September 3, 2000.

Horowitz, David. *Radical Son: A Generational Odyssey.* New York: Free Press, 1997.

Hughes, Langston, and Arna Bontemps, eds. *The Book of Negro Folklore.* New York: Dodd, Mead, 1958.

Jackson, Bruce. *Get Your Ass in the Water and Swim Like Me: African American Narrative Poetry from Oral Tradition.* New York: Routledge, 2004.

Johnson, Joanne. "Rest in Peace: Richard Pryor (1940–1995 [*sic*])." Conspiracy Planet, n.d., http://www.conspiracyplanet.com/channel.cfm?channelid =104&contentid=3031&page=2

Jones, James Earl, and Penelope Niven. *Voices and Silence.* New York: Charles Scribner's Sons, 1993.

Kisner, Ronald E. "Richard Pryor's Richest Xmas." *Jet,* December 29, 1977, 56–58.

Knoedelseder, William. *I'm Dying Up Here: Heartbreak and High Times in Stand-Up Comedy's Golden Era.* New York: PublicAffairs, 2009.

Kravetz, Andy, and Leslie Williams. "North Valley Just the Newest Prostitution Hotbed: Even before the Days of the 'Merry-Go-Round,' Peoria Had a Long History of Sex for Sale." *Journal Star* (Peoria), March 5, 2006.

Lee, Jennifer. *Tarnished Angel: Surviving the Dark Curve of Drugs, Violence, Sex, and Fame.* New York: Thunder's Mouth Press, 1991.

Lees, Gene. *You Can't Steal a Gift: Dizzy, Clark, Milt, and Nat.* Lincoln: University of Nebraska Press, 2001.

[Lester, Peter.] "Richard Pryor's Tragic Accident Spotlights a Dangerous Drug Craze: Freebasing." *People,* June 30, 1980, www.people.com/people/archive /article/0,,20076864,00.html

Levine, Lawrence W. *Black Culture and Black Consciousness: Afro-American Folk Thought from Slavery to Freedom.* 30th anniversary edition. New York: Oxford University Press, 2007.

Littleton, Darryl. *Black Comedians on Black Comedy: How African-Americans Taught Us to Laugh.* New York: Applause Theatre & Cinema Books, 2006.

Luciano, Phil. "A comedic genius — Peoria native had brutal honesty, love-hate relationship with hometown." *Journal Star* (Peoria), December 12, 2005.

———. "As time goes by . . . snidely." *Journal Star* (Peoria), April 14, 2011.

———. "Outsiders' Insight Sheds Light on Pryor." *Journal Star* (Peoria), March 3, 2011.

———. "Pryor Commitment: Despite Illness, Peoria Native Is Making a Comic Comeback." *Journal Star* (Peoria), January 24, 1993.

Marable, Manning. *Malcolm X: A Life of Reinvention.* New York: Viking, 2011.

Maynard, Joyce. "Richard Pryor, King of the Scene-Stealers." *New York Times,* January 9, 1977.

McCluskey, Audrey Thomas, ed. *Richard Pryor: The Life and Legacy of a "Crazy" Black Man.* Bloomington: Indiana University Press, 2008.

McLeod, Elizabeth. *The Original Amos 'n' Andy: Freeman Gosden, Charles Correll and the 1928–1943 Radio Serial.* Jefferson, NC: McFarland, 2005.

McPherson, James Alan. "The New Comic Style of Richard Pryor." *New York Times Magazine,* April 27, 1975, 20–22, 34.

Mitchell, Joni. "Joni Mitchell on Dylan." Bob Dylan's Musical Roots, n.d., www.bobdylanroots.com/mitchell.html#positive.

Monaco, James. *American Film Now: The People, The Power, The Money, The Movies.* New York: Oxford University Press, 1979.

Mooney, Paul. *Black Is the New White: A Memoir.* New York: Simon Spotlight Entertainment, 2009.

Moore, Gilbert. *A Special Rage: A Black Reporter's Encounter with Huey P. Newton's Murder Trial, the Black Panthers, and His Own Destiny.* New York: Harper & Row, 1971.

Mosley, Walter. "The Stage of Life." In booklet included with *Richard Pryor . . . and It's Deep Too! The Complete Warner Bros. Recordings (1968–1992).* Warner Bros. Records & Rhino Entertainment, Warner Archives, 2000.

Mount, Thom. "Richard Pryor." *Andy Warhol's Interview* 16, no. 3 (March 1986), 44–51.

Nachman, Gerald. *Right Here on Our Stage Tonight: Ed Sullivan's America.* Berkeley and Los Angeles: University of California Press, 2009.

———. *Seriously Funny: The Rebel Comedians of the 1950s and 1960s.* New York: Pantheon Books, 2003.

Nazel, Joseph. *Richard Pryor: The Man behind the Laughter.* Los Angeles: Holloway House, 1981.

Oliver, Paul. *Blues Fell This Morning: Meaning in the Blues.* 2nd rev. ed. Cambridge: Cambridge University Press, 1990.

Orth, Maureen. "The Perils of Pryor." *Newsweek,* October 3, 1977, 60–63.

Paar, Jack. *P.S. Jack Paar.* Garden City, NY: Doubleday, 1983.

Parish, James Robert. *It's Good to Be the King: The Seriously Funny Life of Mel Brooks.* Hoboken, NJ: John Wiley & Sons, 2007.

Phillips, Gary, and Jervey Tervalon, eds. *The Cocaine Chronicles.* New York: Akashic Books, 2005.

Pond, Steve. "Lord, Give Me Another Chance." *Rolling Stone,* July 24, 1980, 13.

Pryor, Cactus. "Richard Cactus Pryor — Biography, 2011," http://cactuspryor.com/biography.html.

Pryor, Rain, with Cathy Crimmins. *Jokes My Father Never Taught Me: Life, Love, and Loss with Richard Pryor.* New York: Regan/HarperCollins, 2006.

Pryor, Richard, with Todd Gold. *Pryor Convictions and Other Life Sentences.* New York: Pantheon Books, 1995.

Rabin, Nathan. "Random Roles: Margot Kidder." *The Onion, A.V. Club,* March 3, 2009, www.avclub.com/articles/random-roles-margot-kidder,24554/.

Reilly, Sue. "Bio: Richard Pryor's Ordeal." *People Weekly,* March 13, 1978, 44–49.

"Richard Pryor Joins Grieving Family For Grandmother's Funeral." *Jet,* January 4, 1979, 14–17.

Robbins, Fred, and David Ragan. *Richard Pryor: This Cat's Got 9 Lives.* New York: Delilah Books, 1982.

Robinson, Louie. "Richard Pryor Talks." *Ebony,* January 1978, 116–22.

Romano, Renée Christine, and Leigh Raiford, eds. *The Civil Rights Movement in American Memory.* Athens: University of Georgia Press, 2006.

Rovin, Jeff. *Richard Pryor: Black and Blue.* New York: Bantam Books, 1983.

Sanders, Barry. *Sudden Glory: Laughter as Subversive History.* Boston: Beacon Press, 1995.

Sanders, Charles L. "*Ebony* Interview: Richard Pryor." *Ebony,* October 1980, 33–42.

Scott, Vernon. "Richard Pryor's Recovery Is No Joking Matter." *Sarasota Herald-Tribune* (UPI), June 29, 1980, http://news.google.com/newspapers?nid=1755&dat=19800629&id=p5wcAAAAIBAJ&sjid=3WcEAAAAIBAJ&pg=6498,5956113.

Seale, Bobby. *Seize the Time: The Story of the Black Panther Party and Huey P. Newton.* New York: Vintage Books, 1970.

Shales, Tom, and James Andrew Miller. *Live from New York: An Uncensored History of "Saturday Night Live" as Told by Its Stars, Writers & Guests.* Boston: Little, Brown, 2002.

Slim, Iceberg [Robert Beck]. *Pimp: The Story of My Life.* 1969. Reprint. Los Angeles: Holloway House, 2007.

Smith, R. J. "Richard Speaks! Chasing a Tune from the Chitlin Circuit to the Mormon Tabernacle." In *This Is Pop: In Search of the Elusive at Experience Music Project,* edited by Eric Weisbard, 75–89. Cambridge, MA: Harvard University Press, 2004.

Stein, Charles W., ed. *American Vaudeville as Seen by Its Contemporaries.* New York: Alfred A. Knopf, 1984.

Stone, Laurie. *Laughing in the Dark: A Decade of Subversive Comedy.* Hopewell, NJ: Ecco Press, 1997.

Szwed, John F. *Space Is the Place: The Lives and Times of Sun Ra.* New York: Da Capo Press, 1998.

Tafoya, Eddie. *The Legacy of the Wisecrack: Stand-Up Comedy as the Great American Literary Form.* Boca Raton, FL: BrownWalker Press, 2009.

Tate, Greg. "Richard Pryor, 1940–2005: Used to Be a Genius, I Ain't Lying, Booked the Numbers Didn't Need Paper or Pencil." *Village Voice,* December 6, 2005, www.villagevoice.com/2005-12-06/news/richard-pryor-1940 -2005/.

Trav, S.D. [Stewart, Donald Travis] *No Applause — Just Throw Money, or, The Book That Made Vaudeville Famous: A High-Class, Refined Entertainment.* New York: Faber & Faber, 2005.

Upton, Julian. "Extinguishing Features: The Last Years of Richard Pryor." *Bright Lights Film Journal,* 56 (May 2007), www.brightlightsfilm.com/56/richard pryor.php.

Van Gelder, Lawrence. "Theater Review: Replaying the Days of Black Vaudeville." *New York Times,* January 29, 1999.

Wahl, Greg, and Charles Bobbit. *It Didn't Play in Peoria: Missed Chances of a Middle American Town.* Charleston, SC: Arcadia Publishing, 2009.

Watkins, Mel. *On the Real Side: Laughing, Lying, and Signifying. The Underground Tradition of African-American Humor That Transformed American Culture, from Slavery to Richard Pryor.* New York: Touchstone, 1994.

———. "The Whole Cookie." *APF Reporter* 3, no. 1 (1980), n.p., http://alicia patterson.org/APF0301/APF0301.html.

Weiler, A. H. "Movie Review: 'You've Got to Walk It . . .': Genial Put-Down of Establishment." *New York Times*, September 20, 1971.

Wilde, Larry. *The Great Comedians Talk about Comedy*. New York: Citadel Press, 1968.

Wilder, Gene. *Kiss Me Like a Stranger: My Search for Love and Art*. New York: St. Martin's Press, 2005.

Williams, Elsie A. *The Humor of Jackie Moms Mabley: An African American Comedic Tradition*. New York: Garland, 1995.

Williams, John A., and Dennis A. Williams. *If I Stop I'll Die: The Comedy and Tragedy of Richard Pryor*. New York: Thunder's Mouth Press, 1991.

Wolfe, Tom. "Las Vegas (What?). Las Vegas (Can't Hear You! Too Noisy). *Las Vegas*!!!!" In *Smiling through the Apocalypse: Esquire's History of the Sixties*, edited by Harold Hayes, 201–18. New York: McCall, 1969.

Wolff, Craig. "At Home with Richard Pryor; Still Laughing through the Pain." *New York Times*, February 18, 1993, www.nytimes.com/1993/02/18/garden /at-home-with-richard-pryor-still-laughing-through-the-pain.html?page wanted=all&src=pm.

X, Malcolm. *End of White World Supremacy: Four Speeches*. Edited with an introduction by Benjamin Goodman. New York: Merlin House, 1971.

X, Malcolm, and Alex Haley. *The Autobiography of Malcolm X*. New York: Ballantine, 1965.

Zoglin, Richard. *Comedy at the Edge: How Stand-Up in the 1970s Changed America*. New York: Bloomsbury, 2008.

Recordings

Bruce, Lenny. *The Real Lenny Bruce*. Reissue produced by Ralph J. Gleason. Fantasy Records (F-79003), 1975.

Cosby, Bill. *Bill Cosby Is a Very Funny Fellow, Right!* Produced by Allan Sherman and Roy Silver. Warner Bros. Records (1518), 1963.

Foxx, Redd. *You Gotta Wash Your Ass*. Produced by Redd Foxx. Atlantic (SD 18157), 1975.

Get Your Ass in the Water and Swim Like Me!: Narrative Poetry from the Black Oral Tradition. Recorded and edited by Bruce Jackson. Rounder Records (CD 2014), 1998.

Mooney, Paul. *Race*. Recorded live at the Punchline Comedy Club, San Francisco. Produced by Bill Stephney. StepSun Music/Tommy Boy (3005), 1993.

Page, LaWanda. *Pipe Layin' Dan*. Laff Records (A150). Uproar, 2001.

————. *Preach on Sister, Preach On!* Laff Records (A173), 1973.

Pryor, Richard. "Am I Drunk or Are You Pregnant Raymond." 45 rpm, promotional only. Produced by David Banks. Warner Bros. Records (PRO-S-2089), 1983.

————. *. . . And It's Deep Too! The Complete Warner Bros. Recordings (1968–1992)*. Nine-CD boxed set containing *Richard Pryor, That Nigger's Crazy, . . . Is It Something I Said?, Bicentennial Nigger, Wanted: Richard Pryor — Live in Concert* (2 CDs), *Live on the Sunset Strip, Here and Now* (with previously unreleased interview recorded at the Comedy Store, 6/5/83), and *That African-American Is Still Crazy: Good Shit from the Vaults*. Warner Bros. Records & Rhino Entertainment Co. Warner Archives (R2 76655), 2000.

————. *Are You Serious???* Produced by David Drozen. Laff Records (LAFF A196), 1977. Reissued as Island Records (314-528 064-2), 1995.

————. *Bicentennial Nigger*. Recorded live at the Roxy Theatre, West Hollywood, CA., July 1976. Produced by David Banks. Warner Bros. Records (BS 2960), 1976.

————. *Black Ben the Blacksmith*. Produced by David Drozen. Laff Records (LAFF A-200), 1978. Reissued as Island Records (314-526 213-2), 1994.

————. *Craps (After Hours)*. Recorded live at the Redd Foxx Club, Hollywood, CA. Produced by David Drozen. Laff Records (LAFF A146), 1971. Reissued as Island Records (314-526 214-2), 1994.

————. *Evolution Revolution: The Early Years (1966–1974)*. Original sessions produced by Richard Pryor, Robert Marchese, and David Drozen. Rhino (R2 78490), 2005.

————. *Insane*. Laff Records (LAFF-LP-209), 1976.

————. *. . . Is It Something I Said?* Recorded live at the Latin Casino, Cherry Hill, NJ, May 26, 1975. Produced by David Banks. Reprise (MS-2227), 1975.

————. *L.A. Jail*. Tiger Lilly (TL-14023), 1977.

————. *Live on the Sunset Strip*. Produced by Richard Pryor and Biff Dawes. Warner Bros. Records (BSK 3660), 1982.

————. *Outrageous*. Laff Records (LAFF A206), 1979.

————. *Rev. Du Rite*. Produced by David Drozen. Andasol Records, 1976. Laff Records (LAFF A216), 1981.

————. *Richard Pryor*. Recorded live at the Troubador, West Hollywood, CA, September 1968. Produced by Robert Marchese. Dove/Reprise (RS 6325), 1968.

————. *Richard Pryor Meets Richard & Willie and the SLA!!* Produced by David Drozen. Laff Records (LAFF A188), 1976.

————. *Supernigger.* Laff Records (LAFF A224), 1983. Reissued as Island
   Records (314-528 062), 1995.
————. *That Nigger's Crazy.* Recorded live at Don Cornelius's Soul Train, San
   Francisco. Produced by Richard Pryor. Partee/Stax (2404), 1974. Reissued as
   Reprise (MS-2241), 1975.
————. *Wanted: Richard Pryor — Live in Concert.* Produced by Richard Pryor
   and Biff Dawes. Warner Bros. Records (2BSK-3364), 1978.
————. *Who Me? I'm Not Him.* Produced by David Drozen. Laff Records
   (LAFF A198), 1977. Reissued as Island Records (314-526 215-2), 1994.
————. *The Wizard of Comedy.* Reissued as Island Records (314-528 063-2),
   1995.
Williams, Bert. "Elder Eatmore's Sermon on Generosity." On *Bert Williams,
   The Remaining Titles: 1915–1921.* Document Records (DOCD-5661), 1999.
X, Malcolm. *A Message to the Grass Roots.* Recorded at King Solomon Baptist
   Church, Detroit, Michigan, November 10, 1963. Detroit: AFRO Records
   (AA-1264).

Referenced Films Starring or Featuring Richard Pryor

Bingo Long Traveling All-Stars and Motor Kings. Directed by John Badham.
   Motown Productions, Universal Pictures, 1976. Universal Home Entertain-
   ment (21773), 2002.
Black Brigade (aka *Carter's Army*). Directed by George McGowan. Thomas
   /Spelling Productions, 1970. Westlake Entertainment Group (WLV 3057 S),
   2003.
Blue Collar. Directed by Paul Schrader. TAT Communications Company, Univer-
   sal, 1978. Anchor Bay Entertainment, 2000, with audio commentary by Paul
   Schrader and Maitland McDonagh.
Bustin' Loose. Directed by Oz Scott and Michael Schultz (uncredited). Richard
   Pryor Productions, Universal Pictures, 1981. Universal Studios (61024179),
   2005.
The Busy Body. Directed by William Castle. William Castle Productions, Para-
   mount Pictures, 1967. Legend Films, 2008.
Car Wash. Directed by Michael Schultz. Universal Pictures, 1976. Universal
   Studios, 2003.
Dynamite Chicken. Written, produced, and directed by Ernest Pintoff. Tango
   Entertainment, 1972. Colossal Entertainment (COL #114), 2001.
Greased Lightning. Directed by Michael Schultz. Third World Cinema, Warner

Bros. Pictures, 1977. Warner Home Video, 1992. Reissued as *Comedy Double Feature: "Moving/Greased Lightning,"* Warner Home Video, 2006.

Hit! Directed by Sidney J. Furie. Paramount Pictures, 1973. Olive Films (OF377), 2012.

Jo Jo Dancer, Your Life is Calling. Produced and directed by Richard Pryor. Columbia Pictures, 1986. RCA/Columbia Pictures Home Video (60683), 1996. Sony Pictures Home Entertainment (06673), 2002.

Lady Sings the Blues. Directed by Sidney J. Furie. Motown Productions, Sidney J. Furie Productions, Paramount Pictures, 1972. Paramount Home Video special edition, 2005.

Lost Highway. Directed by David Lynch. Lost Highway Productions, Asymmetrical Productions, CiBy 2000, October Films, 1997. Universal Studios Home Video, 2008.

The Mack. Directed by Michael Campus. Harbor Productions, Cinerama, 1973. New Line Home Video, 2002.

Mad Dog Time. Directed by Larry Bishop. Dreyfus/James Productions, Skylight Films, United Artists, 1996. MGM Home Entertainment, 2004.

The Phynx. Directed by Lee H. Katzin. Cinema Organization, Warner Bros. Pictures, 1970. Accessed at www.veoh.com/watch/v20443766nY2MZZwr

Richard Pryor Here and Now. Directed by Richard Pryor. Delphi Films, Columbia Pictures, 1983. Sony Pictures Home Entertainment (06674), 2002.

Richard Pryor Live & Smokin'. Filmed at the New York Improvisation on April 29, 1971. Produced and directed by Michael Blum. MPI Home Video (MP7233), 1984.

Richard Pryor — Live in Concert. Filmed at the Terrace Theater, Long Beach, California, December 28, 1978. Directed by Jeff Margolis. Special Event Entertainment, Inc., 1979. MPI Home Video (DVD7084), 1998.

Richard Pryor Live on the Sunset Strip. Filmed at the Hollywood Palladium, October 22-23, 1981. Directed by Joe Layton. Columbia Pictures, 1982. DVD released by Columbia TriStar Home Video (40909), 1999.

Silver Streak. Directed by Arthur Hiller. Frank Yablans Presentations, Miller-Milkis Productions, Twentieth Century Fox, 1976. 20th Century Fox (2221490), 2004.

Some Call It Loving. Written, produced, and directed by James B. Harris. James B. Harris Productions, Two World Film, 1973. Video Supply Depot, a division of the Monterey Movie Company (V763).

Some Kind of Hero. Directed by Michael Pressman. Paramount Pictures, 1982. Paramount Home Video (VHS 1118), 1998. Legend Films, 2008.

Stir Crazy. Directed by Sidney Poitier. Columbia Pictures, 1980. Image Entertainment, 2010.

The Toy. Directed by Richard Donner. Rastar Pictaures, Delphi Films, Columbia Pictures, 1982. Columbia TriStar Home Entertainment, 2001.

Uncle Tom's Fairy Tales (aka "Bon Appétit," aka "The Trial"). Directed by Richard Pryor and Penelope Spheeris. 1969. Unreleased. Whereabouts unknown.

Uptown Saturday Night. Directed by Sidney Poitier. Verdon Productions, Ltd., First Artists, Warner Bros. Pictures, 1974. Warner Home Video, 2004.

Wattstax. Directed by Mel Stuart. Stax Records and Wolper Productions, 1973. Warner Home Video, 30th Anniversary Special Edition (34997), 2004. Audio commentaries by Chuck D and Rob Bowman; Mel Stuart, Al Bell, Isaac Hayes, and Larry Clark.

Wild in the Streets. Directed by Barry Shear. American International Pictures (AIP), 1968. Reissued as *MGM Presents Midnite Movies Double Feature: "Wild in the Streets/Gas-s-s-s"* (1004881), 2005.

The Wiz. Directed by Sidney Lumet. Motown Productions, Universal Pictures, 1978. Universal Studios Home Entertainment, 2010.

You've Got to Walk It Like You Talk It or You'll Lose That Beat. Written, produced, and directed by Peter Locke. J. E. R. Pictures, 1971.

Notable TV Appearances

Away We Go. Summer replacement for *The Jackie Gleason Show* hosted by Buddy Rich, Buddy Greco, and George Carlin. Richard Pryor appeared as a guest on the third of the show's seven episodes. CBS. Aired June 24, 1967.

The Barbara Walters Special. Richard Pryor interview. ABC. Aired May 29, 1979, December 2, 1986, http://youtu.be/3MTAQwBLoGw.

Chicago Hope. "Stand." Richard Pryor received an Emmy nomination for his role as a patient suffering from multiple sclerosis. CBS. Aired November 20, 1995.

The Ed Sullivan Show. Richard Pryor stand-up performance as "militant black poet." Included on *The Very Best of The Ed Sullivan Show, Volume One: Unforgettable Performances.* Buena Vista Home Video (1345). CBS. Aired February 8, 1970.

The Kraft Summer Music Hall. Summer replacement for *The Andy Williams Show.* Richard appeared as a guest in 1966 and 1968 when it was known simply as *The Kraft Music Hall.* NBC. Aired August 8, 1966, and July 3, 1968.

Lily. CBS. Aired November 2, 1973. Reissued as The *Lily Tomlin Special — Vol. 1,* Karl Home Video (VHS 054).

The Mike Douglas Show. Richard Pryor (guest host), Juliette Whittaker, Milton Berle, George C. Scott, Trish Van DeVere, and Tuffy Truesdale with Victor the Wrestling Bear. Westinghouse Broadcasting Co. Aired November 25, 1974. Accessed at the Paley Center for Media, New York, June, 9, 2011.

Mod Squad. "The Connection." ABC. Aired September 14, 1972.

NBC's Saturday Night. NBC. Aired December 13, 1975. Reissued as *Saturday Night Live: Richard Pryor, Guest Host.* Warner Home Video (29003), 1989.

On Broadway Tonight. Richard Pryor's national TV debut. CBS. Aired August 31, 1964.

The Partridge Family. "Soul Club." Guest stars Richard Pryor and Louis Gossett Jr. as brothers whose Detroit nightclub is in peril of being taken over by the mob. ABC. Aired January 29, 1971. Sony Pictures Home Entertainment, 2005.

Pryor's Place. Richard's unlikely foray into Saturday morning children's TV featured guest appearances by his friends Lily Tomlin, Scatman Crothers, Kareem Abdul-Jabbar, Willie Nelson, Robin Williams, and Sammy Davis Jr. The show ran for ten weeks and won two Daytime Emmys — for art direction and costume design. CBS. Aired September 15–December 8, 1984. Rhino Home Video, 1998.

The Richard Pryor Show. Indigo Productions, Burt Sugarman, Inc. NBC. Four episodes aired September 13, 20, 27, and Oct. 20, 1977. Image Entertainment (IDO165BMDVD), 2004.

The Richard Pryor Special? Indigo Productions, Burt Sugarman, Inc. NBC. Aired May 5, 1977. Image Entertainment (IDO165BMDVD), 2004.

A Time for Laughter: A Look at Negro Humor in America (ABC Stage 67). Produced by Harry Belafonte. ABC. Aired April 6, 1967. Accessed at the Paley Center for Media, New York, June, 9, 2011.

The Tonight Show Starring Johnny Carson. Guests Richard Pryor and Chevy Chase promote their NBC specials. NBC. Aired May 4, 1977.

The Wild Wild West. "The Night of the Eccentrics." CBS. Aired September 16, 1966.

The Young Lawyers. Pilot episode. ABC. Aired October 28, 1969.